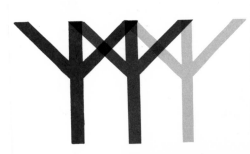

Shade Plants for Garden
and Woodland

By the same author

—

THE PRUNING OF TREES, SHRUBS
AND CONIFERS

Shade Plants
for
Garden and Woodland

*

George E. Brown

FABER AND FABER
London · Boston

First published in 1980
by Faber and Faber Limited
3 Queen Square London WC1N 3AU
Printed in Great Britain by
Latimer Trend & Company Ltd Plymouth

British Library Cataloguing in Publication Data

Brown, George Ernest
Shade plants for garden and woodland.
1. Shade-tolerant plants—Great Britain
I. Title
635.9'54   SB434.7
ISBN 0-571-10377-4

Contents

PART TWO

Illustrations

Acknowledgements

Nos. 1, 2, 4, 5, 6, 10, 12, 17 were taken at Beth Chatto's Nursery, Elmstead Market, Colchester; nos. 9, 13 at the Savill & Valley Gardens, Windsor Great Park (Crown Estate Commissioners); nos. 7, 11 at Bressingham Gardens, Diss, Norfolk; nos. 15, 16 at F. G. Barcock's Garden House Farm, Drinkstone, Bury St Edmunds; no. 14 at Mrs. Dodson's garden, Hill House, Chelsworth, Suffolk; no. 8 at the garden of Mary Alexander, Herb Specialist, Green Farm Cottage, Thorpe Green, Bury St Edmunds.

The above photographs were all taken by Mr Michael Warren: no. 3 was taken by Mr Anthony Carpenter at the Royal Botanic Gardens, Kew.

Figures

The figures were drawn by Peter Styles

Acknowledgements

I am grateful to Mr Peter Styles who drew the diagrams, Mr Michael Warren who took the majority of the photographs and to Mr Anthony Carpenter who took no. 13; also to Mr Richard de la Mare, formerly Chairman of Faber and Faber, whose idea it was that I should write the book, to Miss Eileen Brooksbank, the firm's gardening books' editor, for her help and encouragement and to Mr Frank P. Knight, V.M.H., formerly Director of the Royal Horticultural Society's Garden, Wisley, for the valuable advice he gave me after reading my manuscript.

Finally my special thanks go to my wife Mary, our daughter Sally Annett and our son Robert, for all their help with this book.

Introduction

This book is not intended as a catalogue of plants that will grow in shade; rather the aim is to emphasize the characteristics of plants which can be used to make shady places more effective.

Most plants have peak periods when they are at their best—often when in flower—but many have beauty at other times and other stages. The eye and mind can be trained to appreciate this; for example, there are the rich purple-red shoots of the paeony when they appear above the surface in the spring, or the rosettes of *Meconopsis* before they start to run up to flower. Again, the straw-coloured foliage of *Hosta* as it dies back in the autumn is very beautiful when one appreciates it in relation to the general scene among plants at this time of year. An awareness of such settings brings about a greater love and enthusiasm for plants, and the aim to reach an even higher standard. In shade, foliage effects assume especial importance; the flowers often have softer colours which are better suited to the restful atmosphere that is a vital part of shade where a predominance of very bright colours would be out of place.

The intending shade gardener is advised to build up slowly year by year, working to an overall plan—it is all too easy to attempt too much at the outset and then in later years maintenance becomes a problem. Gardening should not be full of slog, mowing and hoeing and countless other tasks, undertaken on a vast scale and leaving little or no time to look at the plants, to study and enjoy them. There will, of course, be some hard work, but it is enjoyable to allow time also to fuss over plants, encouraging them by watering, feeding, mulching and pruning. This is the way to get pleasure from gardening, and this is where the owner of the smaller garden is lucky, for a high standard is often easier to reach and to maintain where the efforts are concentrated.

Nobody should disregard the possibility of growing shade-loving plants provided there is soil that will grow *something*, no matter how small. Even the very dry site over a thin chalk or gravel will provide a home for some shade-loving plants, perhaps those which come into growth early, such as *Arum maculatum*, the cuckoo pint, and which after flowering die back into bulbs, corms or similar structures before the dry period begins. Reference will frequently be found, particularly in the alphabetical list in Part II, to plants such as this which are part of our native flora, but it is inevitable that many beautiful species have not been given even a mention. These plants grow together to form a community within the limitations of the environment, taking the rainfall and the type of soil and so on into consideration. We should do all we can to preserve at least a part of these habitats and to include them in our garden plan. It will give much pleasure and serve a very useful purpose. It is not necessary to cultivate every part of a garden, or to mow the whole lawn surface. Even in a small garden a corner can be left where our native plants will grow happily, even though it may not exceed the size of a table. What better than to have a shady area for the shade-lovers? I must emphasize that it is wrong to *collect* plants from the wild and the countryside with the aim of establishing them in gardens. In many cases they do not survive for they are often moved or collected when in full growth. Usually it is not the common plants that are taken, thus the rarer ones become even more rare. Should a plant be required there is usually a specialist nurseryman who can help you or give advice. One of the great values of belonging to horticultural societies, specialist or otherwise, is that the members often help one another with plants and seeds; indeed this is often the only way of obtaining some of the rarer species. When required plants are on a demolition site it is a different matter, for their removal may be the only chance of saving them from extinction, but remember that the permission of the owner will be needed.

It would be rewarding to try to preserve some disappearing country crafts and sometimes the garden is the best place for this; hedge-laying, as an example, is seldom met with these days, and yet a laid hedge provides a suitable environment for many indigenous shade-lovers. Again, the old stone walls and derelict cottages and farm buildings found in many parts of the country provide ideal homes for some of our smaller native ferns such as *Asplenium trichomanes*, and in addition are often attractively lichen covered. Such features are nature's gardens and it is well worth our while to preserve at least a part of them as such (maintaining them in reasonable condition) if they form part of a garden. It is surely just as wrong to plant them up completely with wall shrubs as it is to allow them to become completely overgrown with bramble?

One of the rewards of growing shade plants is that they provide shelter for many small animals and birds which love such shady positions. Although woodland is the ideal habitat for wild creatures, even a narrow shaded border against a wall in a town garden can give a little cover, especially for birds which seek out shelter and shade for nesting. Conservation of various forms of wild life is to be encouraged for its own sake but it can also add considerably to man's enjoyment, something well worth bearing in mind when planning a garden.

Readers are referred to the Conservation of Wild Creatures and Wild Plants Act 1975; to the article 'Wild Flowers and the Law' by F. W. Perring in *The Garden* (Journal of the Royal Horticultural Society), vol. 102, Part 5, May 1977, pp. 202–3; and to the article 'Conserving cultivated plants' by Chris Brickell (Director of the Royal Horticultural Society's gardens at Wisley), *ibid.*, pp. 197–201.

Those concerned with shade gardening will be interested to know that recent trials at Wisley have included pulmonarias and fuchsias. Full reports of these trials, which are judged by panels of experts, are published annually in the *Proceedings of the Royal Horticultural Society*. Reports also appear from time to time in *The Garden*.

From every aspect, planning is of great importance and the reader will want to study the plants themselves in relation to the different types of shade available. In Chapter 1 I have defined the main types of shade and much of the book is based on this classification. A thorough understanding of it is essential and it has been set out as simply and as briefly as possible for easy reference.

Part One

Part One

1

Shade and its Influence on Plants

Types of Shade

For the purposes of this book, five main types of shade are defined:

Dappled Shade

Shafts of sunlight penetrate the actual tree canopy or the gaps between trees.

Part Shade

A position with a partial or complete east or west aspect, formed by a wall, building, tree or shrub, or some other object such as a rock or fence. The sun reaches this spot for part of the day.

Shade

A north aspect against a thickly formed tree or shrub, a structure or other feature that does not let sunlight through. The sun never reaches this location.

Full Shade

(i) In summer only, caused by the dense overhanging branches of a deciduous tree when it comes into leaf; for example, the beech (*Fagus sylvatica*). During winter and spring the sun reaches through the branches.

(ii) For the whole of the year, caused by the dense overhanging branches of an evergreen tree such as a holly (*Ilex aquifolium*), or by an overhanging building or archway. The sun never reaches such a spot, and it may be very dry for long periods or the whole of the year (see Fig. 1).

The Behaviour of Plants in Shade

Full sunlight is not necessary to a large number of plants and these will grow well in some form of shade, provided that other conditions such as moisture availability are suitable (see Plate 8). In many cases this is due to the fact that such plants do not manufacture a greater amount of food in the brighter light. In some cases flowering is reduced in the shade.

With true shade-lovers exposure to the sun may not only cause distress, it may result in the tissue drying up and the death of the plant. This is true of some variegated or coloured foliage plants; for example, with *Ribes sanguineum* 'Brocklebankii', a flowering currant noted for its golden-yellow foliage effect, full exposure to the sun results in scorch and a dried crinkling of the foliage.

Sun-lovers grown in the shade often develop into pale and drawn plants, with oversized leaves giving them a completely unnatural appearance; they may often be found in gardens which have become overgrown through neglect. For example *Sempervivum tectorum*, houseleek, forms a tight rosette when exposed to full sun, but in shade it becomes large, open and flabby without the ability to flower. Usually when sun-lovers are grown under shaded conditions they are more prone to such diseases as mildew, rust and botrytis.

Plants growing in the shade of trees and shrubs obviously come into direct competition with them for the nutrients in the soil. However, there is one compensating factor—their fibrous root system is able to benefit from the annual leaf fall, perhaps more readily and earlier than do the tree roots, for the new roots of many shade-loving plants extend during the autumn and winter months, while those of deciduous trees and shrubs in particular renew their activity with bud development in the early spring. The nature of the leaves, however, is an important factor. The large leaves of *Acer pseudoplatanus*, sycamore, lie flat on one another, particularly when they are wet, and in such a condition they can damage or kill some plants beneath, *Cyclamen* species for example, particularly if they happen to be in leaf. By contrast the leaves of *Quercus robur*, common oak, are smaller and do not lie as flat and heavy, and are therefore kinder in this respect.

While a number of herbaceous plants may be grown in sun or shade, the range of shrubs within this category is very large indeed, and it is impossible to make hard and fast lists; some indication of this difficulty will be found in the section dealing with the selection of shrubs for growing on walls and other surfaces. I will cite but one example to illustrate the versatility of some of them: the Chilean shrub *Azara microphylla* is found in full sun, under woodland conditions (where its growth may be thinner), in shaded borders, and on south-facing walls. With this plant the severity of the winter may be the limiting factor, and sufficient shelter is of the greatest importance. This is an evergreen, and a very wide range of evergreen shrubs will grow well in sun or shade. Having justified the omission from this book of many shrubs that *will* grow in the shade, I must point out that shade is essential to some, the woodland rhododendrons for example.

It is sometimes difficult to establish a plant directly under the most shady parts, but observation from nature and among plantings in gardens shows that some shrubs, after being established on the perimeter, perhaps in full sun or dappled shade, are able to branch into badly lit positions. *Cornus mas* is one that will do so, and it will send out branches beneath such dense evergreens as *Quercus ilex*, holm oak, and carry flowers into a dimly lit position. *Parrotia persica* will branch into shade, but will not produce flowers there.

2

Trees, the most Important of the Shade Producers

Bud Break and Leaf Development

The prevailing weather conditions over winter and spring have a great influence on the timing of bud break. Thus a mild winter and spring may bring such trees as the horse chestnut forward to the bud-break stage by a few weeks. This has a great effect on the plants beneath, for the majority have their development linked more directly to the conditions of the soil, and they are slow to respond to milder weather. Thus if the overhead canopy is early they will receive less of the spring sunshine and rain than if the season is a normal one. This has a marked effect on the bluebells, for example, and these may even die out in large numbers if they are in a difficult marginal position, within the edge of a dense canopy. Evergreen plants are less affected by the rate of leaf development of an overhead canopy, although they too welcome the longer period of light and rain.

The considerable variation in the timing of the leaf-break period among the tree species is shown by the following table, which was made up from the world famous collections of trees at the Royal Botanic Gardens, Kew, on 18 May 1973. At this time both the bluebells and the common horse chestnut were in full bloom. The scale 0 to 5 is used to record the stage of development, based upon a visual impression; 0 covers all the stages up to bud break, the figures 1 to 5 indicate the stage of leaf development, with 5 indicating that the canopy is complete. It has been recognized that certain species flower at a very early stage and this has been taken into account. The table also indicates the ultimate density of the canopy later in the season when healthy trees are in full growth and leaf. In terms of the leaf canopy: H = heavy, M = medium and L = light.

Acer campestre	field maple	3	H
A. griseum	paper bark maple	0	L
A. negundo	box elder	3	M
A. opalus	Italian maple	1	H
A. platanoides	Norway maple	4	H
A. pseudoplatanus	sycamore	2	H
Aesculus flava	sweet buckeye	5	M
A. hippocastanum	common horse chestnut	5	H
A. indica	Indian horse chestnut	3	H
Ailanthus altissima	tree of heaven	1	M
A. vilmoriniana		0	M
Alnus glutinosa	common alder	3	M
Amelanchier species	snowy mespilus	2	L
Betula pendula	common silver birch	4	L
Broussonetia papyrifera	paper mulberry	0	L
Carpinus betulus	common hornbeam	4	H
Carya cordiformis	bitter nut	1	H
Castanea sativa	sweet chestnut	3	H
Catalpa bignonioides	Indian Bean tree	0	M
Celtis species	nettle tree	3	L
Cercis siliquastrum	Judas tree	2	L
Cladrastis lutea	yellow wood	1	M
C. sinensis	Chinese yellow wood	0	M
Cornus nuttallii	Pacific dogwood	1	L
Corylus avellana	hazel	3	M
Crataegus monogyna	common hawthorn	4	M
Davidia involucrata	pocket-handkerchief tree	3	M
Diospyros lotus	date plum	1	H
Eucommia ulmoides		1	M
Fagus sylvatica	common beech	4	H
Fraxinus excelsior	common ash	3	L
F. ornus	manna ash	3	H
Ginkgo biloba	maidenhair tree	2	L
Gleditsia triacanthos	honey locust	2	L
Gymnocladus dioicus	Kentucky coffee tree	0	L
Juglans nigra	black walnut	1	M
J. regia	common walnut	1	M
Koelreuteria paniculata	goldenrain tree	0	L
Laburnum anagyroides	common laburnum	4	L
Larix decidua	common larch	3	L

Liquidambar styraciflua	sweet gum	1	M
Liriodendron tulipifera	tulip tree	2	M
Magnolia acuminata	cucumber tree	1	H
M. × *soulangiana*		2	H
M. stellata		2	H
Malus species and cultivars	flowering crab	5	H
Meliosma veitchiorum		0	L
Metasequoia glyptostroboides	dawn redwood	3	L
Morus alba	white mulberry	1	M
M. nigra	black mulberry	1	M
Nothofagus obliqua	robel beech	1	M
Nyssa sylvatica	tupelo	1	M
Parrotia persica		2	H
Phellodendron amurense *japonicum*		2	L
Picrasma quassioides		1	L
Platanus × *hispanica*	London plane	2	H
Populus nigra	black poplar	3	M
P. 'Serotina'		3	M
P. trichocarpa	black cottonwood	4	M
Prunus avium	gean	3	H
P. Japanese Cherries		3	H
P. persica	peach	2	L
Pterocarya fraxinifolia		2	M
Pyrus communis	common pear	3	H
Quercus castaneifolia	chestnut-leaved oak	2	H
Q. cerris	Turkey oak	1	M
Q. phellos	willow oak	1	M
Q. robur	common oak	3	M
Q. rubra	red oak	2	H
Q. × *turneri*	Turner's oak	3	H
Robinia pseudoacacia	false acacia	1	L
Salix alba	white willow	3	M
S. alba 'Vitellina'	golden willow	4	M
S. 'Sepulcralis'		3	H
Sophora japonica	Japanese pagoda tree	1	L
Sorbus aria	whitebeam	2	M
S. aucuparia	mountain ash	3	L
S. cuspidata	Himalayan whitebeam	0	L
S. domestica	service tree	3	H

Taxodium distichum	swamp cypress	2	L
Tilia × *europaea*	common lime	4	M
T. oliveri		o	M
T. petiolaris	weeping silver lime	3	M
Ulmus procera	English elm	4	M
U. × *sarniensis*	Jersey elm	1	M
Zelkova carpinifolia		2	H

Density of Canopy

The density of the leaf canopy, especially during the summer months, is important, for it affects the amount of light reaching the plants and the penetration of the summer rains. Also, of course, the more foliage there is, the greater the amount of moisture taken up in direct competition with the plants beneath. The foliage of a large beech for example is extremely dense and during the summer the amount of light reaching the ground beneath is very small. It is noticeable that the leaves on the lower horizontal branches, in particular, fit very closely together, with comparatively small gaps between them, thus allowing little light beyond them. Rain also stands less chance of penetrating this layer, particularly a light fall. The ash on the other hand has a comparatively light canopy that allows much more light and rain through. Thus a large and healthy beech provides full shade during the summer and little will grow beneath it, while the ash gives a dappled shade, allowing sufficient sun and rain through to support a wide range of plants beneath it (see Fig. 1).

Ash (*left*) during winter, very light dappled shade.
(*right*) during summer, dappled shade.

FIG. 1. A diagrammatic impression of the types of shade cast by two contrasting trees; ash, with a light canopy and beech, with a dense heavy shade.

Beech (*left*) during winter, light dappled shade.
(*right*) during summer, full shade.

The density of the canopy can be reduced by the removal of branches to let more light and rain through, but unless care is taken the tree and the general effect will be spoilt (see Fig. 2).

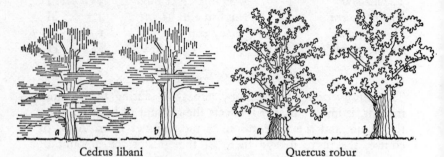

Cedrus libani   Quercus robur

FIG. 2. The appearance of two selected species of trees (a) before the lower branches have been removed to accommodate shade-loving plants and (b) afterwards. It will be noticed how the appearance of the cedar is completely spoilt by this operation. This situation particularly applies to conifers.

Moisture, the Overhead Canopy and the Shade Plants Beneath

Many factors influence the rate at which moisture is withdrawn from the soil by trees and shrubs. Evergreens take some moisture up during the whole of the year, but a greater amount during the growing season. Deciduous trees take up very little during the early winter, but increasingly more as the buds swell to reach a maximum as they break and growth gets under way. During the autumn, as the growths ripen and the leaves fall, the uptake is again reduced to a minimum.

Weather conditions obviously have a great influence on the uptake of moisture, very little being taken up on a wet day compared with a dry, windy one. The age and condition of the tree also have to be considered, the fast grower taking up considerable quantities in proportion to its size (see Fig. 3). The various species also differ considerably, a young *Betula pendula*, common silver birch, taking up much more than a *Sorbus aucuparia*, mountain ash, of equal age.

The view is sometimes expressed that the feeding roots of a mature tree are to be found in a line or circle under the extent of the crown. This is based on the belief that its roots are thus able

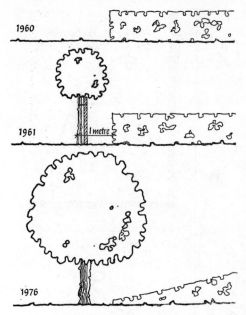

FIG. 3. The effect of planting a young tree—purple-leaved prunus—near a permanent but smaller feature; a cherry laurel hedge. It will be noted how, after a period of 15 years, the hedge has been overshadowed, with resultant deterioration, by the tree. Drought has accelerated the situation.

to benefit from the extra drip which occurs in this area, this being sufficient. This however is far from true, for tree roots will hunt far and wide for food and moisture, often for distances out of all proportion to the size of the tree, or shrub for that matter. Sometimes they will extend most in one direction only if it is worthwhile and particularly rewarding (see Fig. 4). It is not surprising that many shade-lovers come into full growth early, thus escaping this competition for moisture as well as taking advantage of the extra light. Even small tree seedlings growing on the woodland floor break into leaf earlier than the overhead canopy, despite the fact that they are the same species.

Competition for soil moisture among the trees and the shrubs beneath them is very intense during periods when it is in short supply. Often the smaller plant loses and the lack of moisture becomes a limiting factor. This is happening more and more frequently as wells become deeper and deeper, and more water is drained from the surface. There are few plants that will thrive under shade where the soil is dry for long periods, there being no dew to help them. It is also noticeable that there is a wider range of plants under trees on a heavy, retentive soil than on a light one.

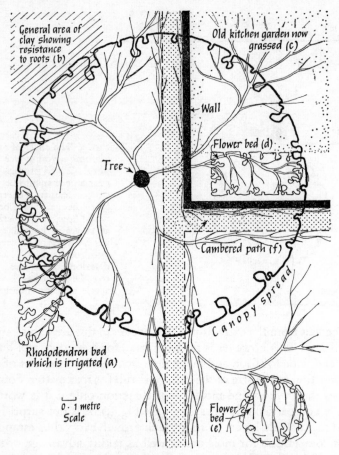

FIG. 4. An imaginary distribution of a main tree root system within a garden setting. Note that the roots will extend well beyond the canopy in some directions. The special features to observe are from (a) to (f). At (b) there is an area of clay which is compact and shows resistance to the roots. This area would be the last to dry out owing to the relative absence of tree roots and the nature of the clay itself. A good position for shade plants. (Notice how the roots follow the edge of the cambered paths for extra moisture.)

To some extent this may be due to the greater availability of minerals on the heavier soil types.

It follows from this that most woodland and shaded sites can be improved by the addition, if necessary, of a retentive soil. An annual dressing of leafmould is of great benefit to all, for it directly increases the food content and the moisture-holding capacity of the soil.

Tree Form and Shade

The type of tree and branching have a great effect upon the amount of light reaching the ground and the plants beneath. The tree with a straight bole or trunk up to a height of perhaps twenty-five metres (about eighty-two feet) and then branching with ascending growths lets through a considerable amount of light and even rain, especially if the trees are widely spaced. On the other hand, a low-branching specimen with growths which go down to ground level will let much less light through (see Figs. 5 and 6). It is often the case that when one is forming a

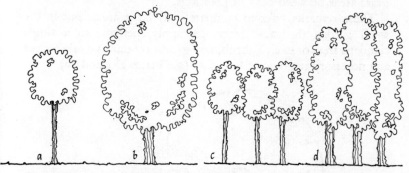

Fig. 5. Tree form and its ultimate effect upon the planting. (a) The young standard as a single specimen at planting. (b) At maturity. (c) The same type, close planted as in a wood or group. (d) At maturity. There is adequate scope for shade plantings with both (b) and (d).

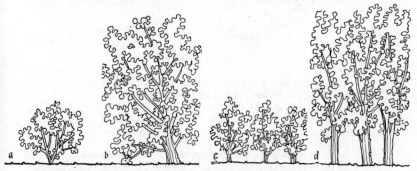

Fig. 6. Tree form and its ultimate effect upon the planting. (a) The young low branching tree as a single specimen at planting. (b) At maturity. (c) The same type, close planted as in a wood or group. (d) At maturity. The scope for plantings beneath is limited with (b) to low growing subjects; with (d) however there is adequate scope.

shade planting beneath and among trees some have to be removed completely, and it may often be beneficial to clear at least some of the lower branches of the remaining trees and thus increase the amount of light and even sun coming through in thin beams. The aim should be to keep the overhead canopy yet allow some light and sun to penetrate through the gaps to form a dappled shade. Oak woodland, in particular, lends itself very freely to thinning in this way. Thinning must be very carefully carried out, otherwise wind will get in and cause severe damage or a 'blow-out'. The tree(s) for a shade garden can, of course, be trained with a central lead, in time forming an ideal tree with a good, clear trunk and high branching. To add to effect and to break up the rather un-natural appearance of a forest of bare trunks, some low-branching specimens may be left untrained, perhaps on the edges of clear grass areas between beds or plantings.

These remarks refer to comparatively large areas, but in the small garden the same principles apply, perhaps to a single standard tree, or even a shrub, and great care must be taken over any necessary removal of branches (see Plates 2, 3 and 10).

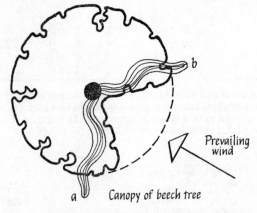

Prevailing wind

a   Canopy of beech tree

FIG. 7. The broken canopy of a large beech and its effect upon the plants and the soil beneath—an actual example as it was found. The side was exposed to the west through the loss of a branch on that side. The rain driving on to the main trunk and branches on this side caused a stream of water to run down between the buttress roots and over the bare soil. This has resulted in the formation of shallow ruts, (a) and (b). These two gulleys have been colonized by *Crocus tomasinianus.*

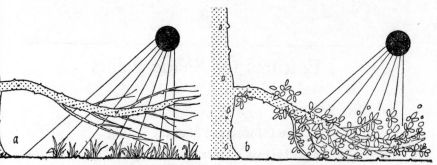

FIG. 8. A low branch of a beech and its effect upon the plants and soil beneath—an actual example as it was found. (a) During the winter and spring the branch is clear of the ground, allowing a growth of bluebells, while the sun and rain penetrate the leafless branch system. (b) During the summer and early autumn, with a full canopy of leaves, the branch is weighed to the ground and in wind its sweeping action would destroy any growth below. There is, however, unlikely to be such growth for no sun or rain is able to penetrate the close canopy of leaves.

Under low-branching trees, the twig growth of which may come down to ground level, the planting is often limited, but we can learn much from nature here. In the wild, provided that the sun does penetrate on one side before the buds break, bulbous plants such as bluebells are found. Obviously this is usually on the south side, while on the north there is often little or no bulbous growth at all, perhaps just a thin covering of shade-loving grasses. This may be in part due to the warming influence of the sun as well as to the light factor, but this side will also receive more rain, particularly through the growing season when the tree is in leaf (see Fig. 7). The angle of the sun also has an effect, for there is often good penetration by the early morning and late evening sun through both low-branching and other types of tree.

There is a final factor to be taken into account: branches are lower with the weight of leaf and growth during the summer than in the winter. This clearly affects the amount of light any ground-floor plants are receiving; moreover, low branching may allow very little headroom indeed, perhaps sufficient only for small plants and bulbous specimens that finish their growth early (see Fig. 8).

3

Features for Shade Plants

The Informal or Natural Setting

The informal garden may consist of one or several different types
of plantings which fit in with the existent features: undulating
ground, stretches of grass, trees—in groups or singly—ponds,
marshes, streams and so on. Shaded sites, large or small, are often
to be found in such features, particularly under or within the
proximity of trees. It is important to study all the factors before
making any choice of plant, and advisable to gain experience over
one or two years, stepping cautiously, for it is easy to make mistakes which cost time and money. It is better to work with nature
than against it, in attempting to alter conditions which are difficult or impossible under the existing circumstances.

A light, acid soil, with an overhead canopy of pines, sweet
chestnuts or oaks, is an ideal one for rhododendrons and other
ericaceous subjects, combined perhaps with lilies and similar
plants, although much will depend on the moisture content of
such a soil. On the other hand, such plants may be more difficult
on a lighter soil, unless some improvement is possible with plentiful supplies of organic material. On such soils the moisture-
lovers may predominate. Thin soils overlying chalk usually dry
out very quickly; most ericaceous subjects are out of the question
since they are mainly lime-haters, but it is an ideal soil for the
early starters such as arums, bluebells and hellebores. Perhaps the
most difficult position is to be found among trees on a gravel
soil, but provided that the overhead canopy is deciduous and not
too dense, again bulbous subjects will be among the most satisfactory plants.

The aim throughout must be to build up an association so that
each will derive benefit from the other, and the appearance of
each and every plant will be improved and in keeping with the
surroundings.

1. (*left*) The young spring foliage of lady's mantle, *Alchemilla mollis*, made even more attractive by the scattering of rain drops which are held on the soft hairy leaf surfaces. The water secretions from hydathodes (water pores) may also be seen on the edges of the younger leaves.

2. (*right*) The strong developing growths of a form of *Hosta sieboldiana* beneath a flowering branch of *Viburnum rhytidophyllum*, with ferns in the background and a ground cover of lesser celandine, *Ranunculus ficaria*.

3. A large scale planting, in informal drifts, of hostas and *Dryopteris filix-mas* beneath a light tree canopy at Kew. *Hosta crispula* with a white leaf margin may be seen in the foreground.

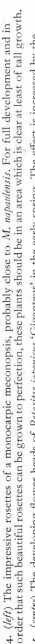

4. (*left*) The impressive rosettes of a monocarpic meconopsis, probably close to *M. napaulensis*. For full development and in order that such beautiful rosettes can be grown to perfection, these plants should be in an area which is clear at least of tall growth.

5. (*centre*) The developing flower heads of *Petasites japonicus* 'Giganteus' in the early spring. The effect is increased by the carpet of fallen leaves and by the fact that the area is clear of other growth.

6. (*right*) The light green developing fronds of the hart's tongue fern, *Phyllitis scolopendrium* with a flowering head of *Euphorbia robbiae*. The small star-shaped flowers, pink in colour are of *Claytonia alsinoides*, an introduced plant which naturalizes freely in damp situations. The informal effect is a delightful one with the fresh spring flowers and growth against the dying fronds.

7. Variation in colour and form from foliage and flower on a partly shaded border. In the foreground is a crested form of *Phyllitis scolopendrium*, hart's tongue fern, backed by the stiff growths of *Gentiana asclepiadea* and the yellow foliage of *Hosta fortunei* 'Aurea'. More variety is added by the sword-shaped leaves of *Phormium tenax* 'Variegatum' in the background, while the effect of contrasts is completed by the hybrid evergreen azalea.

8. A successful planting in part shade, but some of the subjects used are recognized as sun lovers, for example, the rose and iris hybrids. The foliage of the angelica, *Angelica archangelica*, has a golden effect with the low morning sun shining through it. Beside it is the feverfew, *Chrysanthemum parthenium* and immediately behind, the fine foliage of the fennel, *Foeniculum vulgare*.

9. (*left*) An informal drift of Candelabra Primulas among other moisture lovers such as iris. The large central group with deep wine-red flowers is *Primula pulverulenta*. It should be noted how the colours and types are kept mainly together but are mixed on the edges of the groups.

10. (*left*) A drift of *Tiarella cordifolia* in a light woodland setting with other suitable plants such as *Milium effusum* 'Aureum', Bowles's golden grass, and daffodils in the background.

11. (*right*) Where shade and sun meet. An extensive planting of *Pulmonaria angustifolia* as a ground cover subject between the groups of hostas and *Phormium tenax* 'Variegatum' which occupies a central position in the border.

12. The bronze-green foliage of *Rodgersia podophylla*, richly luxuriant and with every detail of the vein system clearly defined, is in distinct contrast to the hard glossy leaves of the rhododendron behind it. Foliage displays like this will last the summer through.

14. (*left*) A scene which will always give pleasure—a drift of *Anemone apennina* at the base of a deciduous tree.

15. (*right*) A striking scene in the early spring—a group of *Helleborus foetidus* in a woodland setting against a conifer.

13. (*facing page*) In dappled shade, the ostrich fern, *Matteuccia struthiopteris*, with the variegated *Hosta crispula* and *H. sieboldiana*, providing a rich contrast in foliage effect to the colourful azalea and primula display.

16. Quite common but beautiful plants in a partly shaded border. *Lamium maculatum* 'Roseum' as the ground cover with hybrid polyanthus and the developing growths of an herbaceous paeony.

17. A delightful planting of foliage and flower combined with *Erythronium* hybrids and *Dicentra formosa*. Most of the woodland floor is now covered and a camellia can just be seen in the background.

The Mixed Woodland

Many lessons can be learnt from nature, and a very useful time may be spent wandering through a wooded area, observing the various trees and plants and trying to understand their distribution. If similar plantings can be observed in different areas of the country, so much the better.

There are many advantages in having more than one, and perhaps many, tree species in a woodland if it is to be used for amenity purposes only. One is the variation in appearance, apparent at all seasons. During the winter, for example, when bark effects and branch and twig formations predominate, a tree such as the hawthorn, with its fine and distinctive light-coloured bark, provides a contrast to the beech, which has smooth bark, or to the sweet chestnut and the common oak whose bark is strongly ridged. Silver birch is another obvious choice for its bark which is such a contrast to that of most other trees. In the spring the variation in leaf break is sufficient to provide interest, and an examination of the table on pages 22–25 will demonstrate what a wide difference there is even among the common species.

It must be borne in mind that the smaller trees will suffer badly or even be killed eventually by the larger ones. The situation in a mixed planting is a very fluid one, and eventually only a few large trees will be left. Some trees and shrubs are able to tolerate competition from large and overshadowing neighbours, and one is advised to give these very careful consideration in any planting to be made, particularly on a light gravelly soil. *Sambucus nigra*, elder, is one such plant that can survive under very dry and poor conditions, which is one of the main reasons why this species is found so frequently in poor and derelict woodlands, on light soils in particular. It breaks into leaf early and is able to put on considerable growth before the trees providing the overhead canopy break into leaf. This species should therefore not be despised, for although common, it can be very useful. There are a number of cultivars of *S. nigra* and a selection of the other species can be considered, for example, *S. racemosa*, red berried elder. *Sambucus* will often spread extensively by seed, but can be kept in check at an early stage. As the bushes age they often become untidy, but will respond well to hard pruning during the dormant season and may, if necessary, be cut down almost to ground level. There are many

B

other trees which can be used, for example, the many species and cultivars in the *Pyrus* (pear) genus; the gean or wild cherry too is a beautiful early flowering subject.

In the autumn the variation in colouring among the various species is often pronounced. The wild cherry colours early, while the beech is much later in colouring and leaf fall.

I have referred only to mixed woodland, but many tree plantings can be treated in just the same way. A mixture of tree species provides a variety of habitats, some plants preferring one type, some another, for the kind of shade under which they can thrive.

The Build-up of Woodland Conditions

The time it takes to establish woodland conditions, whether on a large or small scale, depends upon many factors. If some trees or shrubs are already established, so much the better. The aim must be to provide shelter, humidity and shade, with the best soil and moisture conditions possible. This may mean that an initial planting of trees and shrubs must be given time to become established and grow. It is also necessary to build up the organic content of the soil, preferably in a layer several centimetres thick on the surface and just beneath it; this will be taken down by the worm population and other forms of life which thrive under these conditions.

When started from scratch, perhaps on arable land or pasture, this process will take many years, but some short cuts are possible, for instance by the selection of extra large nursery stock, although it must be emphasized that the right species may not be available in this form. It is always advisable to accept nothing but the most suitable species, for the planting must fit in with the soil and the countryside at large. In a garden setting exotic species or forms can be selected, but great care should be taken in their positioning if they are to be used to provide shade for the plants beneath. It is also possible to introduce undergrowth to speed up the process of providing shade and shelter. *Corylus avellana*, the hazel or cobnut, is very good for this purpose because it is fairly quick growing and starts to produce appreciable shade in four to five years, and it is possible to produce a woodland effect after ten years when the canopy is complete. Furthermore, the hazel will grow on a variety of soils, although it will thrive best on the good retentive loams.

With a completely new planting of trees and hazel, the latter will provide the first real shade. However, as the trees grow they will form the upper canopy, the hazel providing a second layer. Provided that the trees are widely spaced this will prove to be quite suitable for the shade-loving and woodland plants growing beneath, but thinning of both trees and hazel can be done if necessary. The only difficulty with this plan is that thinning, particularly of trees, is seldom carried out! I suggest that to begin with hazels should be planted informally five to six metres (sixteen to twenty feet) apart. They should be encouraged to establish themselves quickly by weeding but after a few years they soon take command of the situation. An alternative to the hazel is *Castanea sativa*, the sweet chestnut, for this (like the hazel) can be coppiced and it thrives on many soils, including the calcareous and lighter ones.

Within the garden it is likely that a more ornamental species would be desirable. There are many shrubs to choose from, including rhododendrons. *Hamamelis*, witch hazel, could be considered if the position is not too shady, but among the best shrubs for acid or neutral soils are the corylopsis. They have the same stool habit of growth as the hazel and the foliage is also similar, but the various species have the most beautiful racemes of flower in the spring before the leaves appear; *C. pauciflora* has the reputation of doing well on a chalky soil. There are many other possible ornamental shrubs for use as undercover.

When the ground shade-loving plants are introduced they will need looking after very carefully until they have become established. Often it is better to plant them in small areas or beds, for if they take very well they will spread. By this method one can build up experience with various species and decide which are likely to be successful. A site may vary considerably even over a distance of a metre or two (a few feet), and knowledge of the limitations this imposes will be acquired. Gradually as the environment is built up, the more exacting species can be introduced. At the same time, ornamental and exotic shade-lovers can be planted in the selected areas once the conditions are right, and it is recognized that particularly in the smaller garden there will be little scope for the native flora to creep in. It is to be hoped, nevertheless, that some space may be spared for these—how much room does one plant of the ordinary lesser celandine take up?

Sometimes a start has to be made on a very exposed and unsuitable site, with poor soil. If it is bare it may be possible to cover parts or the whole with a layer of soil. On such a site it is often better to build up a covering of undergrowth, for this brings shelter with it, even if it is nothing but bramble, *Rubus* spp., and the trees and shrubs can follow. These should be small, only about 500mm. (1 ft. 8 in.) high, and only a limited number should be planted each year so that they can be looked after properly.

Features Involving Water

Many shade plants, if given all the necessary conditions, are suitable for waterside plantings. The shade may be provided by a variety of features including steep banks, walls or rocks, although in most cases the emphasis is on a natural effect with trees or bushes as part of the setting.

A streamside provides adequate scope; there may be, for example, drifts of hostas, and primulas, with ferns overhanging the banks. The planting should be carried out according to the scale of the feature; in a small setting only a few plants should be used, but it can be just as effective as a larger feature. It may be possible to place logs or stones across the stream to impede the flow, thus forming miniature waterfalls. The advantage in sound and effect is at once apparent, and the fact that the water is turbulent adds to the humidity of the atmosphere, to the benefit of many shade-loving plants. Where shafts of light break through in a dappled shade, the occasional gleam and sparkle with the light reflected from the plants make the whole scene alive and refreshingly beautiful.

Much of this also applies to the pond or lake, for some delightful plantings can be made running down the shore, in places to the water's edge. It is desirable for the water's surface to be mostly in full sun, for water overhung by trees tends to become sour through the annual leaf fall, making it unsuitable for plant growth and fish; also most pure aquatics are sun-lovers—water lilies for example. However, trees and shrubs may be within the vicinity of such a setting, providing a home near the water for shade-lovers. Bog or marsh conditions are often found near streams and other water features, and if there are trees nearby, part of these areas may be in some form of shade. This is a situation where such plants as *Caltha palustris*, the marsh marigold, and *Rodgersia* can be used, for they will grow in full sun or shade, thus helping to provide continuity.

The Border Shaded by Trees in a Formal Setting

This type of border may often be found by a path or lawn. If the trees are small, with very little overhang, there is no problem, for a wide range of plants enjoy such a position. Among herbaceous plants there are many, such as *Heuchera americana*, which can be tried with every chance of success. The shade even beneath the trees will be a light one and there may be full sun at certain times of the day. The one problem is competition for moisture, but with small trees this should not be too intense, especially if the soil is improved with organic material before planting is carried out, and mulching is done regularly afterwards.

With large trees there will be more competition, for both moisture and plant foods which, if the soil is by nature a well drained and dry one, may be intense. Much also depends upon the type of tree, and here the reader is referred to the table on pages 22–25. Evergreen trees and many of the conifers may keep off the rains even during the winter, and this will keep the border on the dry side. If there is no overhang there will be direct light from the sky without drip and, with proper culture by way of watering and mulching and the selection of the right plants, many of the problems will be overcome. Such sites may also be cold and draughty, but this can often be improved by a shelter planting. If there is overhang from the trees, drip and bad light may be added hazards. Oak is not such a problem in this respect as beech; the range of plants that will put up with conditions under the latter is limited, but reference to the alphabetical list in Part II will prove that some can do it. One answer to this problem is to thin the trees and even to cut off some of the lower branches. However, if the trees provide a screen or shelter one should be very careful about this for the effectiveness of the original use may be reduced and the feature ruined. Sometimes the problem is best overcome by cutting out the border completely, or perhaps by moving a path. If there is a border, there should be some furnishing in it, and in difficult situations a ground cover of ivy or periwinkle may provide the best solution.

Shaded Dry Retaining Walls

Retaining walls which are very dry do not provide suitable homes
for plants, particularly north- or east-facing ones sheltered from
most of the rain-bearing winds. This is a most important point to
bear in mind—many sun-loving species can thrive under dry conditions, the *Sedum* or *Sempervivum* species for example, but there
are very few shade-lovers that will put up with dry conditions. A
north-facing retaining wall which is dry through overhanging
growth or other sheltering features is very difficult indeed to
furnish.

A retaining wall, of rocks or stones, is built against a bank of
soil. Instead of mortar, soil is rammed in solidly between the
layers, and for stability the wall is generally sloped back 50 mm.
(2 in.) to every 300 mm. (1 ft.) in height.

One is always advised to plant up this type of walling as it is
being built but this, although ideal, is not always possible, and it
can be done when the wall is completed, provided that the plants
are small and rooted, and that care is taken. The autumn or spring
is the time to do this. Some north-facing retaining walls may receive sun during the early morning and late evening in the midsummer period, and if so this will make all the difference to the
range of plants that can be established. Such sites will be warmer,
too, but for some plants it may not be desirable to have even this
small amount of sun (see Fig. 9). Plants growing in east- or west-
facing retaining walls experience similar conditions to those
growing on walls with such aspects, and the reader is advised to
consult that section.

Walls, Fences and Similar Features

As soon as this type of shade is considered, it is apparent that the
orientation of the feature in relation to the sun is of the greatest
importance. Reduced to its simplest form, a wall running east to
west will give full sun on the side facing south, and shade on the
north side, while a wall on a north–south axis will have part shade
on both surfaces. By far the greater number of 'structural surfaces' deviate considerably from such simplified orientation,
however, so a true assessment of the situation can only be made
after a very careful study of the particular feature.

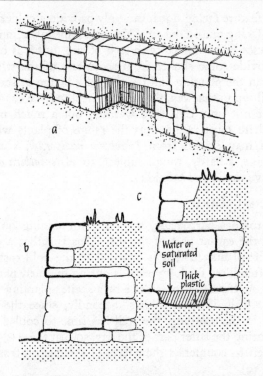

FIG. 9. The dry retaining wall with a built-in recess. This provides shade and moisture and allows a greater variety of plants to be grown. (a) Frontal view of the recess. (b) Sectional view. (c) Shows how an even greater variety of plants can be introduced by the inclusion of a piece of thick plastic sheeting in the base.

THE NORTH-FACING SURFACE

This has no sun, apart from possibly during the midsummer period when the sun rises and sets north of east and west respectively. Much depends upon the proximity of any trees or buildings, for these may reduce or cut out even this short period of sun, but if these brief periods of sunshine do provide an interlude from the shade of the remainder of the year, it makes a surprising difference, perhaps to the ripening of the wood and subsequent flowering of *Chaenomeles*, quince, for example, or to the successful culture of some other plants.

The wall or feature facing north can only provide a colder site than the south-facing one on the same site, and some low temperatures will at times be combined with lack of sun, but it is often possible to provide some shelter from the worst of the winds, which may mean the planting and training of a hedge or screen. If shelter is built up in this way, the environment may be changed completely, for not only can it be warmer, but a much more humid atmosphere must result, thus the range of plants which can be grown may extend from *Jasminum nudiflorum*, winter-flowering jasmine, a hardy, tough subject, to *Asteranthera ovata* which must have shade and humidity.

THE EAST-FACING SURFACE

This feature provides part shade, with the sun shining on the surface during the earlier part of the day. This is rather a cold environment for plants: first, it is exposed to the cold easterly winds which often blow for long periods during the early part of the spring, although much can be done by a shelter-planting well away from the wall, if space allows. Secondly, since the sun reaches it only in the morning, the wall has time to cool down considerably during the latter part of the day, so that there is very little warmth left to counteract the effects of a radiation frost at night (see Fig. 10).

Plants that are frozen are often subject to severe damage if the sun reaches them before they have thawed out; blossoms in particular often suffer from this. Plants against an east-facing feature are very prone to this type of damage; nevertheless a very wide range may be grown in this situation and much depends upon the environment within the particular area and the climate generally. Every gardener should get to know the potentialities of his or her site, and treat all lists of plants for a particular purpose with caution, as indeed their authors intend.

THE WEST-FACING SURFACE

Generally this gives considerable shelter, especially from the east. It is shaded during the early part of the day, which can be an advantage after a period of frost, for the plants have time to thaw out before the sun reaches them, thus minimizing damage. In addition the warming influence of the sun later in the day may be retained until the colder night air returns, when the radiation will

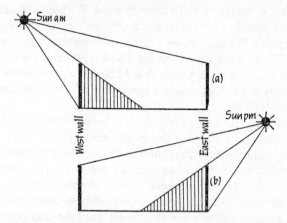

FIG. 10. The effect which the early morning and evening suns have upon east- and west-facing wall surfaces. (a) In the early morning the sun shines upon the east wall while the west facing surface is in the shade. (b) The opposite is the case with the afternoon sun. It will be noted how the soil by the wall is affected, for it is under the warming influence of the sun and is sheltered by the wall. The soil before a west-facing wall tends to be warmer than that before an east-facing one, for the atmosphere is often clearer in the afternoon.

keep off the frost, to some extent at least. There is the point too that the afternoon sun is frequently warmer than it is for most of the morning, for it is often misty to begin with, especially during the winter (see Fig. 10). However, other factors often come into the picture; for example, near the coast a wall may be very exposed to salt-laden gales, and this alone will limit the choice of plants.

Paving and Patio Layouts

Shade of all types is found in many of the features that involve some form of paving. Usually, unless the shade is full and dense, planting is possible between the slabs, and this increases the decorative value and interest, and also gives a more mature appearance. This in turn creates a more restful atmosphere, which is important in a garden and especially so in towns and cities, where more such paved gardens are found.

The success of any planting between slabs depends to a large extent upon the type of rooting medium between the crevices. Plants cannot root down through hard concrete or a sand and cement mixture which is so frequently used. Without disturbing the slabs it is usually possible to drive a mason's chisel through to the soil beneath (wear goggles during this operation to protect the eyes). These gaps may then be filled with soil, most conveniently at planting time, which should be during the autumn so that the plants become established before the following summer's drought sets in.

The use to which the area is put must be carefully considered before the final positions for the plants are decided. They will grow if established successfully, and allowance must be made for this. Remember that it would be heartbreaking to pull a plant out when it is in full growth because it is in the way, and often it would be difficult to know what to do with it. Such creeping plants as *Arenaria balearica* are frequently used for this purpose; they are less likely to get in the way than are taller plants and it is also easier to keep them in check. The Easy Reference Table on p. 216 will give the reader some idea of the range of plants that are suitable for these features.

With any planting it is important to complete the picture and in this case the effect is often achieved by growing suitable creepers against the walls, fences or similar boundary features. It is often advisable to establish narrow borders on the perimeter of the paved area, which may mean lifting rows of slabs. Although the paved area will be reduced, it may enable you to achieve a more effective planting. Suitable low-growing plants may be encouraged to grow over the edges in some places, perhaps being happier and easier to look after there than if growing between crevices.

Tubs of plants standing on a paved area are pleasing, but avoid having too many, which would give a crowded appearance (again the reader is referred to the Easy Reference Table for plants that can be grown in tubs in the shade). Paved areas are usually sheltered, and in an urban climate a surprisingly wide range of plants can be grown.

Stone surfaces in the shade often become slippery through the growth of various forms of algae; this is more likely to happen where there are tubs which are watered regularly through the summer months. Scrubbing with an algicide, bleaching powder or soda will soon put this right, but care must be taken in the region of the plants, to prevent any of the product soaking down into their roots.

Plants in Tubs and other Containers

A large number of plants can be grown in tubs, but most people prefer those that reach fair proportions and will develop into shapely specimens. (The Easy Reference Table, p. 216, gives some idea of the range available.) If the correct choice is made according to the position, the plant should be sufficiently hardy to grow in shade throughout the year if need be; nevertheless, some form of shelter from the north and east is desirable. It is important that the container is sound and has drainage holes of a suitable size in the base. Drainage is very important and any deficiency in this respect will result in a chilled and waterlogged soil, which will in turn quickly result in the death of the root system, and of the plant itself. A layer of crocks should be placed in the bottom, and ample space must be left at the top for watering. It is often advisable to raise the container off the ground by 50 mm. (2 in.) or so, in order to prevent the entry of worms, which will quickly foul up the drainage system.

The plants selected to grow in this way should be a suitable size before they are moved into the tubs, and when this is done, a properly prepared compost must be used for the best results, bearing in mind the soil needs of each plant. The move should be carried out just before the beginning of the growing season. Culture during the summer consists mainly of watering and feeding, and success will depend largely upon these being carried out conscientiously and skilfully. It must be remembered that these plants may dry out at other seasons also and really they should be looked at daily; feeding should only be carried out during the growing season.

A tub or container, being fully exposed, is very much affected by fluctuations in air temperature. This is of great significance during the winter in particular, when the air temperature may drop considerably, often for long spells at a time. To counter this it is of great benefit to protect the container in some way before the winter sets in, for example, with a wrapping of straw; this also prevents cracking of earthenware containers. If it is possible to move the specimens over to a sheltered corner this is a great advantage.

4

Shade Plants and their Uses

Positioning Shade Plants for the Best Effect

On larger sites, particularly in a woodland setting, it is advisable
to arrange the plants in groups or drifts. In this way the planting
will be more effective, and every plant will be used to full advantage. On the largest sites, grouping may be necessary with
really large plants or even trees or shrubs. As an example, a group
of five or six of *Acer griseum*, paperbark maple, would be more
effective in a large setting than just one tree. The same is true of
rhododendrons, a group of five or six of some of the more
common species, would fit in better with a large-scale planting.
On a smaller site the numbers must be scaled down—there should
be only one specimen of the large growers, and the groups of the
smaller plants should also be reduced. On very limited sites even
the small plants may only be set out singly, and although bulbous
subjects may be grouped, these groups too will be small. There
may be few, if any, of the really large growers.

In order to get the best from any planting it is important to
take height into consideration and, generally speaking, the tallest
species are planted at the back, with the shortest in the front, by
the path or the viewing position. However, there can be interesting variations from this, taking the site and its general layout into
consideration. It would be far too formal to have the plants
arranged in tiers and rows according to their height, even in a
setting of straight lines and even proportions. Rather, the tall
plants should be brought forward in some places to form a
promontory, in others the shorter plants may be allowed to run
back to form a valley or ravine (see Plate 11). The natural planting, with a variation in heights, will apply to the woodland
garden in particular—in most cases the most difficult feature to
plant up effectively. Here more than ever scenes in depth are required, with the eye running smoothly over the area, with no
plant in the wrong place.

The variation in height among plants may be used with great effect on a site where there are different levels; for example, should a part be undulating, a grouping of the taller plants may be made on the higher slopes, thus accentuating the differences, especially if low-growing subjects are planted on the low stretches and valleys. Care must be taken with the choice of plants for the higher areas for they may be drier. Some plants are brought into a new perspective when they are grown in a raised area, with the crown of the plant brought to eye level. With *Rodgersia tabularis*, for example, the effect is quite dramatic, giving a view of a jungle of rough stems which vary in thickness according to leaf size. Above this is the heavy leaf canopy, and the whole, when viewed closely, has an almost forest-like effect. Yet how often is this plant seen from this angle? Usually it is in some low-lying swamp so that the eye looks down on a sea of leaves.

The various periods of flowering must also be taken into consideration. In many cases it would be wrong to have two early-flowering groups of plants growing closely together and spread over a large area, unless there are bulbous subjects such as lilies beneath them to give interest and blossom at a later period. Some areas may suit certain types of plant better than others, and this must be taken into account. Bear in mind that a large group of an early-flowering species in the front or near the path leaves a bare space later on, unless care has been taken to provide for a succession. Overall the aim should be to maintain some interest in all parts at all seasons, remembering that a plant need not always be in flower to be interesting (see Plate 3).

The scene can be changed over an area like the views on a kaleidoscope—for example, in the late spring there may be a drift or group of *Primula bulleyana*, running from the front to the back between groups of ferns, with a group of *Rodgersia tabularis* forming the actual background with a tree setting behind. As the primulas pass out of bloom, the ferns will remain, while the rodgersias start to bloom with tall spikes of feathery white flowers, 3 m. (10 ft.) or more in height. Planted up in irregular drifts on the edge of the primulas could be good, substantial groups of a strong-growing lily such as *Lilium pardalinum*. The bold, red and spotted, reflexed flowers would stand out against the plume-like flowers of the rodgersias.

Such a scene, whatever its scale, is built up with imagination, knowledge and love of plants, and there are many variations and combinations that may be considered. The informality and interest can be further enriched by the introduction of bulbous plants, particularly those which will spread and seed. Normally informality is the key word with plants in the shade, even if the feature is in a formal setting. It is emphasized that the outlines to the groups should not be too rigid, and often a mixture of the two adjacent species will avoid a clear demarcation line (see Fig. 11 and Plate 9).

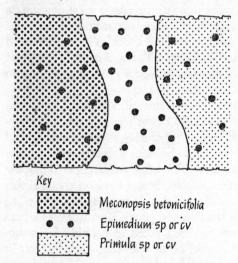

FIG. 11. One method of avoiding a hard outline to groups in a border or bed. An irregular planting of epimediums, a plant with quite a 'hard' and definite foliage, is 'taken in' to neighbouring groups.

Key

Meconopsis betonicifolia

Epimedium sp or cv

Primula sp or cv

Trees often have an important part to play since they usually provide the shade, in an informal setting in particular, but a planting should also make full use of them as a feature. As an example, the base of a tree and the buttress roots are often interesting and if they are, it would be a pity to hide them from view with tall plantings. A distribution of low plants to form a glade or valley of growth running up to the base would show them to good effect. Moreover, such a planting taken round the trunk and beyond it will often introduce an entirely different perspective and bring out new beauties; this technique avoids the often artificial effect which is produced when a low planting is taken up to the trunk and ends at that point.

The effect of the trunks and buttress roots of trees can be extended to the use and appreciation of bark in a shady setting (see

Plate 14). The obvious example is *Betula pendula*, silver birch, too well known to need description, although there are species, forms and cultivars that are considered by some to be superior in their bark effect. Whatever choice is made, it is important not to overdo the bark effect of one type of tree by planting too much of any particular tree over one site. Thus with a birch wood, such plantings as rhododendrons may cover a large number of the trunks up to half way, with just one or two feature plantings of the type already described. For rhododendrons the soil conditions would need to be taken into consideration, but there is a wide variety of evergreens to suit all types of soil. The reader is referred to Part II for information on soil requirements. There are many other trees with an ornamental bark effect and the would-be planter is advised to look closely at the range of species available. One can even go to the extreme of having a very exotic-looking subject such as *Prunus serrula*, which has polished, mahogany-brown bark and is very striking and beautiful; even in a low sun it reflects the light. Thus another effect can be introduced, that of reflection and its opposite, the contrasting and varied depths of shadow. Appreciation of such a planting would depend largely on the setting, for it would be considered by many people not to be in keeping with a wild woodland scene. Again it is stressed, consider carefully before making any planting.

The Use of Colour

Flower colour should be taken into account when grouping and placing shade-loving plants, but generally the quieter tones and shades prevail among them, and usually they combine well with each other. When more definite and bold colours are involved a great deal of care is needed (see Plates 7 and 13). *Lobelia cardinalis*, for example, a perennial which produces vivid scarlet flowers in the mid to late summer period, is sometimes placed on the edge of a shade-planting to give a splash of colour at rather a dull period. This is a good idea, but usually one small group is sufficient. Care is also needed with the bold and clear white blooms. *Rhododendron* 'Palestrina' (evergreen azalea type) has large white flowers in the spring which are very showy and really stand out, but it is inclined to compete with many other plants, particularly those with more delicate colouring. It is not white as such that is being questioned, but this particular intense white.

More subtle is the delicate colour of the giant lily *Cardiocrinum giganteum*, with flowers that are mainly white with shades of light green and maroon, while its foliage forms a wonderful contrast to many of the plants in a woodland setting, a great asset to any planting. Among many others is *Polygonatum multiflorum*, Solomon's seal, which has delicate, white flowers suffused with pale green.

No two people will agree on questions of colour and contrast, and in any case mistakes in colour selection and placement will be toned down by the foliage, especially with shade plants.

Succession of Display and Interest

This is a matter that needs to be considered very carefully, and it concerns the choice of plants as well as their positions in relation to one another and in the plan generally. A knowledge of the capabilities and potentials of the site is therefore important.

It is reasonably easy to have a display during the early months of the year, when growth is green, perhaps with sufficient flowers out to make it colourful in a quiet way. At this time too the trees are breaking into leaf and providing a fresh background. It is later on during the summer, when some of the early plants pass out of flower, that it becomes more difficult to maintain a presentable appearance, yet alone a display. Interest there will always be if the eye and the mind are trained to appreciate it.

A dry site often becomes very difficult later in the year, for the range of plants that will survive and flower or remain in perfect foliage is, in any case, limited. Much can be done by keeping such areas reasonably clean, by cutting off seed heads and by removing plants which have finished their useful life.

On the moister site it is possible to introduce plants which will provide a foliage effect during the summer; hostas or ferns provide suitable examples (see Plates 3 and 13). It is also possible to maintain a succession among groups of plants such as *Meconopsis*, for many species take several years to flower and the collection may be built up year by year. The rosettes, in the different stages, will add to the general effect and the appearance of the group or drift may be enhanced in this way (see Plate 4).

The Use of Contrasts

To a great extent this is a matter of individual taste, but it is important to avoid using too many sharp contrasts in one area. Shade plants, especially in woodland and similar plantings, should promote a quiet, restful atmosphere. At the same time, well-considered contrasting effects make a planting interesting, and can do so much towards improving the general appearance. Many shade-loving plants, when they are well grown, produce lovely foliage effects in both colour and form. The various ferns, with their beautifully dissected and delicate fronds, and the *Hosta* species and cultivars, many of them variegated, may be cited (see Plate 13). When these two groups of plants are used together the result is often very pleasing. To a large extent it is a matter of knowing the plants, when they are likely to be at their best, and what they are capable of; a good result may be achieved after much experimentation.

The scale of the planting also needs to be considered. The two classes of plants already mentioned could be in groups or drifts on a larger scale, or be planted singly on the small site or garden. A large-growing plant needs to be sited very carefully in a small-scale planting, but it is possible to do this successfully. However, really large plants come into their own in the more extensive plantings: *Rodgersia aesculifolia*, with its impressive foliage and feathery spikes of pale cream and green, is in turn dwarfed by the giant *Gunnera manicata*, with its huge, almost rhubarb-like leaves. The two grouped side by side, down a boggy glade in dappled shade, provide a perfect contrast. Rhododendrons and lilies form another lovely contrast in foliage, thus extending the interest well beyond the blossoming period.

Ground-cover Plants

A number of plants which will grow in the shade have been classed as ground-cover plants, but these plantings may take many forms. They copy the conditions which are so often found in nature, with a carpeting of low-growing plants covering the woodland floor, or the ground between shrubs, in a transitional ecology which may be stabilized or reverting back to marsh or woodland. In nature many of these plants will also grow in the sun, and the fact that they are to be found in some areas only in the shade could be the result of their having been driven there, or they may be merely existing on a site which was originally sunny, only to die when the shade becomes too dense.

In the large garden the use of ground-cover plants does allow a more interesting planting, but the extent to which they are used in the smaller garden must depend upon the taste of the owner. Space can be so precious that any one species must be confined to a comparatively small area, in order to grow as great a variety as possible.

Foliage effect is important with ground-cover plants, and for this reason many of the most popular are evergreen, often too with a reflective surface to the leaves. The latter can provide some interesting contrasts, even in the half-light of morning or evening —important for those who leave for work early and return late. Such characteristics are mentioned in Part II. Two of the main points put forward in favour of these plants is that they keep the roots of the larger plants cool and provide more natural conditions, and that when they are fully established they save labour in weeding. Despite these benefits, however, remember that covering may sometimes be invasive, or for some other reason be no longer welcome. It is important to try small batches of likely plants first, selecting those which seem to be the most suitable and trying them on a larger scale before a final decision is made.

It is often claimed that their use reduces maintenance problems, but this is not necessarily true for the first season or so after planting, when additional work may be involved in weeding; watering and so on; only after they have covered in the ground completely is there a significant drop in the time spent on the menial tasks. If a good grower which is well suited to the conditions is selected it will get away quickly after planting, cutting short the time spent in waiting for a full ground cover.

There are two other points to consider if a full coverage is wanted in the shortest possible time. Before planting it pays to clean up the ground as thoroughly as possible; what this will involve depends entirely on the weeds and the problems connected with them—sometimes more than one season's concentrated effort may be involved. The other important point concerns the number of plants of the ground-cover subject used initially. It is surprising how many plants are needed in an operation of this nature, but in most cases plants set at 200 mm. (8 in.) apart are preferable and will give a quicker coverage than those which are placed at 400 mm. (1 ft. 4 in.) from one another. If they are closer than 200 mm. (8 in.) it becomes difficult to weed between them whilst they are becoming established. Propagation is often a problem, and a good ground-cover plant must be easy to raise in large numbers.

There are other, perhaps less important, points to consider; for example the annual leaf-fall from nearby deciduous trees may become a problem with certain ground-cover plants, while others allow the leaves to fall through. For guidance on this and other problems, consult the alphabetical list in Part II.

5

Maintaining a Collection of Shade Plants

Maintenance

Maintenance is an important part of gardening, and it entails not only keeping the garden tidy and beautiful, but also tending each plant, making sure, if this is humanly possible, that it is thriving or growing well. The aim should be to get the best out of the plants and the garden generally. In a natural setting it is important not to be too tidy; it might therefore be felt that such areas are easy to look after without much work, but this is not always the case, and much depends upon the style and intensity of the planting.

It is important to remember this at the planning stage, for it is all too easy to lay out large areas and then to find later that they cannot possibly be maintained. Again it is emphasized that there is much to be gained by taking time to browse and wander around. Plants and their beauty can then be increasingly appreciated through the various seasons, not only when they are in display, and new and improved ideas for making the plants happier or the work easier will come to mind.

It is not necessary to mow grass in a natural setting regularly; indeed such areas are improved and are more interesting if mown only once or twice a year. The stretches of grass can extend beneath trees if these are included in the layout, and many naturalized plants, *Narcissus* spp. for instance, can grow in perfect surroundings. Grass alone is very beautiful, but especially so when it is mixed with grassland species such as *Ranunculus acris*, meadow buttercup. Generally such an area may be mown in late June when the natural grassland coverage is past its best, by which time the bulb foliage will have died down. On the other hand, it will have to be left until the autumn if summer-flowering plants such as *Filipendula ulmaria*, meadow sweet, are present. Specially blended seed mixtures should be used for laying out grass areas in the shade. Accessibility, an important point, can often be achieved satisfactorily by carefully positioned grass paths, regularly mown to keep them short. Shade-loving plants are also grown in the more formal parts of the garden, such as on the edges of lawns, where grass will generally be close mown.

Weeding is as necessary in shade areas as in any other, in fact the growth of weeds may be stronger if the soil is moist and rich. This task is more difficult in the informal garden and among natural groupings of plants, and in addition to being conscientious and careful, it is essential for the weeder to be generally familiar with plants and to be able to recognize which should be saved or discarded. It is an advantage for beginners to learn at an early stage to identify common weeds and time thus spent is never wasted. With completely unskilled labour there is a chance that valuable seedlings may be pulled up and discarded with the weeds. More new and potentially valuable plants are lost each year by careless or indiscriminate weeding than are introduced by skilled hybridization and selection. It is often advantageous to leave non-invasive native plants, for example, *Sanicula europaea*, sanicle, but such pernicious weeds as *Epilobium montanum*, broad-leaved willow herb, should be ruthlessly removed before they spread everywhere. It will be found that certain weeds are difficult to control, no matter how much trouble is taken in trying to get rid of the last one. Sometimes, for example, a bed of primulas will become very weed-ridden over the years, and it is then often preferable to make a fresh start, and allocate the site for a few years to such strong-growing plants as hostas as a means of weed control.

ORGANIC MATERIAL AND ITS IMPORTANCE

An important requirement in the culture of many shade plants is high organic content in the soil. In a natural setting where there are trees, these have a similar high demand, as do shrubs. Organic material is in greatest need over the dry, hungry soils, but it will also decompose more quickly on these. There is also a tendency for organic material to decompose very quickly when it is in thin layers. When, conversely, it is in thick layers, the moisture is held to a greater degree, the material holds together more and compacts. Thus in turn it holds even more moisture, a certain amount of air is excluded and decomposition takes place at a slower rate. This is not a bad thing, for organic matter is usually in such short supply that it can decompose too rapidly; slow decomposition also has the advantage that a supply of whole leaves is built up for the earthworms to take down—they dislike small pieces. A very thick, impervious layer of large, partly rotted leaves is not advocated, for this is harmful, but it is wrong to speed up the process beyond the pace that nature intended.

The organic material for a shade garden needs dividing into two kinds if there are trees present:

Firstly, there is the dead vegetative material which includes the weeds removed during the process of cleaning up—this should be rotted in a properly made compost heap for returning to the soil at a later date. Most weeds, even the pernicious perennial ones such as *Aegopodium podagraria*, bishop's weed, can be included if it is dealt with in the right manner. The one or two species of *Oxalis* which are bad weeds should be disposed of by burning, or burying deeply, as the tiny bulbils tend to fall down the sides of the heap, thus escaping the rotting process. Secondly, there are the leaves which have to be collected in the shade garden where there are trees. These are a valuable source of organic material and should be stored for one or two years in a wire netting enclosure which will keep them together. One or two turns during this period should be sufficient for them to reach a reasonably rotted condition, without breaking the material down too much and thereby losing the bulk.

It is a mistake to rake the leaves from beneath trees for this will deprive them of a valuable mulch and will encourage them to root more freely into nearby beds and borders where there is more food and moisture. It must be remembered too that leaves as they fall from the deciduous trees in the autumn form an attractive carpet, and they should be left for a time, if this is possible, to be enjoyed. Also there is no point in clearing up only to find things as bad soon afterwards, and if it is very wet, considerable damage may be caused to lawn and soil surfaces by raking. Should any special plants be covered, a restricted area may be cleared round them. Most of the borders need be cleared only once, after the bulk of the leaves have fallen, the paths perhaps several times, depending upon their use.

Sheltering trees or shrubs with low branching help to hold in fallen leaves and prevent them from blowing about over vast areas; the planting as a whole will benefit from the extra organic

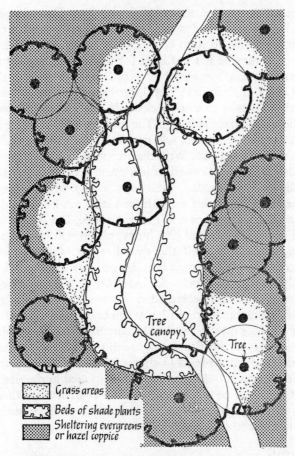

FIG. 12. The conservation of organic material by
suitable plantings. The annual leaf fall may be confined
within a given area with such plantings as evergreen
thickets or hazel coppice.

material and work will be reduced (see Fig. 12). An extensive
planting of such cover is not necessary to be effective, and there
are a few species that will survive under very dry and shady conditions; for example *Sambucus nigra*, elder, will put up with a lot
and it will branch low to hold in leaves.

Mulching is generally best carried out during the early winter,
when most herbaceous plants have died down to the surface.
Often this task can be combined with cutting down the dead

herbaceous stems and the general clean up. On a large scale, especially, there is an advantage in doing it this way, for the task of identifying the position of groups of plants is easier, and certain groups may be left until last for this reason. It may also be necessary to leave some groups until later in order to enjoy the winter effect of their dead but decorative stems and seed heads. As a rule it is easier to work backwards, using a plank if necessary to avoid undue consolidation. The material for mulching should be fine and well prepared, and consist of compost or leafmould, or a mixture of the two. With the stronger growers a portion of well-decayed manure mixed in is a great help. It is advisable to have the various mixtures handy at the edge of the planting so that the requirements of the various plants can be catered for.

All these preparations and care take time, but if this work is carried out carelessly and in a hurry, plants will be lost and the resulting gaps will spoil the overall effect. Often then it is necessary to get right down beside a group and spread the layer carefully with a hand fork—for example, with *Primula* generally the crowns must not be buried. Perhaps among these a 20 mm. layer of fine material would be sufficient, while a 60 mm. thickness of a coarse dressing would be suitable for larger subjects.

Some plants start earlier into growth than others; for example, muscari are above ground in the early winter. This means that early developers should be carefully positioned in the first place, so that they can be attended to at the right time without upsetting the remainder; it can be a mistake to have such early plants in a prominent position or in too large a group.

WATERING

It is difficult to lay down any hard and fast rules about watering because so many factors are involved and naturally much depends upon the prevailing weather. It must be remembered that a drought during the early spring is likely to result in more serious damage and losses than one during the late summer, and that once watering is started it must be kept up if dry weather continues, for the growth will be lush and strong, and the plants will need more water to maintain this. There is one other important point to consider: if watering is carried out, it must be done thoroughly, which means really soaking the soil, otherwise the roots will just develop on the suface in the hope of getting a little and often. One good soak every fortnight or three weeks is usually sufficient for most soils and situations.

Those who have a reliable spring or stream on their property are lucky, but because of deeper pumping for the public water supply, many sources which were reliable years ago are now drying up. The drought of 1976 proved that lack of water could become a serious national problem; there was hardly enough for ordinary household use, and at a time like this plants must at the best take a second place. It is therefore very important to bear this in mind and to select the most suitable species. The planting of moisture-lovers on a site that is likely to dry up during even an ordinary summer, is unwise, but if they must be included, they should be limited in number and concentrated in one area where they can be looked after.

The presence of a particular moisture-loving species on a site is some guide, but on its own is not sufficient. The plant in question may just be clinging on or even dying out, owing to some changed circumstances, for example, a reduction in the moisture availability through a falling water table. Again the moisture-loving species may be found only in certain areas on a site and this can easily be overlooked. To take a simple example, the bluebell can survive on a dry soil and may cover almost an entire area, within which there may be isolated pockets and drifts of *Allium ursinum*, ramsons, the white onion-like flower. This requires a moist soil, and the moist areas can often be picked out this way; sometimes it is difficult to explain, but obviously they are damper for a reason. It is wise to work with nature, and to arrange the planting so that the moisture-lovers go into the damp spots. Not only will they have more moisture as a matter of course, but if it does set in very dry, these should be the areas which it is easiest to water. Sometimes the absence of particular plants should give cause for concern. The male fern, *Dryopteris filix-mas*, is very tolerant of conditions which are dry for quite long periods, but if there are no ferns at all the question must be asked, why? Again, if the epiphytical fern, *Polypodium vulgare*, polypody, is growing freely on the tree trunks and branches it can be taken that there is quite considerable moisture in the atmosphere and that the site as a whole has a medium to heavy rainfall; but this rainfall may not be held to any extent in the soil which may therefore dry out quickly. All this makes it essential to see and watch a proposed site for shade-lovers over a period of a year at least before deciding upon a final plan and the species to plant up.

One of the advantages of concentrating moisture-lovers together on a dry site is that one is able to build up shelter, which helps to conserve moisture and also surrounds the plants with a humid atmosphere. A group of *Meconopsis betonicifolia*, for example, may be flowering beautifully but be completely ruined by a hot dry wind should the site be too exposed. In this case it is not just a question of moisture, for the plants may be very well supplied with this at the roots, but is due to a lack of humidity. In bad cases the blossoms will wilt and become dried and the display will be ruined. The other factor to be borne in mind is that any trees in the vicinity of an area which is kept moist, while the site as a whole is a dry one, will quickly find it and root in extensively for any extra moisture they can pick up; this is dealt with in detail in Chapter 2. Mulching also helps and it is sometimes sufficient to 'bridge over' a dry period—a subject discussed in detail earlier in this chapter.

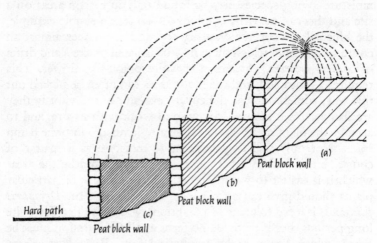

FIG. 13. Where the peat garden is terraced, with a built in irrigation system, it is often beneficial to have the better drained medium at the higher level (a). The closest medium in the lowest level (c) allows a wider lateral movement of moisture, but as it is the furthest away from the irrigation nozzle, it thus receives less water from this source. The hard path allows accessibility, an important point with this feature, where treading feet would destroy the walls.

The removal of dead flowers and unwanted developing fruits is a great help to plants under normal conditions, but the more so when they are under stress during a drought.

If water is given it should be applied gently, and the irrigator or spray provides the best means of doing this. On a small scale, or when sufficient for only one or a few plants is needed, a watering can with a fine rose is suitable. Watering by an open hose may result in some damage to plants and is often not very effective (see Fig. 13). A fine spray with water like a dew, is a great help, even though the plants may be much too dry at the roots, as most plants are capable of absorbing moisture through the leaves, but it is best to apply the spray at night when it does not dry up so quickly.

If there is an adequate supply for irrigation purposes it is often a good plan to water following a light insufficient rain. Often a humid atmosphere prevails for a time, so the extra given as a result of the application will soak in better and do much good. Sometimes it is possible, if a light rain is forecast but is only a possibility, to irrigate during rain. Another effective way of using irrigation is to make up for a low winter rainfall by heavily irrigating among trees, even during the very early spring. In this way the trees more contentedly root in their own area, instead of extending into other areas in search of extra moisture.

Part Two

A DICTIONARY OF
SHADE PLANTS

Introduction

I must emphasize that this 'dictionary' is by no means complete, and there are many plants, some common, some quite rare, that have not been included. A number even of those which are discussed are not easy to obtain, but there is much to be gained by exchanging experiences and plants with others, particularly through the membership of the various societies.

The compilation of the list has not been easy, for a number of plants require shade in the southern part of the country, where it is generally warmer, while in the north they will sometimes do well right out in the open—some *Primula* spp. for example. Even on a local scale the climate, the soil and many other factors come into the picture. The object therefore is to give here some account of the range of plants available for consideration.

Over the years many forms and cultivars of the species mentioned have become available in the nursery trade—indeed, these may be the only ones offered from that source. The intending buyer is advised whenever possible to see the plants in growth and flower before making a choice.

Plants that are growing in the shade of other subjects, be they trees or shrubs, need to be studied and experimented with more than plants growing in the open, because both the shade-producing plant and the plant in the shade itself must grow together. It is hoped that this guide gives some indication of where there is scope for thought and experiment.

Every effort has been made to bring the nomenclature right up-to-date but it is impossible to achieve this in every case, for changes continue to be made. Common names have been included where appropriate.

The method of propagation has been given for many plants, but this has been mainly confined to the herbaceous subjects. Tree and shrub propagation in particular is so specialized that it seems preferable to make little mention of it, rather than to deal with it inadequately.

Alphabetical List of Genera

Acanthus Acanthaceae

The members of this genus, belonging to the large and mainly tropical family Acanthaceae, are valued for their foliage and flower effects. The strongest and best species is *A. mollis*, bear's breeches, a plant with bold, deeply lobed foliage and impressive 1·3 m. (4 ft. 3 in.) high spikes of white and purple flowers with prominent hooded bracts which are coloured green and tinged with purple. The main flowering period is July and August, but odd spikes may appear during the autumn while in a mild winter most of the foliage remains green.

It is a very tough plant and able to grow among other strong plants including coarse grass, thriving as well in a very light, dappled shade or part shade as in the sun. It can be used effectively in shaded herbaceous plantings and is also a good coastal plant. *A. mollis* prefers well-drained and even light soils, which is not surprising when it is remembered that it is native to southern Europe, and is likely to be more successful among trees and shrubs in the warmer positions and localities.

Division in the spring is the normal means of increase, but the seed and root cutting methods of propagation are also successful.

Acer Aceraceae

The maples in general do best in a sunny position, but the so-termed Japanese maples, made up of *A. japonicum*, *A. palmatum* and the various cultivars of each, are an exception. They are often quite happy in a position of part shade where they are sheltered from cold east winds in the spring. They will also thrive in a very light, dappled shade among widely spaced trees, provided they do not meet too much competition for moisture; deep, moist, well-drained soils are preferable. They hate being dried up during the height of the summer and if this happens the foliage shrivels. In a hot dry district *A. p.* 'Senkaki' appreciates dappled shade, which prevents the foliage burning badly.

Aconitum   Ranunculaceae

These popular perennials referred to as monkshoods are commonly found in herbaceous borders, where they are valued for their
spikes of hooded flowers, which give colour late in the season
from July to September when it is most needed. They are at their
best in a deep, fertile soil which has been well manured, and where
irrigation is available if needed. Under dry conditions the palmately lobed or divided leaves, which are carried well up the
flowering stem to add greatly to the beauty of these plants, soon
wither and the appearance generally is spoilt. This is hardly surprising when it is remembered that many genera in the family
Ranunculaceae have a high moisture requirement. They are quite
happy in limy soils. These plants are often grown in full sun, but
in many localities they will do equally well, if not a little better,
with some shade. Certainly the early blossoms will be better
coloured and last far longer in shade.

In addition to the many species that are spread throughout the
northern temperate zone there are a number of well known
hybrids and cultivars. Many of the more recent introductions are
shorter and do not need staking—'Bressingham Spire' for example, with violet-blue flowers, reaches 1 m. (3 ft. 3 in.) high,
while 'Ivorine', with slender spikes of ivory-white flowers, is
even shorter.

Aconitums have a stiff, rather formal appearance, and for this
reason they are generally thought to be better suited to the more
formal parts of the garden where they may be grouped with
other herbaceous plants in dappled shade, part shade or even
shade.

Propagation is normally by division.

All aconitums are very poisonous indeed and there have been
many cases of the tuberous roots being mistaken for a vegetable
and eaten, usually with fatal results. These plants should not be
grown near vegetable gardens or in areas likely to be cultivated
for crops at a later date. It is dangerous also to save their seed,
since they could be mistaken for vegetables.

Actaea   Ranunculaceae

These are perennial herbs suitable for a mid to background planting in a woodland or shade garden. There they add greatly to the

C

effect, especially in dappled shade with light and shadow playing on the foliage and picking out the spikes of white flowers with their prominent stamens; later the shiny fruits reflect light even from the darkest places—so attractive, especially to children, and yet so deadly poisonous.

A. spicata, herb Christopher, baneberry, a rare native of northern England, makes an impressive clump of aruncus-like foliage with leafy spikes, 700 mm. (2 ft. 4 in.) tall, of white flowers that start to open during June and appear over a period of several weeks. Soon the heads of shiny fruits follow—at first they are green, then red and finally, if the birds leave them alone for long enough, a deep plum colour. *A. rubra* from North America has finely segmented foliage which is effective even at an early stage soon after the growths appear above the ground in April. It is very pleasing in a group or drift with the tightly packed buds appearing in spikes above the pleasant green foliage, the stems being darker and thus adding to a charming picture. *A. alba*, from the northern temperate zone, has white fruits, but it is taller, growing up to a metre (3 ft. 3 in.) and really needs support from a few hazel branches thinly positioned.

The baneberries, like so many other plants in this family, must not dry out, otherwise the foliage quickly loses condition; therefore they need a good damp soil and site. If happy they will spread beneath such evergreen shrubs as rhododendrons if there is enough space for them and they are lovers of dappled shade.

They may be propagated by division and of course by seed if it can be obtained.

Adiantum   Polypodiaceae

A large genus of ferns which is mainly tropical and warm temperate. Apart from one native species, *A. capillus-veneris*, which is very rare indeed, there are two species which are grown in the open in this country.

A. pedatum, from North America and elsewhere, has a choice appearance and yet, if happy, is quite a strong grower. At maturity the branched fronds are held on 500 mm. (1 ft. 8 in.) high stems which are thin and very dark coloured. With an established plant the fronds form a thick cluster which may be 600 mm. (2 ft.) or more wide. During mid April when the delicate fronds first appear they are a very pale bronze in colour. This is the stage when shelter from cold east winds is appreciated. The cultivar 'Klondyke' has an even deeper colouring at this stage. *A. venustum*, from the Himalayas, is on the borderline of hardiness and has broadly triangular fronds which are finely branched and delicate, usually reaching little more than half the height of *A. pedatum*. During mild winters the fronds often remain green.

Both species should be grown in shade, for the fronds are liable to scorch if a strong sun reaches them. They are plants for a selected position in a woodland or shade garden near the front or path, where the delicate fronds can be appreciated and the plants can be looked after properly, for they need careful cultivation. Suitable conditions may also be found in shaded rock or stone-work, for which the dwarf forms of *A. pedatum* are suggested, especially in the smaller garden. In addition to shade, a cool and sheltered site with a moist but well-drained and peaty soil is needed.

Propagation is by careful division and replanting in the spring.

Adlumia   Fumariaceae

A. fungosa, climbing fumitory, is a biennial from North America. In the spring the fine parsley-like foliage is very attractive, especially in the early morning as the leaves glisten with dew.

By June plants which are in their second year produce climbing and trailing growths, with reddish stems that extend for several feet. They will ramble quite freely and will cover shrubs up to a height of 1·5 m. (5 ft.) or more, clinging by means of tendrils which are part of a compound leaf system. The pale pink tubular flowers, typical of the family, are borne on short axillary racemes throughout the summer months. It is a plant for the dappled shade where an informal effect is desired, and where the nearby supporting shrubs are not too choice.

Propagation is by seed, but often there are sufficient self-sown ones to supply continuity.

Aesculus   Hippocastanaceae

A. parviflora, a bushy horse chestnut with a height of 3 to 5 m. (10 to 16 ft.), is a popular, July-to-August flowering subject, which is undoubtedly happiest in an open, sunny position. However, it has been chosen to show how some plants are capable of adapting to a situation, making the fullest use of all there is to offer. When grown on the edge of a thin scattering of trees, the suckerous growths which it normally produces will develop between the trees on the shaded side. The growths are long with little branching, but with large, thin leaves, and root shallowly into the surface layer of organic material.

Ajuga   Labiatae

A. reptans, bugle. It is only in more recent times that this lowly plant has found its way into our gardens. Even so, it must have been noticed in earlier days when, during May and into June, some lightly shaded ride or clearing in the woods and forests took on a bluish glow as countless thousands of the lipped blossoms opened, causing the passer-by to stare in wonder at a display which dared to rival even that of the bluebell. Today many of the same rides have become overgrown, but where this plant does abound its displays can quite easily be shown to full effect, simply by cutting tall herbage every autumn and raking the bulk off so that the plant can be seen. This is necessary, for the pairs of leaves have very short internodes, with the result that the plant hugs the ground closely during the winter, colonizing by means of short stolons. A number of coloured-leaved forms, such as 'Purpurea', are available, and it is through these, coupled with the fact that it is a good evergreen ground-cover plant, that it has become so popular in our gardens.

In nature bugle is found on moist but not boggy soils, in dappled shade, part shade and full sun, although in the latter case it is often shaded during the summer by taller plants. In the garden, as a reward for the protection it is given from competition with stronger plants which it experiences in the wild, it is more accommodating, but still prefers a moist position in dappled shade or part shade, and has a distinct dislike of the hot, sunny positions. There are many situations for these plants in the garden if conditions are suitable, including the more formal features such as shrub borders and herbaceous plantings in the shade. The forms with deep-coloured foliage are very much in keeping with patio settings and against other stonework. It is an excellent subject to overgrow a position which is occupied with summer and autumn flowering bulbs like *Orchis purpurea*. *A. pyramidalis* has taller spikes of dark blue flowers.

The propagation of *A. reptans* and its forms is a matter of straightforward division, in either autumn or early spring. With some cultivars the use of a frame may be necessary for propagation purposes.

Alchemilla   Rosaceae

This is a large and confusing genus. *A. mollis*, generally considered to have been introduced from eastern Europe, is referred to commonly as lady's mantle, but that name is also applied to a whole group in this genus. The leaves, palmate with rounded lobes, are silky, being covered with minute hairs, a feature not associated with true shade-loving plants. The effect through the winter is attractive, as the leaves are clustered over the spreading crowns, especially after rains or dews, when the drops are held on the surfaces (see Plate 1). During late May and June the branched heads of pale yellow flowers develop to 500 mm. (1 ft. 8 in.) above the foliage. By August, when it has finished the main flowering, the brown heads remain, heavy with developing seeds, lying on the foliage and looking generally untidy. This is the time to cut these off, for soon afterwards new leaves appear with a few scattered heads of flower which develop later.

It is a plant for the sun, although it will give a very good account of itself in light, dappled shade but does not grow aggressively into a shady position. It will grow in a wide variety of soils, but shows considerable impatience with the drier types. It is suitable for planting in a newly formed shrub border, where it appreciates the more open conditions, and also for a lightly shaded, herbaceous planting. Try it first on a small scale, for example in a group near the front, where it can be tidied up when necessary, without treading over the bed. Propagation is by division during the late autumn or spring but self-sown seedlings are usually available. Plant at 180 mm. (7 in.) apart.

A. hopiana var. *conjunta*, is a small grower for a shady recess in the rock garden, although it will grow well in the sun. Its potentilla-like foliage is edged with a thin strip of white which is most attractive, and it has pale yellow flowers.

Allium   Liliaceae

The vast majority of the species, distinctively smelling of onion or garlic, are sun-lovers, but there are two species worthy of naturalizing in dappled shade.

A. triquetrum, triquetrous garlic, from the western mediterranean region, has white flowers, which are produced during May and June and hang in clusters from a height of 300 mm. (1 ft.). Each petal has a thin green line on the outside, which gives it a most captivating appearance. The innocent, captured by its charms, could easily plant it in a favoured part of the rock garden, but would regret it later during hours of weeding, for it spreads in ever increasing circles. *A. ursinum*, ramsons, is a native which will colonize in damper parts, and will often oust the bluebell in restricted areas on its home ground. Ramsons has clear green foliage which forms a perfect background for the close heads of pure white flowers, which appear at the end of May.

Both species are suitable for planting under 'natural' conditions in dappled shade well away from cultivated areas.

Andromeda   Ericaceae

A. polifolia, bog rosemary, is an interesting little native ericaceous plant, and is available in several forms. Those which are dwarf are particularly suitable for peat beds or peat retaining walls. This plant must never dry out at the roots, and also requires a cool environment, high humidity and an acid soil. In the dry and hot areas of the south, these conditions are best gained by shelter and light partial shade.

Anemone   Ranunculaceae

These plants are often remembered first by spring scenes which have been made up in part by drifts of our native *A. nemorosa*, wood anemone, running through an area of deciduous woodland, and it is fitting therefore to account for this species first. It is found in many parts of the country and on various soils, including those over chalk, but it appears to be happiest on the rich loams and heavier soils. In many cases, drifts will already be growing in an area designed for a woodland garden, but the plant is easily established, provided the soil is right, and may even become a nuisance by appearing in beds and areas where it is not welcome. Sometimes, spreading either by means of the rhizomes or seed, it will appear in quite sunny positions and it does this in common with many other anemones. If found in such a position in the wild, it is sometimes accounted for by the fact that the wood or hedgerow has been removed, the colony having been left to fend for itself. This it will do quite easily provided the surrounding herbage is not too rank.

On unsuitable soils, for example the poor and dry sands or gravels, it is often only necessary to dig in a quantity of clay or heavy soil to bring about success. In some cases, the addition of chalk is sufficient, but this should only be carried out, if at all, after careful thought, for it may upset other plant communities.

A. nemorosa flowers during March and April and the foliage dies down soon after midsummer, but the area can remain interesting by the introduction of such plants as ferns.

There are many forms and cultivars of the wood anemone, but these may be considered for planting on a more limited scale, perhaps in a partly shaded border. The whole range, including the type species, would be suitable for the town garden. Choose the position carefully, for the flowers only open fully when the sun reaches them. The thin rhizomes may be planted during the dormant season, preferably in the autumn.

A. blanda, from eastern Europe, is one of the earliest anemones to flower, and is generally out during March. It is often seen in shades of blue, but the range of colour is much greater, extending to pink and white. There are a number of fine cultivars including 'Atrocoerulea', which produces a strong mat of foliage, finely segmented, 75 mm. (3 in.) high, and large, clear blue flowers, freely produced, on 150 mm. (6 in.) stems. It is attractive, with the blue petals showing up distinctly, even when it is in bud, while in common with the other species it is in flower over a period of several weeks. This is a species which naturalizes even in short, thin grass, and often shows a preference for spreading into quite sunny positions. However, it will grow and flower well in dappled or part shade.

A. apennina, from Italy and the Balkans, is usually in flower a few weeks later, in April (see Plate 14). The growths often appear above the surface in February, however, and it is important to apply any mulching early, to avoid damage to these. As with the former species, the appearance of the first leaves above the surface is interesting. With *A. apennina* the petioles, at first coloured pink, are bent, the leaves being drawn up through to the surface like germinating peas. There is a white form, but reversion to blue often takes place among the seedlings, when the group or drift becomes mixed, which makes it even more beautiful and pleasing to the eye. Both *A. blanda* and *A. apennina* have corms which should be planted in the early autumn.

A. rivularis produces a buttercup-like foliage 100 mm. (4 in.) or more high, while during the early summer it flowers on leafy and branched stems 300 mm. (1 ft.) in height. These flowers are white, similar to those of the Japanese anemone, and they stand out very well against rock or stonework. It is a suitable plant for a moist and shady pocket in the rock garden, also for a narrow, shaded border against a wall. Undoubtedly it would also thrive in a moist area in the woodland, or shade garden, provided it could be cared for and protected against stronger and more invasive subjects.

A. x *hybrida* is a term which relates to a set of cultivars known as Japanese anemones. They flower at a useful time during the late summer and early autumn. Coupled with this, they have a reputation for growing well in a shady position, but this is true to only a limited extent; once established they creep about and will often find a position which suits them better. This may be in part shade, where they get a great deal of sun at times. However, the group will accommodate to a position in shade, although flowering may suffer a little. They will spread through shrub borders. In a rhododendron border a small group here and there will produce some welcome colour at a dull time of year.

How wonderfully the flowers appear against stonework too! There are many fine cultivars, so the best advice is to see them in flower and then to be patient for a year or two after planting, for they are slow to establish. In common with so many of their family, this group prefers a heavy soil which does not dry out rapidly.

Propagation is by division during the dormant season; great care must be taken as the roots are brittle.

Anthriscus   Umbelliferae

A. sylvestris, cow parsley, is a very common native, found by the roadsides, in hedgerows and beneath thinly spaced deciduous trees, for this species thrives in sun or light dappled shade, often with grass. It usually flowers in May and has a much branched and compound umbel a metre (3 ft. 3 in.) or more in height. The myriads of small white flowers of a large colony throw a thin mist-like veil over the herbage beneath—bluebells, arums, woodland grasses and so on. Such an effect will be appreciated in areas, large and small, where our native plants are encouraged.

As the flowers drop and the seed matures the plant assumes a brown and dried appearance. By this time the flowering grasses and other plants will hide it until the annual cut is made. During the autumn the rosettes of light green, parsley-like leaves develop to produce an interesting and pleasant effect through to flowering time.

Should this plant be considered to be too plentiful it may be discouraged by slicing off the developing growths in the spring, using a Dutch hoe or sickle, thus allowing the other plants to remain and flower. On the other hand, a delay in making the general cut until the seed has been scattered will prove an encouragement.

Antirrhinum   Scrophulariaceae

This is regarded as a genus of sun lovers, and the alpine species in particular must have sun. However, the various strains and selections of snapdragon commonly grown in our gardens for display and bedding purposes are not quite so demanding and although they thrive best in the sun, they will flower in the shade provided that the position is not cold and draughty. There are dwarf strains which are suitable for window-boxes, but there are many others, all for varied uses and beautifully described and illustrated in seedsmen's catalogues. They usually thrive best in a neutral or alkaline soil.

Aquilegia   Ranunculaceae

This group, so well known as columbines, have effective foliage as well as a charming, fresh and colourful flower display. Many of the species and cultivars have glaucous, segmented leaves, on which the raindrops glisten and hold together intact.

A. vulgaris, a native, is sometimes successful when introduced into the dappled shade of light woodland, but there are many hybrid strains which are available from seedsmen. They may be raised from seed sown in an open bed in June, and after being pricked out into nursery rows, are planted out in their flowering quarters in October. They flower during the following June–July. These types are suitable for herbaceous plantings, not as part of a natural layout. Although they are usually given a sunny position, they will often thrive even better in the coolness of dappled shade or part shade. They are even successful in shade, are attractive against stonework, and are well suited to the town garden. They thrive best in a deep, rich soil to which lime is added if necessary.

Many of the species are alpine forms, and are exacting in their requirements. Some, such as *A. glandulosa*, do well in a shady part of the rock garden.

Arabis
Cruciferae

A. caucasica (*A. albida*) is most commonly grown and generally (and quite rightly) a sunny position is selected by choice. Nevertheless it will grow in part shade or even shade, either on a dry retaining wall or in a well-drained formal border, and under these conditions it will flower and keep surprisingly neat. Overhanging trees may cause rot through drip and leaf-fall, and such positions should be avoided. *Arabis* is suitable for shaded window-boxes.

Arctostaphylos
Ericaceae

A. uva-ursi, red bearberry, is an evergreen carpeting species from the northern hemisphere which spreads by means of growths extending over the soil surface during the growing season. From these a close branch system develops, the white and pink flowers being produced during the spring and early summer. Often these are followed by a crop of red fruits. The foliage is dark green, the new growths produced during the summer being lighter in colour, which provides a pleasant and interesting effect.

This species should be planted approximately 200 to 300 mm. (8 in. to 1 ft.) apart in groups or drifts. Plenty of peat should be added, for it is an ericaceous subject and a lover of acid soils. It will grow in the open, but is equally at home in light shade, and will extend into denser shade, beneath and between even the smaller rhododendrons.

Propagation is by seed or late summer cuttings.

Arenaria
Caryophyllaceae

A. balearica is a prostrate plant, closely related to the sandworts and pearlworts. Its habit is to creep over damp and shady rock or stonework, with minute much-branched stems and leaves forming a close and pleasant carpet of green. During the late spring and early summer the mat of foliage is covered with small, white, star-shaped flowers on short thin stalks.

The plant is perfectly at home in many parts of this country and has occasionally become naturalized. In neglected and over-grown gardens it often remains thriving on rock and stone surfaces, while the majority of the once cultivated plants have disappeared beneath the encroaching thickets.

The Balearic pearlwort must have a shaded and damp position, and the softer sandstones suit it better than rocks and stones with a very hard surface. The fine roots gain a good foothold on the porous surface of the former types, which does not dry out quickly. This little plant may be grown on rocks, walls, and also in paving, and wherever it is successful the feature assumes a more mature appearance. It is suitable for the town and patio garden.

Establishment of *Arenaria* over a rock or wall-face may be brought about by planting rooted pieces at the base, in either spring or autumn. It will then creep over every possible surface and position in the vicinity.

Arisaema   Araceae

A. candidissimum, from western China, never disappoints, and it is just the type of plant one would expect to find in some quiet shady place. It is often found in a woodland setting but why not in shaded town gardens? One never tires of it. The large tri-foliate leaves, often a full 500 mm. (1 ft. 8 in.) in height, have an interesting venation pattern of parallel veins from the midrib, and also a marginal pattern. In the early stages of growth they are a pleasant, glaucous green, very effective among other shade lovers.

However, often the first sign of life, even before the appearance of the foliage, is in June when the arum-like flowers appear. These are white with green veinal markings on the outside, and a flush-ing of pale rose inside nearer the base of the spathe. There is also a form which has a pure white spathe.

The foliage dies down in the autumn, often with a crop of bright orange-coloured fruits which can be used for propagation, but the tuberous roots can also be divided when dormant. A good posi-tion is just off the path or edge, where the plants can be ap-preciated. They require dappled shade and a moist soil well stocked with organic material.

There are a number of other beautiful species in this genus which are worth growing outside, for example. *A. sikokianum*, from Japan, which has a white spathe striped with green and purple. *A. triphyllum*, from North America, is the Jack-in-the-pulpit which has been grown in this country for centuries. The spathes, which have the hooded appearance so typical of many of this genus, are green and white on the outside, brown and white within.

Arisarum   Araceae

A. proboscideum, a strange, low-growing plant from Italy, is well worth a place in a light woodland setting. It loves a moist soil in dappled shade, and should be planted by a path or edge where it can be inspected closely.

The early appearance of the tiny and crowded leaves spearing the surface, often in late February, is attractive, as is the tight canopy of intensely green, pointed, arum-like leaves, which develops soon afterwards. Interest is added to this when blossoming takes place a few weeks later, for the flowers are hidden by the leaves, except for narrow tips or tails which protrude above the general canopy. They are green and brown, but white at the base. By July, the foliage has died down completely.

An easy method of propagation is by division during the dormant season.

Armeria   Plumbaginaceae

The species and cultivars known commonly as thrifts are ideal for hugging rocky faces and stone-work. Usually found in a sunny position, they can also be grown successfully in the shade; while there is less flower, the tight tufted habit remains. They are ideal for providing a contrast in habit of growth, and for furnishing a north-facing dry retaining wall.

Arum   Araceae

Arums with their foliage effect can add much to the atmosphere of a woodland setting. The native, *A. maculatum*, known to most as lords and ladies, or cuckoo pint, is most commonly found in hedgerows and woodlands and, with the bluebell, will grow in all but the shadiest of places, being beaten only by the ivy, which will survive under evergreens.

The place for this plant is in the uncultivated parts of the woodland garden, where it will grow very well in dappled shade or part shade. The triangular leaves, produced from a tuberous root in the early spring, are sometimes spotted black, a variation which invariably stimulates interest. The very pale green spathes produced in the late spring are not showy, but again they add to the general effect, which is so important. Finally come the heads of scarlet fruits, which mature in the late summer—very effective, but unfortunately poisonous to man. It is not suggested that this arum should actually be brought in to grow with such plants as primulas and meconopsis, for it may become a nuisance by establishing itself where it is not wanted; but if a little informal corner in a town garden can be found for it, it will introduce a breath of the country.

A. italicum, from south east Europe and other places including the Canary Islands, comes into foliage late in the autumn and survives the winter in leaf, and despite the fact that it becomes limp during frosts, it will survive. The venation is the attraction with this plant, and with a good form—'Pictum' for instance—the colouring can be most attractive. Often the main veins are lined with yellow, while the remainder of the leaf is a glossy green. During the spring the clumps grow taller and bolder, reaching a height of 500 mm. (1 ft. 8 in.) or more. The spathes are again a pale green, but the heads of fruits, a shiny green at first, are quite conspicuous, especially if the old dead foliage is cleared away. Before the summer is out, the birds will have eaten the 'berries', often while they are still green. Then just the main stems are left standing with the white 'berry' stalks remaining, a curious effect. A plant for dappled shade, part shade, or shade, in the woodland, shade garden or shade border.

Propagation is by division during the dormant season.

Aruncus   Rosaceae

A. dioicus (*A. sylvester*, *Spiraea aruncus*), is a stately herbaceous plant which produces strong flowering shoots which grow up to a height of 2 m. (6 ft. 7 in.) or more. The tiny, white flowers are held on branched plumes with a medium green foliage running well up the flowering stems. The leaves themselves are broken up into leaflets—a perfect combination giving just the right atmosphere for the dappled shade of the woodland or wild garden—

even in grass it will hold its own. This plant loves a moist situation, and for the most luxuriant growth and flowering, a deep, rich soil is best. However, it thrives on the clays and although these can crack and be very dry at times, it appears that the promise of wet conditions for long periods in the future is sufficient for it. If planted in a group, the plants should be at least a metre (3 ft. 3 in.) apart. It will readily divide during the dormant season. A magnificent plant for the right setting, not to be packed in an odd corner.

Arundinaria   Gramineae

Bamboos are very confusing because they are so much alike at first sight. The purpose of this small account is to describe and emphasize the characteristics and qualities of two species only, from a large number which can be grown in various degrees of shade.

A. nitida is a very graceful bamboo from China, with canes 3 m. (10 ft.) long or more, these being flushed with purple-black in places. As the leafy branches develop, the stems arch over in a most attractive manner. It is a vigorous grower and forms a thick and spreading clump. The species is a good one for furnishing among trees, in dappled shade or part shade, and will act as a good contrast to other foliage plants, such as rhododendrons.

This species, with others, is a fine one for growing in tubs which are to stand in shady places, but under these conditions care must be taken to see that they do not dry out. Again with others, this bamboo is most effective against brick or stone-work, relieving the harshness and making the area more acceptable.

A. vagans, from Japan, is a creeping species which often reaches no more than 500 mm. (1 ft. 8 in.) in height. It will grow equally well in sun or shade, making the most of the site available to it; it will even creep under beech or holly in places, and in its habit of growth it is most aggressive. It is a plant for the informal woodland planting in the larger garden.

There are a number of other species which are suitable for use in an informal woodland or tree planting, including one giant which reaches 5 m. (16 ft. 4 in.) in height—too large for a small garden. This is *A. fastuosa* from Japan, but it needs a sheltered position, otherwise it is blown about badly.

Bamboos generally will grow on a wide variety of soils, but it is

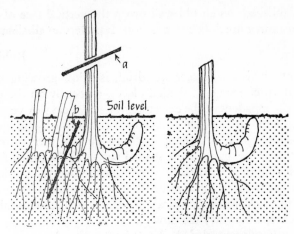

FIG. 14. The propagation of bamboos. (*left*) The portion
is removed from the parent clump at (b), so that it is
made up of a mature cane formed during the previous
season, and a shoot which will develop into a cane in
the forthcoming season. The cane is then shortened as at
(a). (*right*) The piece or 'culm' is planted with the
growing tip just beneath the soil surface.

advisable to add plenty of leafmould to give them a good start as
the site is being prepared. All are impatient of being dried out,
particularly on a light soil.

Most bamboos are best propagated by division in early May,
taking pieces from the outside of the clump. These consist of the
lower end of a cane made during the previous year, to which a
new developing cane is attached (see Fig. 14). These are referred
to as culms, and are planted in a prepared site at 300 mm. (1 ft.)
apart. At this early stage, when they are widely spaced, they are
very prone to the attacks of water fowl which love to eat the
young shoots as they break through the soil. A wire netting protection may be necessary to keep out the birds until the clumps
thicken.

Asarina   Scrophulariaceae

A. procumbens, from southern Europe, is a trailing plant closely
related to the genus *Antirrhinum*. The greyish leaves are heart-
shaped and lobed, while the large, pale yellow flowers are
produced throughout the summer months. This plant will thrive,

once established, on an old wall or on the vertical face of rock-work, even in a north-facing position. It prefers an alkaline soil.

Asperula   Rubiaceae

A. odorata, bedstraw, sweet woodruff, is a low-growing native perennial, often found in shaded places, especially on the chalk. It is a little impatient of the extremes, the very heavy or very light soils, but with care and encouragement it can usually be success-fully established. If it is happy, it will quickly form extensive drifts, usually seeking out the shaded parts. The whorled foliage on slender stems is an attractive green, while the younger leaves, produced after the heads of sweetly scented white flowers in May, are of a lighter colouring, a pleasant effect which remains into the late autumn, when they die down.

A plant for the dappled shade of the woodland garden, or for a shaded border by a path, and ideal for a shaded, dry, retaining wall.

A. orientalis is a low-growing, hardy annual with lavender-blue flowers. It is suitable for shaded borders in more formal sur-roundings, and for shaded window boxes and tubs.

Asplenium   Polypodiaceae

A. trichomanes, maidenhair spleenwort, is a native fern found in shaded walls and rocky outcrops in many parts of the country. It prefers a moist and humid climate, and is less frequently found in the drier parts of the country, particularly in towns and cities where the whole environment dries up rapidly especially during the summer. The evergreen fronds, which vary in length, are generally about 120 mm. (5 in.) long, with the small and light green pinnae held along the length of a dark and thin, wiry rachis, which is curved or twisted, lending much to the appeal of this little fern. An established fern produces short rhizomes, which will creep along the rock crevices or the gaps between the bricks or stones of a wall. Thus in time small colonies develop and give the feature a mature and pleasing appearance.

A. ruta-muraria, wall-rue, is another native often found huddled and clustered in the crevices of old stone walls where it appears to enjoy the crumbling mortar. A humid atmosphere and some shade are important to it, but undoubtedly it is able to extract a little moisture from the rooting medium. Although small, the light green fronds are not extensively divided, and this gives the plant an appearance which is hardly fern-like. In addition to providing interest, established colonies give a feature a more mature effect.

There are many other species, a few of which are hardy and native to this country. However, rather than describe them I propose to give an account of the establishment of these two species alone. The methods can be adapted for many of the other species.

The plants should be obtained in the first instance, from a nursery or garden, but if they are planted out directly they may be lost—there is only one chance with each plant. The original stock should be established in pots or pans, using a very open medium made up almost entirely of old bricks or sandstone, broken down to pea or walnut size, with the addition of a small proportion of leafmould, or peat and coarse sand. With *A. ruta-muraria* a proportion of old broken mortar rubble should be added. The plants should then be grown on in a moist and shaded frame with the object of collecting spores in due course for propagation. Eventually the young plants, which may be easily raised by this method, are planted out from the small pots in which they have been established. The early spring period is suitable for this, and a variety of likely positions in the shade should be selected. Be prepared, however, for some surprises—like so many plants they will often thrive where you hardly dare to think mere survival is possible.

Proof of this was found in a garden on the outskirts of London, where *A. trichomanes* was to be found thriving in a shaded border with a rich soil, while another example was in a small, unheated but sunny greenhouse at half a kilometre (547 yds.) distance. Both plants were thriving and colonizing in a wall facing the sun. In both cases high humidity was maintained by irrigation and watering, and undoubtedly this was the reason for their success. The exposure to the sun in the greenhouse may appear to be contradictory, until it is remembered that the glass does not allow the whole of the light from the suns rays to penetrate. In nature too the presence of these ferns in some positions seems at first sight difficult to explain, but there is always a reason—either shade or part shade, or high humidity—possibly both. Thus they may be found growing happily in a sunny wall—a puzzle until it is noticed that overhanging stones are giving enough shade for their survival. Again they may be found in full sun on high ground, hills and mountains, which is baffling until it is realized that such elevations are often shrouded in mists and clouds or drenched by driving rains. The strangest of all combinations was found on the wall of a West Country town: *A. trichomanes, Polypodium vulgare, Sedum acre* and a colony of seedling hybrid wall-flowers (the latter two recognized sun lovers), all growing side by side. The wall is 1·5 m. (5 ft.) high, by quite a busy street and in part shade—how confusing!

Asteranthera   Gesneriaceae

A. ovata is a plant to which the correct environment matters a very great deal. Even to grow this creeper from the cool, moist temperate forests of South America, is considered to be a great triumph, but for it to flower is a much greater one. The blossoms, sometimes produced freely during the summer and autumn, are spectacular, being tubular and a deep, intense pink. The chances of success in this country are greatest when it is provided with a very sheltered corner which is always cool, moist and humid, and where the sun never reaches it. Such conditions are perhaps more likely to be found in the south and west, but there is a tendency for gardeners to 'open out' such damp and dark corners where it would thrive. A suitable environment for *Asteranthera* could be built up round part of a north-facing wall, for it will climb or creep on stone or brick walls. Alternatively a very small clearing in damp woodland, where it is sheltered by evergreens, mossy and humid, has possibilities, allowing it to climb over an old, decaying tree stump. Plenty of leafmould in the soil will help it to feel more at home.

Astilbe   Saxifragaceae

These popular, herbaceous perennials are happy in shady conditions, although they will also thrive in full sun. A moist soil with a high organic content is the key to their cultivation. So vital is moisture to them, that they will succeed in very wet, boggy conditions by the waterside; under very dry conditions they will wilt and even die unless the deficiency is remedied. Thus in common with other moisture lovers, on soils which have a tendency to be dry at times, especially on a site full of tree roots, some form of irrigation may be necessary, and this should be taken into account when deciding upon the size and position of the groups. The flowers, in prominent, feathery plumes, are produced during the summer, some species and cultivars earlier than others, while the colour range is not only from white to pink and red, but to even deeper shades which are near purple. In foliage too the variation in colour is extensive—the green, copper and bronze tones extending to a purple, which for comparison is as deep as that of any *Dahlia* or *Coleus* cultivar. Their height varies from 120 mm. (5 in.) to well over a metre (3 ft. 3 in.).

Before the final choice is made, it is worthwhile taking the autumn and winter colour effects into consideration, for dried inflorescences turn to rich shades of brown or red-brown according to the variety. This display, left to glow through the winter months, will be appreciated until the first snowdrops and winter aconites appear. Then with all haste every herbaceous stem which has been left standing should be cut down.

There is a wide choice for the group or drift in the dappled shade of the woodland, or for the streamside, where colour matters a great deal. However, unless an almost foolish boldness is to creep into the stillness of this feature, be careful: choose the softer shades, plant on a small scale and keep each variety together. If more than one colour is used in a drift, make sure that they blend.

If the results are pleasing and an increase is desired, a careful division during the dormant season is the best means. On the other hand, an overpowering effect may be remedied by planting them elsewhere, perhaps in more formal features where the colour selections can be more riotous.

A. simplicifolia, a pale pink flowered species from Japan, which is only 150 mm. (6 in.) high, is suitable among other smaller growers for a shady part of the rock garden.

Astrantia   Umbelliferae

In this genus of herbaceous perennials the inflorescence is made up of lightly coloured bracts surrounding a cluster of inconspicuous flowers. Although they will grow well in a sunny position, provided that there is sufficient moisture, good results are also obtained in the shade, where drier conditions can be tolerated. They are plants for drift planting in the dappled shade of the woodland where their quaint flowers can be appreciated, especially during the summer when many shade lovers are past their best. They are also effective in shaded herbaceous plantings or in mixed borders.

A. major is the most common species and possibly the easiest to establish. It is 500 mm. (1 ft. 8 in.) or more in height with palmate foliage, the bracts being green, faintly stained with purple. The cultivar 'Rubra' has quite a deep purple colouring, and a random mixture of this and the type plant produces a very pleasing effect.

The usual method of propagation is by division. Plant at 400 mm. (1 ft. 4 in.) apart.

Athyrium   Polypodiaceae

A. filix-femina, lady fern, is a native commonly found in the moister parts of the British Isles, mainly on acid soils. This fern is at its best in dappled shade, part shade or shade, but it is very adaptable and is found often, although generally more stunted, in the dry and exposed parts of the country.

As the common name suggests, the light green fronds, which appear in the late spring, are delicate in appearance. They reach 1·5 m. (5 ft.) high by midsummer but die back in the autumn, when for a time the fronds assume a rich brown colour before bending over and collapsing, although in a mild winter they remain green for a long time. It is a good subject for stabilizing the autumn leaf-fall, and the fronds should be left until the spring to serve this purpose, when they may be cut down to the crown just before mulching.

There are a number of forms with fine plumose or deeply segmented fronds; for example 'Magnificum Capitatum' has parsley-leaved fronds, and 'Plumosa' has dark cristated fronds.

These are very desirable ferns for shaded places, in both large and small gardens, but the dwarfer forms are suitable for shaded parts in the rock garden, or for a position near the front or edge of a planting—for example, the cultivar 'Minimum', which has a rather crowded but delicate appearance, is only 300 mm. (1 ft.) high.

Normally the various forms and cultivars should be propagated vegetatively, by division in the spring.

Aubrieta   Cruciferae

Aubrieta cultivars and strains are usually associated with a sunny and well-drained wall or bank, and undoubtedly they are at their best in such a position. In the shade, flowering is often later and very much reduced, but nevertheless they will often succeed where many other plants fail. Thus they are worth trying on a north-facing dry retaining wall, provided the feature is well drained. Should they become untidy and bare at the base the plants may be cut back hard after flowering. Aubrietas are not happy in shade which is caused by overhanging trees, as the drip and leaf-fall cause the foliage to rot. Variegated forms may keep their colour better in shade.

Aucuba Cornaceae

A. japonica, comes from Japan, and there are few shrubs, evergreen or deciduous, which will tolerate density of shade as well as this does. It will grow even beneath holm oak, provided that there is some sidelight, but such situations can be so dry that this becomes a limiting factor. The fresh green growths in the spring above the evergreen foliage make it very attractive, as later does the scarlet fruiting display borne by the female plants.

This shrub is obtainable in a number of good varieties and will grow equally well in the open; continuity is therefore possible if the planting covers both sun and shade areas.

Berberidopsis Flacourtiaceae

B. corallina, coral plant, is an evergreen for the milder parts of the country, where it succeeds best when trained against a north wall, in a sheltered position. Soil suited to the rhododendron, well-drained, acid, peaty and moist, suits it best. When grown well, it produces during the latter part of the summer long growths, full of pendulous crimson flowers, with clean, holly-like leaves. It is one of the earlier introductions from Chile.

Berberis Berberidaceae

The belief that *Berberis* is well worth having just to push in some odd corner to fill it up or to place on the boundary to keep children out, is unfortunately still too widespread. Even the evergreen types seldom do well in situations where they are completely overshadowed by trees even if these are deciduous. *B. julianae* is probably the most satisfactory, often growing thinly, but succeeding where most fail completely or are very untidy and miserable. Many of the evergreens will grow well in light, dappled shade, but the selection needs to be studied carefully, especially on dry, sandy soil; in shade, perhaps on a north-facing border with no overhanging trees, many will be successful, taking hardiness and exposure into account, while in part shade there is no problem, and the range may include the deciduous species and cultivars.

Bergenia   Saxifragaceae

These low-growing perennials, with large glossy leaves up to 300 mm. (1 ft.) high which remain green or tinged brown and red through the winter, are suitable for use as ground-cover, for example in shrub borders, or among rhododendrons and mixed plantings in light woodland and in areas beneath trees. They are also effective in a shaded herbaceous planting. Surprisingly they are happy in full sun, in dappled shade, part shade or shade, and their soil requirements are very modest, though they dislike the very light soils.

At first it might appear that the many species and cultivars are much alike, but there are many important differences which should be taken into account to provide variation, if more than one group or drift is to be made; they should not be mixed within a group. With *B. crassifolia*, for example, the large, crowded leaves change to dull shades, red on the edges and at times over the whole surface; this foliage loses its condition during April when the spikes of pale rose flowers appear. By contrast *B. stracheyi* is a smaller and neater grower, and usually flowers a month earlier, when the heads of white flowers are attractive against the new, rosy green foliage. In June the old seeding heads on *B. crassifolia*, held at a height of 600 mm. (2 ft.), well above the fresh green foliage, look bold, dark and impressive and provide a slowly changing display and effect against a background of reflective surfaces as the large leaves catch the light. What wonderful plants they are, and all the better for a little attention such as the removal of the old heads of flowers and withered leaves after all their displays have finished! When doing this, to prevent undue consolidation avoid a wet period, also of course step carefully, otherwise the leaves or the rhizomes may be damaged.

There are many other species and cultivars to look out for. To the trained eye they all vary so much and they need to be seen at all seasons before a choice is made. The rhizomes, with leaves attached, may be separated during the late autumn or in early spring and in mild weather in the winter. Plant at 250 mm. (10 in.) apart.

Billardiera   Pittosporaceae

B. longiflora is a tender evergreen climber from Tasmania, but there are many people with warm gardens in the west or south west who could grow this plant very well. It is suited for a north-facing, low wall 1·5 to 2 m. (5 ft. to 6 ft. 7 in.) high, where little or no sun ever reaches it. It must of course be sheltered from cold northerly and easterly blasts. This may be difficult, but if one is successful in meeting the challenge, perhaps by carefully posi-tioned screen plantings, the results can be very well worthwhile. The effect is interesting enough during the summer, when the slender growths shyly hold the pendulous, yellow flowers, but the real display is in the autumn, for provided the 'set' has been a good one, the dark blue fruits hang down in masses.

Blechnum   Polypodiaceae

B. spicant, our native hard fern, is to be found in great abundance in moist, acid woods and valleys, in the hedges or banks, over moors and among the rocks of hills and mountains. It is found in full sun, but seems to be happiest where it is at least in some shade and in places which are misty at times as a result of drench-ing, low cloud.

In the garden it is not often possible to copy these conditions exactly, but it can still be grown, given certain essentials. It should have a moist, acid soil with plenty of peat added, shade, part shade, or dappled shade, and shelter. The latter condition ensures the maximum humidity, giving the foliage a better chance of remaining green over the winter and late into the spring, when the new fronds appear. The entire pinnae, dark green in colour, are placed on either side of the very dark midrib—simple but very effective. Many of the older fronds lose condition and turn brown and the plants sometimes have a dejected appearance, but not for long, as the new fronds, a light and delicate green, are produced in a rosette from the centre of the crowns. If it is intended to cut the old fronds off, this should be done just as the new ones appear.

The first to appear are the sterile fronds, which may grow up to 400 mm. (1 ft. 4 in.) in length and arch over or lie close to the ground. The fertile fronds are more upright, in complete contrast, and will often reach 700 mm. (2 ft. 4 in.) in height.

It is a very good fern to have in any collection, and if it can be grown successfully will add much to the appearance of the woodland garden, introducing an atmosphere of maturity. It is effective in the background, with a few plants brought to the front in places where they can be seen more closely. It is a good marker plant to use for indicating the position of plants or groups which are hidden beneath the surface at some time in their growth, for example *Primula nutans*.

B. chilense, from Chile, is often wrongly termed *B. tabulare*. It is a striking fern with fronds often a metre (3 ft. 3 in.) in length. They stand out boldly from neighbouring plants, being a rich, dark green, the pinnae having undulating edges. In a moist and sheltered position the fronds remain green through the winter, a perfect contrast to an autumn carpeting of fallen leaves. As the new fronds appear the old ones turn a rich brown—another contrasting effect which can be left to be enjoyed for a time, before they are cut off. A very desirable fern for grouping in some sheltered valley or bog in the dappled shade, or shade of the woodland. It is not a plant for very cold exposed areas.

Bletilla   Orchidaceae

B. striata (*Bletia hyacinthina*) is a terrestrial orchid, from China, certainly hardy in the south and west of the country, and probably in many other parts too if it is positioned carefully. It is a very desirable species and one which is surprisingly easy to grow, but it prefers an acid soil that has been enriched at planting time with peat, or even well-decayed farmyard manure. It also prefers shelter and at least some shade, and is suitable for the border in shade or part shade, in addition to the woodland or wild garden in dappled shade. A group planting is advisable, for it is then that the broad and pointed leaves with their prominent, parallel venation can be seen to good effect. The light purple flowers, produced in the June–July period, are held loosely among or just above the leaves, the overall height being 300 to 400 mm. (1 ft. to 1 ft 4 in.). Once a clump is established it quickly fills in, and if propagation is desired, the required material may be carefully removed in the spring, as growth starts, with the small, swollen roots or pseudo-bulbs attached, so that the clump as a whole is left undisturbed. Plant at 250 mm. (10 in.) apart.

Boykinia   Saxifragaceae

B. aconitifolia, a woodland plant from North America is not in the least demanding provided that it has a soil which is usually moist and lime-free. One of its attractions is the pleasing effect of the foliage. In late March to April the bronze growths appear on the surface but they gradually change to green as they emerge. When it is planted in a drift, with the developing foliage in clusters or clumps, the bronze and green tones give the whole a delightful sense of informality—just the atmosphere that should reign in the woodland or shade garden. Later the round and palmately lobed leaves assume a fresh, green colour—this sense of continuity and development with the seasons is just what is required. The small, white flowers, which open in July, are held on 600 mm. (2 ft.) stems, but the foliage remains in good condition until the autumn, long after the petals have fallen. Even after the growths have died down for the winter, the dead flower stems remain, 'holding' the fallen leaves from neighbouring trees, thus serving a useful purpose in preventing them from drifting on to plants such as meconopsis, which would easily rot under such a layer. It is also useful as an indication of the size and extent of the drift, when the annual clean-up is undertaken during the winter.

It is a valuable plant for the dappled shade of the woodland and shade garden and as ground-cover among shrubs, for it spreads very freely and is propagated quite easily by division in the early spring, when the growths first appear.

Brunnera   Boraginaceae

B. macrophylla is a tough perennial for planting in groups or drifts in the dappled shade of the woodland, and also as a ground-cover plant in the shrub border. It thrives as well in the sun, although in shade the leaves are often much larger, 150 mm. (6 in.) or more in length.

Early flowers are always welcome and this is often bright and interesting in February with its heart-shaped leaves and 'forget-me-not' flowers (it is closely related to *Myosotis*), of the brightest blue. A few weeks later, a planting will become a river or sheet of blue, the flower stems elongating as blossoming continues. By the early summer there is a thick canopy of foliage 400 mm. (1 ft. 4 in.) high, with the flowering stems held another 300 mm. (1 ft.) above this. When the flowerheads become unsightly they should be removed, being cut well down to the crowns. This encourages the production of a second crop of flower in the autumn —sparse, especially after a dry summer, but very welcome. Soon, as the winter sets in, the leaves turn to a dark brown, the largest changing first. This stage is interesting too, for with many of the younger leaves from the centre still green, a wonderful almost mottled effect is produced. It then becomes very apparent that there is great variation in the size and age of the leaves.

This plant grows well on most soils and it is one to plant up where the soil is well drained, hungry and light. Plant at 250 mm. (10 in.) apart. It is a rapid spreader and can easily be divided during the winter.

There are also variegated forms.

Buxus   Buxaceae

B. sempervirens, box, is a well-known native evergreen shrub or small tree found naturally over chalk and limestone formations, in open and partly open positions, in addition to the lighter parts of beech woods. For hundreds of years it has been used in gardens for a variety of purposes, but mainly for hedging, usually in full sun. Despite the fact that a very definite soil preference is shown in the wild, it is not at all particular in the garden, provided the drainage is good.

The box and its cultivars will grow in dappled shade once established, and provided that it is left to grow freely. Often growth will be thin, by comparison with that produced in the open, and there may be some dead twig growth after a dry season, but the trunk and bark effect as the specimen ages will be more apparent, and will compensate for this.

As a formal, clipped hedge plant it is not good in the shade of trees, for grown as such it is usually clipped annually during August, a period when it is often too dry in this situation for a good response. In part shade it is a different matter, and whether clipped or allowed to grow freely it usually thrives, and a good variegated form will brighten a dull shaded border.

B. *balearica*, from the Balearic Isles, is normally grown in a sunny position, but it will grow very well in dappled shade and make a shapely pyramidal tree.

Caltha   Ranunculaceae

C. palustris, marsh marigold, king cup, is a native, herbaceous plant, commonly found in boggy positions, wet pastures and by the waterside. This species is often abundant in areas fed by rivers and streams that run through chalk or limestone. It is early flowering and has large golden blossoms; its rounded leaves are rich, green and glabrous—with running and sparkling water as a background the plant is very appealing. It grows to a height of 300 mm. (1 ft.) and is best described as a giant buttercup.

Although it is often found in full sun, it is also plentiful in dappled shade and in part shade. Thus we have a very beautiful plant which is ideal for a group or drift planting in a natural situation—in sun or shade. Grouping should be completely informal without regularity or pattern, for early flowering subjects (early March), are very distinctive, since the majority of the neighbouring plants are only just starting into growth. An error in planting is therefore very evident. There is a double form, *C. palustris* 'Flore Plena', which is striking in blossom, and will not form viable seed. This is an advantage, for the pure species sets seed very freely and may sometimes germinate where it is not wanted, but the double form lacks the charm and beauty of the single-flowered plant.

C. palustris sub.sp. *minor* is smaller, spreading freely by creeping and rooting stems once it is established.

Camellia   Theaceae

These ever popular shrubs are at home in the light dappled shade of the woodland, or in a cool position on the north side of a wall or building. They will grow and flower well in full sun, but during a hot summer in the southern part of the country, particularly in urban and town areas where there is considerable reflected heat, extensive leaf scorch may be experienced. These risks also apply to wall plantings in these areas with a south or west aspect.

Shelter is very important, in particular from the north and east, for while camellias are very hardy when completely dormant, the young growths, a very light green and tender, are subject to damage from cold winds and frosts. The blossoms are also subject to frost damage, and shelter from the early morning sun will help to prevent this.

Camellias thrive best in a light, acid soil to which plenty of peat or well-rotted leafmould has been added. There are a number of species, hybrids and cultivars to choose from, including the wonderful cultivars from *C.* × *williamsii*. Selection should be made after studying growth, as well as flower colour, for habit and foliage effect are important. The fact that it is an evergreen with such bold and reflective leaves, is an important point to consider when selecting the plant and deciding upon its position. Finally, camellias are well suited to planting among rhododendrons, having the same requirements, and they introduce a greater variety and interest. The *C.* × *williamsii* selections are ideal for this purpose, as they often flower during the winter months, but there are many others that could be used.

Campanula   Campanulaceae

Many campanulas do well in sun or part shade, but they need to be introduced into the smaller or more intensive part of the natural woodland or shade garden with care. *C. lactiflora*, from the Caucasus, growing from 1 to 1·5 m. (3 ft. 3 in. to 5 ft.) in height, freely produces pale blue flowers in July, and often a lighter sprinkling in the autumn. It is ideal for group planting in the larger, more natural garden where it has sufficient space to develop, perhaps in part shade against, rather than under, trees, but it will compete successfully against the strongest herbaceous growth. *C. latifolia*, a native, is in some ways similar, but is not as large, growing generally up to 1 m. (3 ft. 3 in.), with flowers of purple-blue. It is a species that will naturalize, if conditions suit it. In the overall effect these two species are very different from each other, and in cases of doubt over the most desirable one for a particular planting, they should be tried first in prepared beds. Both are suitable for use in shaded herbaceous plantings.

C. persicifolia, from Europe and from western and northern Asia, grows to about 900 mm. (3 ft.) in full sun, but often less in shade. It is ideal for herbaceous plantings near trees or part shade, but it will flower well in shade where the sun never reaches it, for example in a border against a north-facing wall. It is ideal for shaded town gardens, where the winter's foliage, neat and clustered at ground level, is especially appreciated.

C. rapunculoides, from Europe, Asia Minor and the Caucasus, is very much at home in this country and has spread extensively, especially on the lighter and well-drained soils. It grows up to 500 mm. (1 ft. 8 in.) high, producing spikes of the most beautiful blue flowers, but it is a very rampant grower, spreading by means of thick roots which over-winter as tubers. Once it is established and happy, it is very difficult to eradicate, especially in rock gardens, and will quickly take over, unless much patient work is undertaken to keep it down. If it must be grown, a good position is in grass among fruit trees, perhaps with naturalized crocuses. First the crocuses, then the grass herbage, and finally the campanula—most effective, but beware!

C. latiloba, from Siberia, is a good plant to have among rhododendrons in a woodland. Just a thin distribution in the form of a drift here and there is most effective. The cultivar 'Highcliffe' is suitable, producing spikes of blue flowers 2 m. (6 ft. 7 in.) or more high, during the summer and autumn. After flowering, the stems should be cut down to the rosettes, which remain an attraction.

C. poscharskyana is among the smaller species, reaching 200 mm. (8 in.) high with light blue, star-shaped flowers. It is very accommodating, growing equally well not only in full sun and part shade, but also in some shady crevice in the rock garden, where the sun's rays never reach it. The flowering heads are produced from a pleasant carpet of green in the early summer.

There are many more species and cultivars which can be used in shade—*C. portenschlagiana* (*C. muralis*), for example. This will actually grow in old walls and in other impossible situations, in shade or sun, but it must have good drainage.

Finally, a plea for our own native harebell—*C. rotundifolia*—which is being driven from our pastures to survive only in small colonies in odd places, often in part shade. It should at least be preserved in these areas.

Cardamine   Cruciferae

C. pratensis, cuckoo flower, lady's smock, is a native found in wet and boggy areas, especially those overlying clay. It is a perennial, with flower stems which rise to a height of approximately 300 mm.

(1 ft.). The simple, four-petalled flowers, generally coloured the purest pale lilac, are held in a head which extends as the flowers drop and the fruits develop. A drift or even a single plant has all the grace and charm of spring, as it stands well above the developing grass, fresh and green, darkened in places by clumps of rushes. The beauty of this plant is that a drift will often extend from sun to dappled shade or even shade, provided that sufficient moisture is available during the growing and flowering season.

It is not suggested for planting in beds within a shade garden, for it passes out of flower leaving nothing for a few weeks, until unimpressive rosettes of cress-like leaves prepare for the next season's flowering. Rather it is a plant for the outer reaches of a shade garden where it may already be established—if it is, the area should be conserved, for this and many plants associated with it are being driven out by relentless large-scale drainage schemes.

If it is decided to introduce this species, the best method is to obtain a small stock from a nursery and establish plants in a small bed in the selected area. If the position is suitable they will soon spread.

Cardiocrinum   Liliaceae

C. giganteum, a monocarpic species, closely related to the genus *Lilium*, is ideal for group planting in light woodland, perhaps on the sheltered side of a clearing or cluster of trees. For such a distinct and shapely plant to be seen at its best, the setting and the scale of the planting are important. At flowering stage a healthy plant has large and impressive foliage, with a stout flowering stem of up to 2·5 m. (8 ft.) in height, holding well above all other shade-loving herbage a dozen or more large white trumpet-shaped blooms, stained with purple within and beautifully scented.

For a plant to reach this stage, conditions must be perfect for its growth and development over a period of four to seven years from the time of planting—some shade, shelter with a cool and moist root run, are essential. In addition, the species loves an acid medium with a very rich organic content, for it is a heavy feeder. With such demands, it is hardly surprising that good specimens of this massive lily are seldom seen. Often a good start is made for young plants when a bed is prepared, but within a year or so neighbouring trees have rooted back in, causing impoverishment and at times excessively dry conditions.

Usually, the bulbs from any one planting reach maturity and flower over a period of several years, but this is all the more interesting. The growth dies down each autumn to a bulb which is very close to the surface, needing the protection of a covering of bracken over the bed in winter. Each spring a generous mulching of well-rotted farmyard manure should be given, and watered during the summer, if it becomes dry. As new growths appear each year, they should be fatter and stronger, developing foliage which is ever bolder and more distinctive, to be admired for its own sake but with the promise ultimately of a two- to three-week period of glory before the plant sets a crop of seed and dies. This always seems very sad, and there are times when, as the moving patterns of light from the nearby canopy play on the reflective surfaces of the glossy leaves, the thought crosses the mind that it is a pity it ever flowers, so beautiful is it even in these early stages. Yet the wise gardener who can grow this lily well plans for the future and has a succession to gap-up old beds and for planting new ones. The planting distance should be 1 m. (3 ft. 3 in.) apart.

During the spring of flowering the rate of growth is very rapid and by early June the stem may be a metre (3 ft. 3 in.) or more high, with large sheathing olive-green leaves which are left behind one after the other, until the clustered buds appear at the tip. Soon these too separate, as the stem reaches its ultimate height when the flowers finally open, depressed at a gentle angle, doubtless to protect the vital organs from the dripping rains of the Himalayas, its native home. Growth in the final season is really exciting, just as it is with any other rosetted plant which is running up to flower, perhaps after a wait of many years.

In the autumn the foliage often turns a rich brown, while the stiff and dried flowered stems proudly hold the large capsules aloft to scatter their seeds. There is beauty even at this stage.

The stock is normally maintained by detaching offsets, which are found around the base of plants which have flowered, and are best planted directly into the beds. If required, stock can also be raised from seed.

Carex
Cyperaceae

The sedges make up a very large genus. *C. pendula*, pendulous sedge, is one of the most distinctive, and if it is not present as a native, it is worth introducing, provided the soil is boggy or wet throughout the year. It will grow well in light, dappled shade, and even a solitary plant on the edge of a clearing is most distinctive, with a strong clump of broad foliage and prominent spikes which have pendulous branches. It will reach a height of 1 m. (3 ft. 3 in.).

Propagation is by division.

Carum   Umbelliferae

C. petroselinum is the common parsley, but no excuses need be made, for it is a fine plant for spring bedding displays where it will provide good cover beneath such bulbs as tulips, and will grow in part shade or shade. The foliage remains a dark green from the autumn into the winter and spring and, if a good variety is chosen, it is closely curled and attractive. It is also suitable in towns for window-boxes and tubs which are often in the shade, especially during the winter.

Parsley must have a deep, rich and moist soil. The seed may be sown *in situ* during July if it is used for border furnishing, and finally thinned to 150 mm. (6 in.) apart. For use in bedding schemes, window-boxes and tubs, sow in boxes or pots, pricking plants out singly into 70 mm. (2½ in.) pots; they are finally planted out in the autumn. Parsley being a biennial, a new sowing must be made each year.

Cassiope   Ericaceae

This genus is made up of beautiful but difficult plants which can be grown with real success only in the cooler areas of the British Isles. In those parts they may usually be grown in the open, or full sun, but in the warmer south some form of shade is desirable to keep the plants cooler. Usually dappled shade is the best, but some very fine plants have been grown in shade. At one time a very comprehensive collection was grown successfully in a cool, aired and shaded greenhouse, where the air was kept moist and humid. Humidity appears to be the critical factor with these plants, and they must never dry out at the roots. An acid soil is essential and if necessary a good portion of peat should be added.

Caulophyllum   Berberidaceae

C. thalictrioides, from North America, is one of the herbaceous perennials in the family Berberidaceae, in some ways close to the genus *Epimedium*. Being rather choice and pleasantly light in appearance, it is just the plant for a secluded position in dappled shade, or in a shady corner of the rock garden. It is an interesting and uncommon plant, with foliage that is almost certain to contrast well with the surroundings. From the moment when it appears above the soil in mid spring it will give pleasure and satisfaction. First there are the dark green growths and folded leaves which give a thalictrum-like appearance. Then as the compound and segmented leaves unfold, the effect is both delightful and exciting. Many of the leaflets are trilobed and of the most delicate green colour possible. The inflorescence, held on 400 mm. (1 ft. 4 in.) stems and consisting of small, pale purple flowers which are above the foliage, is cloud-like. During the late summer the yellowing foliage provides yet another display.

A deserving plant to grow singly or as a small group in a moist situation. Well-decayed leafmould should be added to the soil at planting time.

Cephalotaxus   Cephalotaxaceae

The few conifers which will thrive in shade are seldom used in such situations, which is a great pity, for they are so valuable as furnishing under these conditions. Although it resembles the Yew, *Cephalotaxus* is in a separate family. In all forms of shade the trees are much superior to yews and will even thrive in a long, dry period on a light soil and in competition with large trees. In shade they are best grown on as a large bush, when the main branches and growths spread out from ground level. The new growths, which are light green during the summer, arch over in a most attractive manner. These forgotten plants will grow on a wide variety of soils, but in common with the yews, show a distinct dislike of the really heavy clays.

Cercidiphyllum   Cercidiphyllaceae

C. japonicum is a tree renowned for its autumn colouring, this often being in shades of pale yellow. It will thrive in part shade on the edge of a clearing or group of trees, and on a good growing soil. In areas which are dry and hot during the summer, for example the Thames Valley, shelter and a cool, dappled shade are essential to its well-being, otherwise the foliage becomes badly scorched.

D

Chaenomeles Rosaceae

C. speciosa, flowering quince, is a shrub at its best in the sun, and it will flower most profusely when trained on a wall with a southern aspect. It will, however, flower well in the part shade on walls with an east or west aspect, and even on a north-facing wall, although this will lead to later and reduced flowering, with thinner growth.

Chamaecyparis Cupressaceae

C. lawsoniana, Lawson cypress, is one of the few conifers that will grow reasonably well in light dappled shade, especially on a heavy soil, where more moisture is likely to be available under otherwise dry conditions; the furnishing growths are thinner, however, in shade.

There are many named varieties, but strong-growing seedlings are likely to be better in difficult situations.

Chamaedaphne Ericaceae

C. calyculata, an evergreen ericaceous shrub from the northern hemisphere, is an ideal subject for planting with rhododendrons, vacciniums and other shrubs with a similar requirement—a moist but well-drained acid soil with a high organic content. Although this species will succeed in full sun, it will thrive in dappled shade, in fact in the southern part of the country, where it is often hotter and less humid, a little shade is welcome.

The plant forms a compact bush, 0·5 to 1·0 m. (1 ft. 8 in. to 3 ft. 3 in.) high, with box-like foliage and neat lily of the valley type flowers produced in short axillary spikes in April. As the flowering period ends, the new growths appear and by the autumn form buds for next season's display. During the winter the foliage is bronze and the flower buds are pink.

This shrub should be planted when young, to enable it to grow into the position and space. A mature plant will not adapt itself in the same way, and will always appear to have been moved from elsewhere. It is effective in a small group of 5 to 6 plants, set at 600 mm. (2 ft.) apart.

Chamaepericlymenum Cornaceae

C. canadensis (*Cornus canadensis*), creeping dogwood, is a little creeping plant without which no work on shade plants would be complete. It grows to no more than 150 mm. (6 in.) high, producing new growth each year from a mass of creeping stems. During the summer the white flowers are produced on the colonies of growths, to be followed in the autumn by the bright berries.

It is a plant for the dappled shade, but it is not an easy growing, tough subject. A light, well-drained, but moist soil, which is well stocked with decayed organic material, is necessary; but in addition there should be a layer of natural leafmould or peat through which the rhizomes can spread easily.

Chelidonium   Papaveraceae

C. majus, greater celandine, a perennial herb, is a member of the poppy family, and a doubtful native. Like the stinging nettle, *Urtica dioica*, it is often near buildings and neglected gardens, and will suddenly appear following disturbance of soil, giving the impression that the seed has lain dormant for many years, until brought nearer to the surface. The plant will grow on a wide variety of soils, rich garden soil conditions suiting it best, but it will also thrive in areas and pockets made up almost entirely of builder's waste and rubble. The only soil it appears to dislike is a badly drained one.

The leaves are segmented and form a neat rosette during the winter months, while the flowers produced throughout the growing season are bright yellow, being held prominently on much-branched stems, which reach a height of a metre (3 ft. 3 in.) or more. The thick, orange, almost latex-like sap is poisonous. The plant has an attractive appearance after rain as the leaves hold the drops.

This is not a subject to introduce into the garden or light woodland where the plants are cultivated and weeded, for it reproduces from seed very rapidly. However, it is such a good colonizer of vacant ground that it would be worth trying it for this purpose on spoil heaps or rough ground, whether in the sun or beneath trees. These are places where a start has to be made, and other species can follow as the organic content is built up.

Chionodoxa   Liliaceae

C. luciliae, from Asia Minor, is a small, spring-flowering bulbous plant, little more than 100 mm. (4 in.) in height, bearing clusters of striking star-shaped flowers. Sometimes it is in flower in February, but more often in March or April. There may be as many as twelve flowers to a stem and the effect, especially when it is seen in large numbers, is both conspicuous and pleasing. As with its related species, it will grow in a variety of soils, in grass or border, in sun or shade, including the full shade of a tree such as beech, for in this latter position the foliage reaches maturity and even starts to die back before the leaves of the tree cut out the sun completely. It is also good, in common with many other early flowerers, for planting among low, clump-like plants such as epimediums and hostas but it is important that these are cleared of all old leaves by the end of December, well before the bulb shoots even penetrate the surface. By this means interest is increased with a more natural effect, the bulbous plant completing its flowering and growth before the leaf growth of the main subject is complete. However, this is not always necessary—for example, a planting of chionodoxa can be made between clumps of *Speirantha gardenii*, a Chinese plant with stiff, evergreen foliage and spikes of tiny white blossoms in May, when the new foliage appears a pleasant fresh green; the bulbs flower when the speirantha foliage is tarnished and past its best.

This may give the impression that the chionodoxa is only fit to 'push in' to extend the season and interest, but this is not so— it is a display plant in its own right. Few people could fail to be impressed by the sight of an irregular blue drift stretching across a grass surface, green from early spring growth and lit by the softened rays of a strengthening sun. It is then that its common name, glory of the snow, seems to be most inappropriate.

There is a pink form, *C. luciliae* 'Rosea', which is to be admired, but the colour is just not suitable for a naturalized setting. *C. gigantea* has large flowers which are a gentle, pale blue, and if naturalized will give a misty bluebell effect. With *C. sardensis* the blue is very intense.

Cimicifuga   Ranunculaceae

This genus of herbaceous perennials produces small and dainty white flowers with many stamens on tall, slender spikes during the late summer or autumn according to the species. Although they are often to be seen in herbaceous borders, they thrive so well in a lightly shaded position that many consider them better suited for the light dappled shade of the woodland. Certainly they have a quiet charm and simplicity, which is lost in the colourful herbaceous border. Shelter is advisable, in order to avoid any form of staking which would tend to spoil the appearance. All the species prefer a deep, rich and moist soil. Lack of sufficient moisture during the growing season results in poor flower spikes and a miserable appearance generally.

Of the species, *C. racemosa* is one of the earliest to flower, in late July to August, with the spikes up to 2 m. (6 ft 7 in.) high. Even in early July the white buds are prominent on the spikes, which have by then almost gained their full height. The foliage is quite dense, up to 1 m. (3 ft. 3 in.), but one of the beauties of this species is the way some leaves are produced higher up the flowering stems. There is no better plant for producing pleasing light and shade effects.

C. cordifolia (*C. americana*) may reach a height of 2 m. (6 ft. 7 in.) with beautifully slender spikes on dark purple and green stems. The large leaves, being almost palmate, are most impressive and remain in good condition until the winter sets in. Even at this stage the old dried flower spikes are attractive in their way and need not be cut down until the spring. By March the display from this plant starts once again when the nodding and folded leaves break the surface. There are a number of other beautiful species and cultivars—all are suitable for the dappled shade of the woodland or shade garden, but cimicifugas may also be grown successfully in the shaded herbaceous planting, provided there is sufficient head room, and in the shade of a north-facing border.

Propagation is by division as growths appear in the spring. Plant at 1 m. (3 ft. 3 in.) apart.

Circaea   Onagraceae

C. lutetiana, enchanter's nightshade, is indeed an enchanting plant, with opposite leaves and 300 mm. (1 ft.) spikes of small, white flowers which light up a dark corner or piece of woodland in the June–July period when most other plants are over. Even a few plants are very pleasing, while a large drift produces a hazy effect from the hundreds of small blossoms.

However appealing and enchanting it is, be not fooled! Once it is introduced into a planting where conditions are suitable it will quickly become a nuisance, spreading extensively by means

of creeping rhizomes. It will seek out all the shaded places, rami-
fying through the roots of shrubs and failing even to flower in
its greed for territory. The simple answer is to leave it to be
enjoyed in the wood where it will come to no harm. It could be
introduced into areas which are in the process of being established
as 'natural' woods or copses, where moist positions in dappled
shade should be selected; choose the dormant season for planting.

Clintonia   Liliaceae

Given the right conditions, these plants are quite easy to grow.
They love an acid, sandy and peaty soil which is moist, and of
course shade, for they are woodlanders. They like dappled shade,
but even a shaded corner where the sun never reaches them is
suitable. Many shrub plantings provide suitable conditions.

C. borealis, from North America, is perhaps the easiest species
to grow. The foliage effect is bold and pleasing, being in tightly
packed rosettes. The broad leaves are 200 mm. (8 in.) long and
edged with fine hairs. By early summer the heads of pale yellow
flowers are produced on stalks 300 mm. (1 ft.) long. The colour
is pleasingly restful and is ideal for a shady setting—it should be
in a group near the front where its charm and simplicity can be
appreciated. As the foliage dies down the developing fruits, on a
head similar to that of ivy, become prominent, especially if the
patch is carefully cleared of fallen leaves. As they ripen the fruits
turn blue.

C. andrewsiana, from California, has shapely, shining, fresh green
foliage which is very attractive and provides an interesting variation to other plants. The crowded heads of deep rose flowers,
which have an interesting placement on the 500 mm. (1 ft. 8 in.)
high stem, are followed in August by clear blue fruits. The largest
cluster terminates the stalk, but there are tiers or whorls lower
down, which are the last to ripen. Finally the fruits turn to a
violet colour. Again, a plant which should be near the front.

Clintonias are propagated by division in the early spring just as
growth begins.

Codonopsis   Campanulaceae

A genus of small, trailing or climbing plants which is at home in
the cool conditions of mottled shade. The nodding flowers are
bell-shaped, but if you look up into the centres their star-shaped

appearance is quite striking; then, when their beauty has been fully appreciated, their campanula-like formation is apparent.

C. vinciflora, from western Asia, has thin, almost opposite-leaved growths that appear above the soil during April. Soon a mat of these slender growths develops; they twine together and creep forward beneath and through any nearby clumps of such plants as hostas, but also climb through shrubs which have a definite branch system, sometimes reaching a height of a metre (3 ft. 3 in.) of more. By July and until the autumn the small blue flowers appear above the carpet of green, held on 70 to 90 mm. (2½ to 3½ in.) stems. The petal tips are turned back to form a lip, while the centres within are beautifully spotted. When the first frosts appear the growths are killed to the ground.

C. pilosula, from China and Korea, has hairy stems with foliage which is unpleasantly scented when crushed, or on a hot day. The flowers, green and inconspicuous with a prominent calyx, are seen when closely inspected, to be of great beauty.

Codonopsis are not woodland plants, but the odd plant in a border or planting of shade-lovers brings a riotous informality into the scene. However, should a more orderly appearance be preferred, they can be given pea-sticks to climb upon. They thrive best of all when grown in a well-drained and rich soil.

The usual method of propagation is by seed, finally planting out from pots.

Colchicum   Liliaceae

These are sometimes wrongly termed autumn crocus, a group which is actually in the genus *Crocus*. However, colchicums do flower in the autumn, and what a joy they are! They emerge at a time when there is a growing realization that summer is at an end, with the last failing blossoms and the first of the warming colours that precede leaf-fall, growing daily in intensity. The shapely flowers are bold, but very beautiful, being of the purest and palest colours in the rose to mauve range, and with one or two white forms which are very desirable. When they are seen in flower one feels at once that such beautiful plants should be more widely grown. Some gardeners have tried them many, many times, but not always with success and often with disappointment where they do thrive, because they have been expected to behave like crocuses and have been treated in the same way. The foliage is

expected to be grass-like and manageable; instead, the leaves, produced in the spring, are broad and spreading, growing on into the
summer. If the plant is hampered at all or excluded from the
light, the flowering and the corms deteriorate. Even as the foliage
yellows towards the latter half of the summer, the process must
not be hurried in any way, or the corm will not ripen properly
again, to the detriment of the plant. There is also the soil requirement to consider: a moist but well-drained neutral medium
is needed, but it must be rich in organic material, preferably well-
decayed leafmould. This is in contrast to many of the genus
Crocus, which are very accommodating in this respect and will
thrive where colchicums will fade out completely after a few
years. The reason for this may be connected with the foliage
which does not hold its own when in strong and rank grass;
crocus foliage on the other hand is grass-like, and is produced
early enough to compete with grass for light, food and moisture.
In addition, many regard the yellowing and ripening colchicum
foliage as untidy, with only a short period when the flowers are at
their best, especially if the weather is rough.

Although colchicums thrive in the sun, many will also do well in
light dappled shade or even part shade. They should be used
sparingly in small groups, certainly to begin with. The plantings
may be increased later if desired. Suitable positions may exist
between shrubs, or beneath larger ones that are not low spreading.
Beds set in very light woodland or areas of trees can also be
successful. They should be carefully positioned with a background
of shrubs, and a little off the beaten track so that a special journey
or effort has to be made to see them when in flower. Even the
smaller garden or town garden could find a place for them in this
way; if they were not in a prominent position their period of
untidiness would go unnoticed. What a joy it would be to find
them in flower when one returned from a late summer holiday!

C. speciosum, from the Caucasus, is one to try in the first instance. The 180 mm. (7 in.) high, rose to purple flowers are produced in the September to October period. The colour variation
is a wide one; of a number of very good cultivars, 'Album' is
among the best, and the effect when it is in flower in a woodland
setting is really exciting, for the white blossoms stand so boldly
that from a distance they can be mistaken for a group of the
toadstools that abound at this season.

There are a number of other species, cultivars, and large-flowered hybrids which can be tried—the last group including one or two double forms. The range of flowering can be extended by their inclusion, but the advice must be to tread carefully, building up the numbers and variety in easy stages, remembering that not all by any means will do well in shade, which must in any case be light.

Colchicums take several years to flower from seed, but a good method of propagation is to lift the corms as soon as the foliage dies down completely, when they may be separated and replanted.

Convallaria   Liliaceae

C. majalis, lily of the valley, is a well-known and much-loved plant. A native, it is common in gardens, particularly old ones, while as a cut flower it frequently appears in shops and on market stalls. As a shade-lover it has much to commend it, but might prove to be too aggressive among choice subjects. As with all other plants, therefore, the position should be chosen carefully.

The thin green leaves appear in late March to April, to be followed by racemes of tight buds. Often growths are more forward in a sheltered or sunny position, but this makes it all the more interesting. By early May the flowers open with a thickening mat of foliage which forms an excellent ground-cover and weed suppressor. After the flowers have dropped, the foliage remains often thicker and a darker green, until finally it dies in the autumn. Even at this stage the dead foliage is useful, for the position of the drift in relation to neighbouring plants, which may be hidden on or under the surface, is clearly defined—a great help when mulching and clearing up. The fruits usually drop at the green stage, and few actually reach the light red stage of ripeness, when they are quite prominent.

The cultivar 'Fortins Giant' has large flowers and leaves, which form a thick and full mat of growth and stifles even the most pernicious weeds. The variegated form has pale yellow lines marking the venation, and although it is interesting, it is less vigorous than the type, often flowering later. There is also a form 'Rosea', with rose-coloured flowers. Most will agree that the ordinary type species is the best and most effective one for naturalizing, with the possible exception of 'Fortins Giant'. All are suitable for shaded borders and for window-boxes and other features in town gardens where the wonderfully fragrant bells, hanging in simple, nodding racemes on their thin stalks, with the clear, light green foliage as a background, bring a breath of the countryside into the surroundings. The species, forms and cultivars prefer a well-drained and light soil. They are more difficult to establish on cold, wet, clay soils, partly because the roots and rhizomes have difficulty in penetrating such an unkindly mass but also because they prefer to rest during the dormant stage in a soil which is warm and even on the dry side. One answer on heavy soils is to raise the bed above the general level with a mixture of light soil and leafmould before planting.

If the plant does establish and get away, given the chance it will creep through into the shade of deciduous subjects, even low-growing bushes and in drifts which extend along the edges of woods among brambles. In gardens it will even colonize the gaps between paving slabs. It is also suitable for growing beneath rhododendrons, provided the canopy is sufficiently open.

The crowns should be planted when dormant with the tips just beneath the surface. Plant single 'tips' at 60 mm. (2½ in.) apart.

Cortusa   Primulaceae

This genus is made up of two species from the mountains of Europe and Asia.

C. matthioli has rose or magenta-coloured flowers during the early summer period. However, from the time the growths develop from the crowns, which are just beneath the surface, the appearance of a plant or drift is both interesting and appealing. First tufts of delicate, frond-like leaves appear during March and, being a bright green, they look particularly attractive against a dark brown mulching of leafmould. As the foliage develops, it becomes more and more primula-like, in fact it could at first sight be mistaken for that of *Primula malacoides*, a popular pot plant. The leaves have a delicate crinkled surface, serrated edges and hairy petioles. By the time they are fully developed they form a carpet of rich green, 150 mm. (6 in.) in height. The heads of the nodding flowers, on stems 300 mm. (1 ft.) high, open during May and most of June. After flowering, the fruiting heads and dead foliage should be removed, when the plants will remain presentable until the autumn. The white flowers of the form 'Alba' are particularly attractive against the intensely green foliage, while they stand out in the fading light from some darkened corner.

It is a fine plant for the dappled shade of the woodland or shade garden, where the soil is moist and rich in leafmould and is perhaps most effective in irregular groups or drifts running from the front, where it can be seen and admired from close quarters. The planting should be no more than 2 m. (6 ft. 7 in.) wide, with marker groups, perhaps of hostas, on either side to facilitate top dressing and weeding; treading on the area occupied by the cortusa can then be avoided, which is very desirable. A thin dressing of leafmould should be made in early winter.

Propagation is by division when the growths appear in the spring, or by seed sown soon after ripening.

Corydalis   Fumariaceae

It seems natural to include *Corydalis* among the shade-lovers, but most species will thrive well in full sun, although perhaps they do not appear to be quite as happy as in some shade.

C. lutea, yellow fumitory, is a perennial herb, from southern Europe, with pinnate leaves, which have an almost fern-like appearance, and short racemes of yellow flowers produced throughout the summer. It is a plant that most people appreciate having in their gardens, particularly on or against old buildings, rock-work or a dry wall. Corydalis are accepted as plants for such positions and who would be bold enough to disagree? Whether in foliage, or with the flowers, their appearance is just what is needed to give an appearance of maturity and completeness, wherever they are growing. Once established, *C. lutea* seeds and colonizes freely, which is fortunate, for the plants should appear to be there by chance where no human hand could have planted them. They should never be allowed to grow too thickly, however, for without the surrounding background of stone or brick the effectiveness of this plant is much reduced. When flowering it reaches a height of 300 mm. (1 ft.). It will grow and flower where the sun never reaches it but there must be moisture within reach.

C. solida is an extraordinary little plant, from the Continent, reaching no more than 200 mm. (8 in.). Growth appears above the soil in early March, and within a fortnight it is in full leaf, with dull purple flowers. Flowering lasts for only three to four weeks, and at this stage the aquilegia-like foliage forms a thick carpet. Such beauty is very short-lived however and by the onset of summer the plant is at rest once again in the form of a rounded tuber.

It is happy in the dappled shade of the woodland or shade garden, where it should be in narrow drifts between ferns, for example, which will cover the bare soil completely during the summer and autumn. This plant would also be a joy in a shaded town garden.

Cotoneaster   Rosaceae

In this very large genus of ornamental shrubs are a number that will grow and flower well in a light, dappled shade, part shade, or even shade; although if a direct comparison is made, the majority would flower and fruit better in full sun. The one out-standing species for growing against a north-facing wall is *C. horizontalis*. The fan-shaped growths press against a vertical face with such force that they will spring back into position when pulled away. However, as the bush becomes older a considerable amount of growth develops out from the wall and may in time weigh the main branch system down, unless supporting ties are made. Even though this is a species that will do better in the sun, because it is hardy and tough it may be given this cold and sunless position. Many other cotoneasters would do just as well, except that they do not have such a marked 'spring action' when against a wall. The ability to withstand a sunless position is made use of with *C. dammeri*, a prostrate evergreen which will grow between shrubs and down shady banks, to provide a dense cover that will suppress weed growth.

Crinodendron   Elaeocarpaceae

C. hookerianum (*Tricuspidaria lanceolata*), is a wonderful plant to grow in the milder areas, where the atmosphere is also more humid. Usually it is best against a wall in a position of part shade or dappled shade, while shelter from the north and east is de-sirable. There are gardens which can supply just these conditions, together with the essential neutral or acid soil. The reward is an attractive, dark green foliage and dull-red flowers which open finally in the late spring, having survived the winter as immature 'pips' on long stalks.

Crocus   Iridaceae

This large and well-known genus is made up mainly of sun-lovers, but many are very adaptable and will thrive in light shade or part shade. Thus many places can be found for them—in the woodland garden, in grassy areas with widely spaced tree plantings, in shrub plantings, to mention just a few.

So far as soil is concerned, while they have a preference for a well-drained medium, most crocuses are very accommodating and will succeed on a wide range of soils from the heavy clays to the very light, sandy loams and chalky soils. A number of the easier and stronger growers will even increase by seed on their own account, if the conditions and soil suit them. There must be at least some drainage; they will not grow on a permanently boggy site, while the earliest flowering in the spring often occurs on a sunny and well-drained bank. There are many species, cultivars and hybrids to chose from, but only the more robust and accommodating should be considered for the types of shade already mentioned, certainly to begin with.

C. tomasinianus, from Yugoslavia, is among the earliest of the spring-flowering crocuses, and is often in flower in February. The thinly-stalked flowers, pale lilac or purple in colour, are held well above the developing leaves. On the lighter soils this species will seed and colonize extensively in light shade or sun, in border or grass. It will even eke out an existence beneath heavy and low-branched beech trees, where the canopy is so thick in the summer that even grasses are unable to survive. Crocuses in this position must flower and complete the formation of the new corm before the canopy has fully developed, when there will be little rain and no sun reaching them until the leaves fall in the autumn. See Fig. 7.

Among the many other spring-flowering crocuses, the choice is a wide one and includes the large-flowered hybrids, but they must be robust and able to survive under competition from trees, shrubs and grass. This also applies to some species that would not tolerate any form of shade. Groups or drifts of the stronger growers are fine if naturalized in grass, and it is preferable for each planting to consist of one colour only. They can be established in an area with an open, sunny position extending beneath deciduous trees, especially if these have high branching or start late into leaf. Crocuses planted in this way will introduce a new dimension into the scene for a period of two to three weeks when they are out (narcissi similarly distributed will provide another display of this nature a few weeks later). There are many other planting positions for these spring-flowering crocuses; for example, they may be taken into the part shade of buildings, but it must be remembered that the flowers will only open fully when the sun is on them.

The autumn-flowering species are sometimes confused with *Colchicum* (see p. 103). *Crocus speciosus*, from Persia and elsewhere, is one of the easiest to establish and will spread freely by seed to form large colonies in sun or light shade. This species flowers in late September. It has pale blue petals with deeper coloured veins, while the stigma is red. The colour is variable, and there is at least one white cultivar.

Crocuses are so little trouble that every effort should be made to accommodate them. There are a few important points to remember—in common with bulbous and cormous subjects generally, they should be left with their foliage intact until it dies down naturally, after the new corm has formed. Fortunately when the grass is finally cut and removed, the crocus seed is left behind to ripen and some of the species will, in consequence, spread and naturalize.

In a large or a small planting the positions should be selected carefully; always bear the maintenance of the area in mind. In addition, with the autumn-flowering species it should be remembered that the annual leaf-fall often collects or is blown into some areas or corners during a wind or gale, and these should be avoided for planting. Remember too that mice will greedily eat the corms, particularly during the dormant season, and should if necessary be controlled.

Many *Crocus* species may be raised quite easily from seed sown in prepared beds, and this affords a good means of building up stock in the first instance.

Cyclamen   Primulaceae

The hardy cyclamen are much admired and are becoming even more popular, possibly because at long last it is being realized that a number of the species and forms are quite easy to grow. Although they will thrive in the sun, they are associated with shady conditions and are at home at the base and among the buttress roots of large trees, on shady banks or in drifts beneath small trees. They should be near the path or at the front where they can be seen easily, for they are mostly dwarf and often reach little more than 100 mm. (4 in.) high. To get the best from them, they should have a background and be grown where a little scene can be built up. All the species seem to enjoy some sun, and this may be provided by dappled shade or part shade—probably they enjoy the baking and dry conditions which they often experience if the sun reaches their location when they are dormant through June and July.

C. graecum requires a position in full sun. All the species must have a well-drained soil stocked with well-decayed leafmould. Clay soils should be improved with an addition of grit; the plants do not seem to mind whether the soil is acid or alkaline.

C. hederifolium (*C. neapolitanum*), from central and southern Europe, is probably the easiest species to grow and is outstanding for its foliage effect during the winter. This develops in the late autumn after the flowering period; the leaves have a deep green centre with an ivory marbled edge—the perfect contrast to the autumn colours and winter scenes which follow. The foliage also blends well with rhododendrons, particularly the tight-growing kinds such as *R. yakushimanum*. The foliage thickens year by year as the corms, which are very close to the surface, enlarge. Self-sown seedlings also thicken up the effect. The foliage dies down completely during May, and the corm remains dormant until the flowers appear. It is always exciting to find the clusters of dainty, pink flowers, and there is a variety *C.h. album* which is equally good; the two may be mixed together quite effectively. Seed is set very freely, this being evident from the fruits which lie on the surface with their curious coiled stalks.

C. coum, from Greece and Asia Minor, is also an accommodating but variable species, which flowers from January to March and generally has little mottling on the leaves.

C. repandum, from southern Europe, flowers with thin, twisted petals during April and May.

Propagation is by seed, which should be sown as soon as it is ripe, certainly by the following spring. Once it is sown the seed must never dry out—a rule which is of great importance with most plants, but is vital to this and other members of the family Primulaceae. The cyclamen should be planted out when large enough, as leaf development begins, ensuring that the corms rest just beneath the soil surface.

Cypripedium Orchidaceae

This genus consists of the lady's slipper orchids, which in nature live only in the upper layers of the soil, made up mainly of decayed organic material. It is because of this that they are so demanding: the upper layer must be rich in organic material—preferably leafmould—it must be open and thus contain sand or grit, and yet it must remain moist and cool, even during the hottest and dryest of summers. It is no small wonder that there are so many failures with these beautiful plants, but unless the basic requirements can be met, they are better left alone. The best advice which can be given is to choose a site in dappled shade, preferably towards the base of a north-facing slope, where there is likely to be moisture with cool conditions, and then to add decayed leafmould, sharp sand and loam. It is emphasized that the site must be well drained. One should avoid planting near trees which have a vigorous and aggressive root system, for they will rob the plants of food and moisture. Sheltering shrubs are beneficial and at the same time provide a suitable setting.

C. reginae (*C. spectabile*), from North America, is the most beautiful species. Growth begins in late May. The pale green leaves are strongly ribbed by the parallel venation; the leaf edges and stems are hairy. The flowers, produced on 300 mm. (1 ft.) stems in the June period, are white with a rose 'pouch'. Even after flowering and for the remainder of the summer a group or clump remains attractive, for the leaves, which sheath the stem, provide such a perfect contrast to other foliage. This period between flowering and dying down for the winter is vital, for it is important for the foliage to keep in good condition in order that the plant builds up for next season's growth. A very weak liquid feed, for example manure water, is helpful after flowering. During the winter, after clearing away the old stems, a very thin dressing, about 20 mm. (¾ in.) in depth, of a fine mixture of three parts leafmould and one part of very well-decayed farmyard manure should be made. The position of the plants when dormant should be carefully noted, for the shoots lying in wait for the spring are very close to the surface.

C. pubescens, from North America, is the easiest species to grow.

It has twisted, lemon-coloured 'petals' which are finely marked and a deep, yellowish 'pouch'.

Propagation is by division in the spring just as growth begins. Mycorrhizal activity may have a great part to play in their successful culture, and for this reason a small quantity of soil from a site on which they are growing successfully should be added.

Cystopteris   Polypodiaceae

C. fragilis, brittle bladder fern is a native often found in rocky places and more rarely on old walls. The fronds develop from the dormant crowns in April, with an ultimate height which varies from 150 mm. (6 in.) to three times this measurement. Such a beautiful fern, so neat and with such light green, finely divided fronds, is obviously a desirable species to grow among shade-lovers. It is a plant for the front or near the path, perhaps on a rocky bank, but well away from other ferns, where it can be appreciated in contrast to other foliage and flowering shade-lovers.

Although this is the easiest and most suitable species to grow in this small but interesting genus, in dry and hot conditions the delicate and rather sensitive fronds will quickly lose condition.

Propagation is by spores, although in the first place plants should be bought from a nursery.

Danae   Liliaceae

This small genus contains only one species, *D. racemosa*—a near relative of the butcher's broom—which should be grown much more widely. It is from northern Persia and Asia Minor, and is an evergreen, similar in appearance to the genus *Sarcococca*, and at a glance may be mistaken for it, which may explain why it is so little known. The foliage is a fresh green, and is willow-like, while the shoots, extending like suckers from the base, are green and give the shrub a vase-shaped outline, reaching a height of a metre (3 ft. 3 in.). The whole appearance of the shrub is one of grace, and although the flowers are small and insignificant, these are often followed by a thin scattering of bright red berries. It is a plant to grow either singly or in a group, in dappled shade, choosing a moist position. It will also thrive in shade.

Propagation is by seed, or division in the spring just as the new growth starts.

Daphne   Thymelaeaceae

The correct soil types are most important to this genus. Taking
one of the British species, *D. laureola*, spurge laurel, as an example,
it is found in light woodland, on the damper of the calcareous
soils and on the heavy clays. *D. mezereum*, another native, will
grow well on most good soils, but where it is really happy, often
on the heavy clays, it will naturalize freely among other shrubs,
and in very thin tree groupings, especially if there is encouragement from good mulching. *D. pontica* is among the easiest species
to establish in light dappled shade, and it will certainly grow well
where the spurge laurel flourishes. The very light, warm and dry
soils are the most difficult for all three species, and an attempt to
make these more acceptable by the introduction of leafmould or
peat is advisable. It is most interesting that these three species will
die on a light soil in prolonged drought, while on the heavier ones
they will survive, although with the latter the clays may be
cracked and dry. Part of the answer in the successful culture of
this group is to transplant into the final positions early in life. The
soundest policy seems to be to try *D. laureola* and *D. pontica* first
if a position in dappled shade is being considered, building up with
a number of other species after gaining more experience.

Daphniphyllum   Daphniphyllaceae

D. macropodum. This evergreen shrub is rarely seen in gardens,
but it is reliable and will thrive in dappled shade beneath deciduous trees. Reaching up to 6 m. (20 ft.) high, the habit of
growth is similar to that of a rhododendron, and it may easily be
mistaken for one. However, it can be grown on a wide range of
soils, including those of an alkaline nature, and although the
flowers are inconspicuous, good forms make up for it in part at
least, for some of the petioles are coloured deep red and are quite
showy. Also, in the early summer this shrub is quite attractive,
with spikes of setting fruits standing erect beneath the new
foliage, which is fresh and green.

Dennstaedtia   Polypodiaceae

D. punctilobula, from North America, is an unusual fern, which is,
however, quite easily grown in a light, acid soil, provided there is
sufficient moisture within easy access to the roots.

The small, hairy, bracken-like growths appear in the late spring and by midsummer they reach a height of 500 to 700 mm. (1 ft. 8 in. to 2 ft. 4 in.), with fronds of a pleasant light green.

At this stage they need the support of a few hazel twigs, to prevent their arching over on to neighbouring plants. Usually the fronds are laid flat by the first severe frosts.

It is a desirable fern for the mottled shade of the woodland or shade garden, where its invasive and spreading habit helps to create a natural effect. The soil must be moist but well drained, so add peat at planting time. It is most effective in a group in the mid distance or background.

Propagation is by careful division in the spring.

Dentaria   Cruciferae

This genus is closely related to the cardamines, and is in the same family. However, unlike the majority of this family, which like the fields and sunny places, either growing naturally or as commercial crops, these two genera show a preference for coolness and dampness. *D. bulbifera* is a native, but is quite rare and localized, mainly in woods over chalk. It is a strange plant with a fleshy rhizome and a head of purple or pinkish flowers, but it relies upon bulbils in the axils of the leaves as the means of increase.

D. pinnata, from Europe, is white to purple flowered, with the foliage a fresh green; the leaves have a horse chestnut-like appearance, the edges being coarsely serrated.

D. enneaphylla, from Europe, has creamy-yellow flowers and foliage which brings to mind that of ground elder or bishop's weed, *Aegopodium podagraria*. Both these and the other species are plants to have near the front, in dappled shade or part shade, where it is cool and moist. In the main the heavier soils seem to suit this plant best, but as a guide, wherever the cuckoo flower or lady's smock—*Cardamine pratensis*—is thriving these plants should also succeed.

Dentarias are not by any means common in our gardens, but this is probably because they have frequently been mistaken for weeds and have been pulled up. The task of weeding through a mixed collection of plants is a very skilled one, for without knowledge many rare plants may be lost.

Dicentra   Fumariaceae

This genus is closely allied to *Corydalis*, to which it is similar in
many respects. The best-known species is *D. spectabilis*, from
China, Japan and Siberia, a plant which has many common names
including bleeding heart, lyre flower and Dutchman's breeches.
From the time the shoots break the surface in March–April, until
it dies down in the autumn, this plant is very decorative. First
the pale shoots, when they appear in the spring, are flushed pink
and brown, and with its delicately folded leaves it is distinct
among herbaceous border plants at this stage. The flowers, which
follow quickly as the growths gain their ultimate height of
600 mm. (2 ft.), hang from nodding racemes and consist of two
inflated, intensely rose-coloured petals with white-purple tipped
ones between. The lowest flowers on the racemes open first, with
the remainder in order of development—a beautiful effect, enhanced by the maturing foliage which is much divided—perhaps
the most beautiful stage of all. Even after flowering has finished
a few weeks later, the foliage remains in good condition until it
dies down in the autumn.

The plant loves a good, deep garden soil and one that does not
dry out rapidly, especially if it is in the sun. It is better really
when it gets some shade, especially during the hottest part of the
day, perhaps under or near apple trees with other herbaceous
plantings. Propagation is by division in the early autumn or
spring. The fleshy roots are brittle and the plant does not like
disturbance.

D. formosa, from North America, is better suited to the dappled
shade of the woodland or shade garden, or a position of part
shade in the rock garden and in other places where it is likely to
be cool. Like *D. spectabilis*, it is beautiful in all stages of growth
through the season. The leaves, folded and looped over as they
break the surface by early March, have a delicate appearance, being
finely segmented and fern-like, with a pale blue-green colouring.
By the time that spring is established, the whole clump or drift
is a mass of foliage 300 mm. (1 ft.) or more high, with the arching
spikes of rose-coloured flowers above this (see Plate 17). By the
early summer the flowering is reduced and the foliage begins to
lose its fresh appearance, particularly if a dry spell sets in, but any
substantial rains soon revive it, with the production of new foliage

and possibly a late flower display. Often an odd flower spike is found in the autumn. A fine plant to have for effect among other foliage and flowering shade plants; it is also a good marker plant. There are, in addition, a number of beautiful cultivars.

D. macrantha, from China, has most lovely foliage, the leaves being divided, with serrated edges and pale green and yellow colouring. The yellow flowers are produced in the spring. The autumn colouring is often pleasing as the older foliage is dark brown while the youngest leaves are still green.

Both *D. formosa* and *D. macrantha* may be propagated by division.

Digitalis   Scrophulariaceae

D. purpurea, the foxglove, is too well known to need description, so common are the spikes of purple flowers, often in their hundreds, in woodland clearings, by hedges and in many other situations. This species will thrive on a wide range of soils, provided that the drainage is reasonable. The only limiting factor which prevents it from growing everywhere in the northern temperate region, is that the minute seedlings, which appear in such vast numbers, must have good growing conditions. There must be sufficient light, in the form of full sun, dappled shade or part shade, and the soil must be reasonably free of other herbage— better still if it is bare or almost completely so. These conditions are to be found in semi-natural, light woodland or shrub border plantings of a varied nature. The plant can easily be established, either by sowing directly on to the border in the spring, or by planting seedlings which have been raised elsewhere. It is usually biennial, forming rather a coarse rosette in the first season of growth, and flowering from this during the next year, usually in the early part of the summer.

The question of whether or not it should be introduced can only be answered when personal choice is taken into consideration. The rosette will be appreciated for many months, for they are evergreen, while the effect of a spike as it comes into flower is very beautiful. However, as the procession of opening flowers moves towards the tip of the spike or raceme, the lower ones fade and the seed vessels develop. The plant then loses much of its beauty, particularly when viewed as closely as it is in a garden. This is the time when one should harden one's heart and remove it, certainly before the bulk of the seed is dispersed. This timely action will save hours and hours of work in pulling out the thousands of seedlings, which otherwise develop everywhere. Also the heavy drain on moisture and nutrients taken from the soil as the plant develops this heavy crop of seeds will be ended, to the benefit of other plants in the immediate area.

A number of strains are available from seedsmen if these are preferred, but they are perhaps more suitable for flowering borders. The simple white form creates a welcome variation, even in a naturalized planting, and is especially appreciated in the twilight hours after a tiring day.

Diphylleia Podophyllaceae

D. cymosa, from North America, has every appearance of being a woodlander, and in such a situation it will not disappoint, for it creates just the right effect. The first exciting stage is when the growths appear above the surface during late April, for the young leaves are copper coloured and very much like *Podophyllum*, to which it is closely related. The flower buds are also apparent at an early stage, almost at ground level.

The plant develops rapidly, and within three or four weeks the foliage has a coarse appearance and consists of enormous, rounded, cleft leaves on 600 mm. (2 ft.) high stalks. In early June, interest is in the flowers, which are held in umbel-like clusters 300 mm. (1 ft.) above the foliage. They are white with prominent yellow stamens—just the pure and simple flowers one would expect to find in a woodland. Another interesting display follows four to five weeks later when the fruits ripen to a powdery blue, unusual but effective, especially if the light green, irregularly lobed foliage remains in good condition. It is a plant for the dappled shade of the woodland or shade garden, but it must have a good growing, moist soil. A drift in the mid-distance or background is very effective.

Propagation is by seed or division just before growth starts in the spring.

Disanthus Hamamelidaceae

D. cercidifolius is a beautiful shrub, reaching up to 3 m. (10 ft.), with as much spread. It has a most charming effect during the summer, with its thin and slender branching and light foliage.

During the autumn it assumes the most fantastic colourings, ranging from orange to purple. It is, however, difficult to grow well, unless the conditions are perfect in every way—shelter, coolness and dappled shade, with a good growing, but moist and acid soil. It is a big challenge to those who try this plant in the hot Thames Valley.

Disporum   Liliaceae

This is a small group of herbaceous perennials, with a distinct likeness to Solomon's seal, to which they are closely related, being in the same group and family.

D. smithii, from North America, forms a thick clump of growths 500 mm. (1 ft. 8 in.) high, the thin, wiry stems growing into one another to form a carpeting mass. The leaves clasping the stems are nicely oval-shaped and tapering at the tips with parallel venation. The hanging, bell-shaped flowers are greenish-white, and are produced in early June on the branch tips. The fruits which follow are berry-like, yellow-green at first, but orange when fully ripened by early August, with the foliage remaining in good condition, provided there is sufficient moisture. In the autumn and early winter the light brown growth looks attractive, and is worth leaving for as long as possible. *D. pullum*, from Asia, is similar, with dull blue clusters of fruits which often hang until the autumn, when the foliage turns to a copper colour.

There are a few other species, and all have a delicate effect if used as a contrast, especially between groups of bolder plants. They should be near the front where their beauty can be appreciated. These plants thrive in a dappled shade and a moist, woodland type of soil which is well stocked with organic material, especially leafmould.

Propagation is by division as the growths appear in the spring, or by seed sown as the berries are about to fall. Plant small clusters of roots 230 mm. (9 in.) apart.

Distylium   Hamamelidaceae

This genus is in the same family as the witch hazel, one which is generally recognized as preferring neutral to acid soils, with sun or, at the most, part shade. *D. racemosum* will, however, grow quite well in dappled shade beneath deciduous trees, while it can be taken on to soils which are definitely alkaline, provided that plenty of organic material is added. It is a slow-growing shrub with a spreading habit which is extended to the laterals, but the main units of branching remain distinct under shaded conditions, for the growth is naturally thinner.

During the early spring the clusters of flowers, which are held in the axils of the leaves, open to display the red-purple stamens. Soon the bushes become dusted with pollen, almost as if a thin scattering of lime had been applied. Later the branches are heavy with the developing fruits and new growths, which have pale green leaves, and a second crop of intense cerise-red flowers. An unusual shrub to grow.

Dryopteris   Polypodiaceae

D. *filix-mas*, male fern (see Plate 3), is a native with an almost world-wide distribution and how beautiful it is—our hedgebanks and woods would be the poorer without it.

In late April the crowns start into growth with the appearance of the fronds, at first in the form of a coiled midrib, which is a woolly light brown. A week or so later the pinnae on the lower part of the fronds have developed, while the tips are still folded within the midrib which at this stage appears like a shepherd's crook—fascinating indeed, particularly in the early morning when the hairy midribs reflect and glisten in the low sun.

The ultimate height is a metre (3 ft. 3 in.); the colouring light green which deepens with age. An established group will form a thick covering by June, and the foliage remains in good condition until early November when it usually turns a light brown, autumn colour. In a mild winter the fronds may remain green until the new ones develop, but in any case they should be cut down to the crown, to allow the new fronds to be seen as they appear in the spring.

A plant for grouping in the dappled shade of the woodland, or the larger shade garden where it can be grown as a contrast to other foliage or flowering subjects. It is suitable too for shaded borders where the sun never reaches, but it will also grow in part shade, provided sufficient moisture is available. When a natural woodland flora is being built up, following the establishment of trees or coppice, this species may well be introduced at an early stage, for as soon as the layer of leafmould and other organic matter has built up to a sufficient level, it will spread and colonize quite freely. It will be pleasing enough by itself, but in all probability a host of other beautiful native plants will arrive.

There are numerous cultivars, too, many with crested fronds which are very beautiful; these are more suitable for the 'cultivated' part of a shade garden or a border. There are also other species: for example, *D. dilatata*, from the north temperate zone, has an intense green colouring, and *D. borreri*, a native, which remains fresh and green until December or through the winter. Most of these are large and substantial enough to hold a mid-border or background position, but *D. spinulosa*, narrow buckler fern, a native, should be near the front where the delicate fronds, 300 mm. (1 ft.) high, can be seen quite closely.

Propagation is normally by detaching side growths in the early spring and if necessary establishing these in a nursery bed before planting out. Spore propagation is also possible with the species, although some hybridisation may occur.

Endymion   Liliaceae

E. nonscriptus (Scilla nonscripta), bluebell, wild hyacinth, is a well-known bulbous plant likely to be found in almost every part of the British Isles—in woods and copses, beneath deciduous trees, and in the shelter of hedgerows. It is perhaps most at home on a light, acid or neutral soil, where it will sometimes colonize into open stretches of long grass, and in beds and borders which are filled with more permanent plantings such as shrubs. It is noticeable that it will often thrive in a soil which is too dry and well drained for snowdrops and primroses, and where our native wild daffodil—*Narcissus pseudonarcissus*—does little but hold its own, flowering, but without additional colonizing by seed.

The bluebell starts into growth very early, and the clustered shoots can often be found beneath the canopy of fallen leaves during December. As the shoots break out into the open they often serve a very useful purpose in spearing the leaves, thus holding them in position while they rot. Starting its growth so early, this species is able to complete most of the flowering period and the build-up of the bulb for the next season before the overhead leaf canopy is at full growth and competing for light and moisture. Even so, bluebells sometimes suffer from lack of moisture during a dry spring. Such trees as the horse chestnut—*Aesculus hippocastanum*—complete their leaf canopy so early in the season that even the bluebell is unhappy, or will not grow beneath it.

E. hispanicus (*Scilla hispanica, S. campanulata*), is a stronger grower than the bluebell and the spike stands erect; the flowers are larger and a paler blue. This species is ideal for naturalizing in the dappled shade of the shrub border, but there is one drawback: the soil surface cannot be cleared properly of weeds until the bulb foliage dies down. An effective answer to this is to mulch with rotted compost or leafmould during the early winter so that the surface is kept relatively weed-free until the bulb foliage dies down. The two species will grow side by side, but while *E. hispanicus* often dominates in a particular bed or border, the bluebell remains undisputed in its wild territories.

Both species may be propagated by lifting the bulbs during the dormant season, and by seed.

Epimedium   Berberidaceae

This genus of perennials is of importance to the shade garden. Epimediums are regarded as being shade-loving plants, but they are very accommodating and will thrive in many types of shade, including dappled shade, part shade or shade. Although these plants show some preference for the heavy loams, they are happy on a wide range of soils, especially if some improvement is carried out if it is needed.

So far as their use is concerned, they are suitable for informal features such as the woodland or shade garden, but also for borders with a more formal outline, for example shrub or shaded herbaceous borders. If the setting is an informal one they are very good in groups or drifts, although great care is needed in planning this. They have such a thick foliage effect that the clump and its outline can be too evident and striking. If it is considered to be so, the edge may be broken up a little by planting a few at random away from the main clump or drift. On a small scale individual plants are effective and they will serve as excellent markers for other subjects. Height is an important factor to take into account and generally this varies from 300 to 500 mm. (1 ft. to 1 ft. 8 in.). This means that they are substantial enough to carry a mid-border position, while a planting may be brought right to the front where it can be seen to full advantage.

When a selection is made it is important to remember that a

group or drift should consist of one species or variety only. Epimediums are grown mainly for their varied foliage effects through the season, for they are in flower for only a brief period. However, the flowers are appealing, charming and dainty, and lend much to a woodland atmosphere. Often they have two definite colours, the inner set of petals being spurred to contain the nectar. At this stage it should be emphasized that epimediums are in the main quite hardy, but some shelter from cold winds is preferable, particularly for the flowers and the evergreen species.

In the following brief account the emphasis is upon the various foliage effects.

E. alpinum, from Europe, in which the young foliage, with folded leaves bent over on a delicate pale red leaf stalk, appears in late March and presents a colourful picture, especially in a low morning or evening sun. An early morning dew or hoar frost also gives an unusual effect since it is held by the fine hairy growths. As the leaves unfold they are a pleasant light green, edged with bronze before they turn to a darker green. Younger leaves develop later from time to time and then the contrast in colour among the old and the new makes a very pretty picture. In the autumn the foliage turns to shades of bronze, brown, yellow and green, the delicate venation being more obvious at this season. This assembly of colouring forms a wonderful pattern with the fallen leaves.

A number of the remaining epimediums produce this attractive foliage in the spring, but *E.* × *versicolor* 'Versicolor', from Japan, is often outstanding. First to appear in late March are the deep pink and lemon-yellow flowers, an attractive feature, but the young leaves a few weeks later are red-bronze over much of the surface with a light green patch at the base which reaches up as a margin to the main veins.

E. × *perralchicum* and *E. perralderianum*, from North Africa, are evergreens and are sometimes harmed in a severe winter. The former species is usually bronzed, even during a normal winter. The latter has leaves with a spiny edge and is worth growing for the foliage effect alone. A few show a tendency to become almost evergreen during a mild winter; for example, *E.* × *warleyense* sometimes turns a good reddish copper-bronze colour on the exposed foliage as late as December, while the inside leaves remain green. *E. pinnatum colchicum*, from Georgia, and *E. sagittatum*, from China and Japan, also have this tendency, the latter having leaves which are mahonia-like in texture and appearance.

Many epimediums have reflective leaf surfaces, but none more so than *E. grandiflorum* 'Violaceum'.

The foliage of the deciduous epimediums may be cut back to 100 mm. (4 in.) during February, or even earlier, when all trace of colouring has gone and before the flowers and new leaves appear. At the same time a thin annual mulch may be applied.

Propagation is by division during the dormant season.

Eranthis   Ranunculaceae

E. hyemalis, winter aconite, is indigenous to southern Europe, but is naturalized in many places in this country. Who can resist it? The low crowded cushion of pale yellow, buttercup-like flowers is a true herald of spring, for the growths often peep through during January. It comes into blossom quickly after this, needing only the faintest rays from the low winter's sun for the petals to open and expand to their fullest extent. Even as the flowers open, the pale green and deeply lobed leaves develop, giving support to this bold and early display. By late March the fruits are well formed, and, with the foliage forming a perfect pattern over the clump, the whole effect remains attractive. The fruits are pod-like and open to release their seeds in May when the foliage dies down to small tuber-like structures.

It is an ideal plant for dappled shade in rough grass which is mown fairly short 40 to 50 mm. (1½ to 2 in.) in the late autumn before the winter sets in. A planting can also be considered for the smaller garden, for example among fruit trees set in grass.

Winter aconite thrives well on a wide variety of soils, including the clays and the chalks, but it shows a distinct dislike of soils which dry out rapidly during its short, but very active, period above ground. It is suggested that to begin with a few small patches are tried, for if the plant is happy it will spread quite readily from self-sown seed. On sloping sites the lower and damper areas should be tried first, while on dry sites the addition of a 100 mm. (4 in.) layer of clay beneath the top 50 mm. (2 in.) of soil may be sufficient. A useful guide: where the lesser celandine, *Ranunculus ficaria*, grows the winter aconite is also likely to succeed. It can also be grown in part shaded borders, or beneath deciduous shrubs—it hates evergreens and conifers. What joy it would bring to a town garden or window-box. For the partly shaded pocket in the rock garden, the other species and hybrids should perhaps be considered, but for naturalizing most prefer *E. hyemalis*.

The corms may be planted when they are dormant, 60 mm. (2½ in.) deep; clumps may be lifted, divided and transplanted successfully when in full leaf just after flowering, but it must be done quickly, before they wilt. The advantage of this latter method is that the clumps can be located easily at this stage.

Erythronium   Liliaceae

These choice spring-flowering plants are often looked upon as being difficult, but this is not so if they are given the right conditions. They prefer the shade, and the flowers last for much longer if the position is a cool one. For the best results the soil must be moist but well drained, with plenty of organic material in the form of peat or leafmould. A small amount of well-rotted manure, mixed in as a top-dressing each winter, is also helpful. Erythroniums are impatient of the extremes in soils—the clays, the sands and gravels, unless much is done to improve them.

E. dens-canis, the dog's tooth violet, a name which refers in part to the shape of the bulb, is found in Europe, also in parts of Asia including Japan. Growth appears in the early spring, the foliage being pale green with chocolate and deeper bronze blotches. It is particularly attractive with rain drops resting on the surface, as are the leaves of so many plants. By late March the flowers are about to open; they reach a height of 150 mm. (6 in.). In bud they have a cyclamen-like appearance, but when fully open the petals are recurved, with a colouring which varies from white to rose and purple (see Plate 17).

In order to see the beautiful marking in the centre, often a primrose-yellow with a narrow zone of deeper colouring, it is necessary gently to lift up the nodding blossoms. By late April flowering is complete and a few weeks later the foliage dies back. Being variable, a number of cultivars have been selected, for example, 'Rose Beauty' and 'White Splendour'.

The American species are very beautiful, and a number of cultivars have also originated from these. *E. tuolumnense* 'Pagoda', a cultivar sometimes listed as a hybrid, is outstanding, with nodding pale lemon-yellow flowers, often two or three on a stem.

This excellent plant will reach a height of 400 mm. (1 ft. 4 in.), well above the bright green, tulip-like foliage which has paler but distinct markings. *E. revolutum*, 'White Beauty', has creamy flowers, with lemon-yellow centres which have a deeper orange marking. These and a number of other species and cultivars can be grown quite easily, but it is advisable to gain experience by starting with a few, having them in selected areas near the front where they can be looked after properly. Undoubtedly the best time for planting is during the late summer or autumn, as soon as the growths have died down. In common with plants of the family Liliaceae in general, they should not be allowed to dry out when dormant. Should the bulbs you have bought arrive in a dried condition, it is advisable to place them between layers of moist peat for a week or so to 'plump up' before planting out, 100 to 150 mm. (4 to 6 in.) deep according to size.

Many of the species and cultivars produce offsets once they are established, and it is therefore advisable to leave them undisturbed for a few years. When offsets do arise, this method of propagation may be used, choosing the early part of the dormant season to lift them. Seed sown in the autumn after ripening is another means, but it is very slow.

Erythroniums are plants for the dappled shade or shade of the woodland, the shade garden, a shady part of the rock garden or the shaded border; fine too in the quiet of the town garden.

Escallonia   Escalloniaceae

Usually a position with at least some sun is recommended for these beautiful flowering, evergreen shrubs, yet in the milder south-west of the country good plants can be found thriving in shade beneath trees, and in north-facing positions. *E. rubra* var. *macrantha*, a strong grower with rosy-red flowers is outstanding for this purpose, but only in the milder areas. In a sheltered position *E.* 'Iveyi' which has large panicles of white flowers, could also be tried in shade.

Euonymus   Celastraceae

In this genus are a number of very accommodating evergreen shrubs which will thrive in the sun or in most types of shade, except full shade. *E. fortunei* has a great variety of forms including 'Kewensis', a good ground-cover for shrub borders, provided that the soil is weed free when it is planted, as it is slow to get away. Like many others, such as 'Silver Queen', it will also climb, even through a small tree provided that the canopy is a light one, *Acer negundo* 'Variegatum' for example. *E.f.* 'Variegatus' has a beautiful, white variegation, which is toned with shades of pink, especially during the winter and spring. This is a wonderful shrub for growing beneath a light canopy of evergreens.

There are also many good cultivars of *E. japonicus*, including the stronger growers. The cultivar, 'Albomarginatus', has a narrow white margin to the leaf, while 'Aureopictus' is very showy with a golden centre. Although they will grow in the sun, these are suitable plants for training against a north-facing wall in the warmer areas. They are also ideal for a sheltered and shady corner against stone or brick-work. *E.j.* 'Microphyllus' develops into a small and compact bush, very slow growing and suitable for a narrow border in shade, or for a shaded corner in the rock garden.

Euphorbia
Euphorbiaceae

The vast family Euphorbiaceae can claim to have representatives in many of the 'fields' in which plants are grown, either for ornamental or commercial purposes. However, in the genus *Euphorbia* alone there is wide variation, with approximately 1,600 species distributed throughout the temperate and tropical regions.

E. robbiae, from Asia Minor, has proved to be one of the best ground-cover plants. The spurge-like flowers (see Plate 6), a rich but soft yellow, are produced mainly during mid to late spring in heads which may eventually reach 800 mm. (2 ft. 7 in.) high. Later the flowers, as they fade, turn to green, but still hold interest, being slightly tinged with bronze. Even as late as November the spent inflorescences are prominent above the dark foliage which is held in a rosetted head. With the onset of wintry weather, often most severe after Christmas, these old flower heads turn to a drab colour and have an untidy appearance, and may be carefully removed with secateurs, working backwards because the milky juice which follows a cut is rather messy and will soon spoil clothing. In the early spring, when growth restarts, the youngest terminal foliage is a lighter green, and is a perfect contrast to the older and darker foliage. This plant will thrive on a wide variety of soils, in sun, dappled shade, or part shade. It will creep forward by means of short stolons, and can be readily divided in the early spring; choose the smaller piece.

E. griffithii, 'Fireglow', is another splendid plant with an informal or 'natural' effect. It will grow in full sun, dappled shade, or part shade, and is excellent for planting among trees and large shrubs such as rhododendrons. Planted on either a large or small scale, it should have a suitable background and setting to look its best. It will thrive on a deep, woodland type of soil which is well stocked with organic material. The foliage is a bright green, while the heads of flowers, which are produced in late April to May, are a dull, glowing, salmon-red. In all, the plant at this stage is often a metre (3 ft. 3 in.) or more high, hence the need to grow it only between the largest of shrubs. If it is happy it rapidly produces a thick, clump-like growth, which rises rapidly from ground level each spring, the more exposed stems being a striking red-bronze.

Propagation is by division in the early spring, just as growth commences.

× Fatshedera   Araliaceae

× *F. lizei* is believed to be *Fatsia japonica* × *Hedera helix*. This interesting bigeneric hybrid is a tough evergreen that will thrive in dappled shade. The glossy foliage is quite attractive, being lighter green through the summer with the new growths. In the late summer the sterile panicles of yellow flowers are produced. Under poor conditions it is not such a good grower as ivy.

Fatsia   Araliaceae

F. japonica, which often grows to the proportions of a small tree, is a sparsely branched evergreen, with large, palmate, glossy leaves. In the autumn it is most impressive, each mature growth having a large terminal inflorescence consisting of prominent branching and rounded heads of white flowers, very similar to those of *Hedera*.

This is a good 'key' plant to grow in a sheltered position, in various degrees of shade, but not full shade. It is a good subject with an evergreen tree as a background, or with stone or brickwork, in a sheltered corner.

Filipendula   Rosaceae

Many members of the Rosaceae venture close to shady places and, in company with *Aruncus dioicus* and at least a few others in the family, this genus of herbaceous plants is quite prepared to live contentedly under a light, leafy canopy. *F. purpurea*, a Japanese species which reaches over a metre (3 ft. 3 in.) in height, even prefers a light, dappled shade. It has light green and palmate foliage and by midsummer has an almost raspberry-like effect. However, as the flower heads develop and open a crimson colour, this similarity quickly disappears.

F. ulmaria, meadowsweet, a native, is common wherever there are water and silty deposits, but is not found where the soil is very acid. It will quite happily leave the sun if there is not sufficient moisture, and grow in the dappled shade or part shade if the ground is wetter. This is sufficient justification for introducing *F.u.* 'Aurea' which has intense yellow foliage during the summer months. The leaves when they first appear are yellow, tinged with bronze, and form rosettes which lengthen into flowery heads, but these can be removed as they are often very poor. Although this variety will lose some of its deep colouring if the shade is too intense, it may scorch in hot and dry periods when under a full sun.

Propagate by division during the dormant season. Plant at 300 mm. (1 ft.) apart.

Fragaria   Rosaceae

F. vesca, wild strawberry, is a little native, most frequently found in shaded places on the heavier soils and over chalk. It thrives best where there are abundant supplies of organic material, preferably leafmould. It is a nice plant to have in the background, beneath trees—perhaps in a wilder and semi-natural part of the garden, where it will contribute so much towards the desired effect. It is happy in dappled shade, part shade or shade.

The cultivar 'Variegata' has a white variegation on the leaf which is bright and irregular, but it is a plant for cultivated areas for it is not such a strong grower as the type. A bed in the shade garden or a shaded border is suggested. It will also brighten a town garden.

Propagation is by the runners as they root into the surrounding soil.

Fritillaria   Liliaceae

The native species is *F. meleagris*, snake's head fritillary. Growing

E

up to 300 mm. (1 ft.) high, with grass-like foliage, the flowering
stem forms a complete U-bend, and the bell-shaped blossoms
hang down to protect the nectaries, overflowing with a welcome
to visiting bumble bees. There is a purple and white pattern over
the petals.

This species prefers the moist, heavy loams and, provided that
conditions are suitable, it will spread and naturalize quite freely,
going into beds and grassy areas in sun or dappled shade wherever
the wind-borne seed is carried. The variety *F. m. alba* is even
more adaptable to cultivation and naturalization than the type
species.

This genus contains some of the most difficult species in the
whole family Liliaceae, but generally this is because they are sun-
lovers and in these islands we do not get enough to suit them.

Propagation is by separation of bulbs during the dormant
season, or by seed.

Fuchsia   Onagraceae

Fuchsias are usually associated with full sun or part shade, and
undoubtedly many of the species, hybrids and cultivars are at
their best in such a position. However, they will grow and flower
well in dappled shade or shade, provided it is not too dense.
Fuchsias are suitable for a shaded border, with other shrubs, but
generally, unless the warmer and more favoured localities are
being considered, only *F. magellanica* and the hardier forms and
cultivars should be grown and even these should not be attempted
in the colder parts of the country. *F. magellanica alba* is particularly good in shade, for the white flowers stand out so clearly in
the dusk of a summer's evening.

The larger flowered and more tender cultivars are fine subjects
to grow in tubs or window-boxes, for example in a town garden,
and they will also flower in shade, provided it is not cold and
draughty. If the plants are in tubs or pots, it is sometimes possible
to turn them occasionally so that all sides receive an equal amount
of light, giving in turn a more balanced growth and flowering.

It is important to remember that fuchsias flower from the leaf
axils on the current season's growth during the summer and
autumn as it is being produced. The better the growth, the more
will they flower. In too dense a shade, growth will be drawn,
with longer internodes and subsequently less flower. Cold,

draughty or exposed positions will mean little growth, and thus poor flowering. Another point concerns moisture availability, for while these plants must have a well-drained soil, they are impatient of drought—again little growth means reduced flowering.

F. procumbens, from North Island, New Zealand, is a prostrate species that will grow well in a moist, shady position, for example creeping beneath such shrubs as rhododendrons. It has tiny leaves which are light green, a small flower with yellow sepals but no petals, and a pink, egg-shaped fruit. An interesting, little plant, but it should only be tried in the warmer localities as it is not fully hardy.

Fuchsias are easily propagated by softwood or semi-ripe cuttings.

Galanthus   Amaryllidaceae

G. nivalis, snowdrop, is considered to be a native, but it also has a wide distribution over the Continent and beyond. For shade gardening this species is unrivalled. It is found growing wild in dappled shade, part shade, shade—sometimes too in full sun, but it appears to prefer the shade. The species shows a marked preference for a moist soil, and one which is not too freely drained. The heavy loam and clay soils suit it very well, particularly if it is to grow under naturalized conditions, fending for itself among tree roots, grasses and other strong-growing plants, including blue-bells, which are all eager to make their way in the spring.

Planting is best carried out immediately after flowering, when clusters of six or more bulbs should be set in prepared holes, forming irregular drifts. The work must be carried out carefully, ensuring that the bulbs do not dry out during the operation. Care should be taken with the roots, in order to avoid damage and disturbance as much as possible. This is another reason for planting in clusters, which should not be broken down too finely unless there is need to cover a large area.

Dormant bulbs, available during the summer, should also be planted in small clusters, for they grow well together and form a clump of foliage which is substantial enough to withstand competition from other plants. However, the ground is often hard during this period and then the work will be very difficult. In nature the period of dormancy is a very short one, lasting only a few weeks at the most. Undisturbed bulbs, at rest in the soil, develop new roots with the onset of the autumn rains, so it is preferable for bulbs moved during this period to be planted before the new rooting takes place. Should the planting of dormant bulbs be delayed for too long the moisture is lost and they wither. As a result the bulbs suffer—perhaps just for one season, but often for far longer. This is a pity, because it is not always possible to obtain many of the species and hybrids other than in a dried state; lucky is he or she who has a friend willing to part with pieces of growing plants—all correctly named. The best method of nursing withered bulbs is to place them between layers of moist peat for a week or so, in order that they may plump-up. Then they may be planted without delay and watered if necessary. Feeding with fertilizer or liquid manure is also helpful at this stage. It is also a good plan to remove the flowers at an early stage in order to conserve energy.

If the soil is very light and well drained, the establishment of this species under naturalized conditions may be more uncertain. The addition of a quantity of clay should be tried, either digging this in over the site for the drift or, better still, by excavating soil 300 mm. (1 ft.) deep, and using the clay or heavy soil as a complete or part filling.

The common snowdrop is available in single and double forms, but there are many other species and cultivars. They should be grown to begin with in selected beds within the rock garden or the shaded woodland garden, where they can be looked after properly, with careful weeding and the application of an annual dressing of leafmould. If they seed and spread through the bed into other parts, all well and good, but often they remain where they are, perfectly healthy, but in need of all the care and skill in cultivation which can be bestowed upon them. Some require a drier soil than others, with more sun to ripen the bulbs so that they flower well; *G. graecus*, from the Balkans, is an example. An important point in favour of introducing a greater variety is that the flowering period is extended. *G. nivalis* sub. sp. *reginae-olgae*, from Greece, is in flower in the autumn, while *G. ikariae*, from the Greek island of Ikaria is one of the last to be in display in the late spring.

Galax   Diapensiaceae

G. aphylla, from North America, is not found as frequently as it should be, for, given a cool, moist position on an acid soil it will, being an evergreen, quietly give pleasure and satisfaction the year through. It is low-growing and forms a close hummock of round or cordate leaves, which are a shiny green. During the June–July period there is a pleasant scattering of small white flowers which are held in simple racemes occupying the upper half of thin, leafless stalks, which may be 150 mm. (6 in.) or more tall. If the plant is happy and supplied with sufficient moisture, the leaves remain in good condition through summer, autumn and winter, until the new foliage is produced in the late spring. Not only this, but during the winter the leaves are edged with a dull crimson colouring and at times these shades, toning down to bronze, run through the green towards the leaf centres. The old dead in-floresences are also attractive during the winter.

The species is ideal for a bank by a path or stream, or in some corner where it can be seen easily, producing just the right effect and adding greatly to the charm and mystery of the woodland garden. It can be equally charming in the more formal garden, but its requirements must be met with the right soil and moisture at the roots, remembering that it is happiest in shade or dappled shade. Many town gardens too could provide just the right conditions for it.

Propagation is by division in the early autumn.

Galeobdolon   Labiatae

Galeobdolon luteum (*Lamium galeobdolon*), yellow archangel, is a native found in quite dense colonies in dappled shade, or part shade, on the heavier and moist soils. Under suitable conditions it will increase rapidly by seed, and the runners, which spread out and arch over, reach the surface at some distance from the mature plant. The foliage of the cultivar 'Variegatum' is marked with a prominent silver zoning, and this makes the plant most con-spicuous. In common with the type species, the yellow flowers are produced in the late spring and early summer, but it is for foliage effect, combined with quick coverage, that it is so widely grown. Without doubt it is the most successful ground-cover plant in the family Labiatae, for it will grow into even denser shade, whereas so many others tend to draw away from it. This is a great ad-vantage, as it will loop into and shine forth from the darkest of corners, even during the winter; for the foliage is retained at least until the new growth appears in the spring, although it is often weather-beaten.

There are some disadvantages to this plant; it is so strong that the runners will loop over and swamp smaller shrubs; to thrive, it must have a cultivated bed with a good soil and it dislikes dry conditions, wilting badly if subjected to long periods of drought.

Propagation is easily achieved by cuttings during the summer, and by planting up rooted pieces in the early spring. Another method is to cut out and dig up the parent plants in the early spring and replant them in another selected spot. In this way the rooted layers are left behind to complete the coverage of the bed.

Garrya   Garryaceae

G. elliptica, although at its best in a sunny position in the warmer parts of the country, has proved a surprisingly adaptable shrub. It can be grown in dappled shade, or shade, and even against a north-facing wall in the milder areas. The male plants have the most conspicuous catkins, and the selected clone 'James Roof' is a very good one.

× **Gaulnettya**   Ericaceae

In this bigeneric group is a set of hybrids which have arisen between *Gaultheria* and *Pernettya*. Among these is × *G.* 'Wisley Pearl' (*Gaultheria shallon* × *Pernettya mucronata*, sometimes known as × *G. wisleyensis*). This grows to about a metre (3 ft. 3 in.) high and will thrive in quite dense dappled shade, running right up to the trunks of low-branching deciduous trees by means of suckers, which it freely produces. The soil must be well drained and acid, but in common with one of the parents—*P. mucronata*, to which it is similar in many respects—it is not happy in a soil which dries out rapidly. Perhaps another plant will appear one day of the same cross which has more of *G. shallon* in its constitution, for this is a much tougher plant under dry conditions. In addition to its attraction when the close clusters of flowers are produced in the late spring, this hybrid has an interesting appearance with its clusters of reddish developing fruits, and the light green of the younger growths which develop above the older and dark leaves.

Gaultheria   Ericaceae

This genus consists of shrubby species, some of which are very
dwarf, and contains a number that will thrive in dappled shade,
conditions similar in fact to those sought after by many of the
rhododendrons.

G. *shallon* is one of the strongest-growing species, reaching up
to 2 m. (6 ft. 7 in.) high, and forms a very dense mat of growth.
Being evergreen is an added advantage, and with white racemes
of flower during the late spring and early summer it becomes very
attractive. Afterwards, and right through the winter, the withered
flower-remains show up distinctly against the dark green foliage.
The fleshy fruits are purple when ripe. When this subject is combined with other strong-growing plants, such as *Mahonia aquifolium*, the contrasts and general effect can be very pleasing
indeed. It can also be planted beneath larger plants, for example
deciduous azaleas, where the winter effect alone justifies such a
combination. At this period the rich but light brown of the old
seed cases and the pale green of the swelling buds on the azaleas,
have a perfect background in the dark green gaultheria foliage.

G. *procumbens* is another good evergreen, but it produces an
extending carpet which is no more than 150 mm. (6 in.) high.
This species requires more shade in the south of the country
than in the north where it is cooler. The autumn colour over a
clump often varies in a strange way, for some leaves remain green
while others turn to shades of bronze, orange or scarlet. The
fruits are bright red.

This is a very short account of a large group, many members
of which will grow best in open situations, and are suitable too
for the peat garden. They must have an acid soil.

Gentiana   Gentianaceae

At one time the family Gentianaceae included opposite-leaved
land plants and alternate-leaved aquatics, but the latter group,
including *Menyanthes* and *Nymphoides*, have been transferred. This
has still left a great assortment, even in the genus *Gentiana*. A
number of its members are easy-to-grow, while others, in particular some of the species from mountainous areas, are very
difficult. There is, however, one very good and easy-to-grow
woodland plant among them—G. *asclepiadea*, willow-leaved gen-

tian (see Plate 7), from Europe. Growing to a height of 700 mm. (2 ft. 4 in.) or more, the flowers, which are held in the upper leaf axils, appear from July into September, and are a beautiful blue. There is also a good white form—*G. asclepiadea alba*—which is attractive as a contrast to have near the front, and it is also very beautiful in the fading light.

This species starts into growth in the early spring, the opposite leaves being narrow, and in four distinct rows on the fast developing stem. Unless the site is very well sheltered, early staking with hazel twigs is often an advantage, otherwise the arching stems may be damaged in rough weather. In the autumn the faded flowers and upper leaves turn a rich brown, while the lower leaves are still green. This display is sufficient justification for leaving them until later in the year before cutting them down.

This plant prefers a moist, humus-laden soil in dappled shade, or part shade, but it is very adaptable and will even tolerate a limited dry period. Besides being an important woodland plant it is also suitable for grouping in shaded borders, while the foliage and growth are attractive against stonework; an ideal plant for the town garden.

Established clumps should not be disturbed, and the best method of propagation is by means of cuttings taken as the shoots appear in the spring. Plant at 500 mm. (1 ft. 8 in.) apart.

Geranium   Geraniaceae

Horticulture and the world of botany are full of misunderstandings, but this is one which will go on and on, for the ever popular geraniums grown in our greenhouses, windows and summer flower beds are pelargoniums—mostly cultivars of *Pelargonium zonale*. It is a pity that there is this confusion, for many must shy away from geraniums, believing that they are tender or difficult to grow. Although some *Geranium* species require scree conditions, there is quite a range of them which are among the hardiest of herbaceous perennials and grow well in ordinary soil without any trouble at all. Many thrive in sun, dappled shade or part shade, but with such a large group it is only possible to mention a few.

G. nodosum, from southern Europe, will flower from early summer until late autumn, thrive in shade, and will put up with drought conditions for a limited period. The rose-pink flowers, as thinly held as the pale green foliage, will peep from beneath quite dense canopies that would be shunned by the vast majority of flowering plants. In the spring the fresh green and delicate foliage is edged with bronze, while the petioles are deeply pink. The height is 300 mm. (1 ft.).

G. endressii is one of the toughest of all, growing quite well in sun, dappled shade or part shade and withstanding quite a degree of drought. The tight clump of bright green leaves is produced in early spring, and this alone gives a very pleasant effect. Some would consider the bright rose-pink flowers, which are produced for months during the summer, to be a little too harsh for an informal setting. This species, from the Pyrenees, grows to a height of 400 mm. (1 ft. 4 in.).

G. macrorrhizum is from Europe, but is naturalized in the south west. It is recognized as an excellent garden plant, superb for ground-cover and able to grow well in all but full shade. It is from 100 mm. to 300 mm. (4 in. to 1 ft.) high, the foliage being deeply cut or lobed, while the flower colour of the type plant is pink. Among the available cultivars there is quite a wide range of colours.

G. phaeum, mourning widow, from Europe, is one of the first to open its flowers in the late spring and early summer, these being a deep purple. The light green foliage, which is produced from the crown in the early spring, is deeply lobed with a marked and interesting serration, while the blossoms are held in a short spike above this, a most unusual appearance.

The prize for the strongest grower must surely go to *G. procurrens* (formerly *G. collinum*), from the Himalayas. After planting it devotes a year or so to establishment, rooting freely at the nodes on decumbent stems, and giving nothing but pleasure with its attractive foliage and rose-pink flowers. Once this period is over, and if conditions are suitable, it will show what it is really capable of, extending rapidly with growths and flowers, high among the shrubs and over the smaller ones. It is a plant to grow among larger shrubs such as rhododendrons, where it will thrive in the organically rich and moist soils to be found among these plants. It will not creep into shady places beneath heavy and dense canopies.

For quality one should go to *G. renardii*, from the Caucasus. It has grey tomentose foliage which is produced in the late spring, and large, white flowers in June, these being beautifully veined with purple. However, there are many others which are just as beautiful—*G. wallichianum* 'Buxton's Blue' for example, semi-prostrate with red stems, the foliage buttercup-like with prominent white blotching. The flowers when they open are a beautiful blue with a white centre; surprisingly the underside of the petals is rose-pink.

The plant for a shady crevice in the rock garden is *G. pylzowi-anum*, from Tibet. It has attractive foliage which is somewhat similar to that of a creeping buttercup, but is blotched with white, and the rosy-pink flowers are borne above this.

The species and cultivars listed may be propagated by division.

Gillenia   Rosaceae

G. trifoliata, from North America, is surprisingly, a herbaceous perennial in the family Rosaceae, although the foliage is somewhat spiraea-like. The small growths appear above the soil in mid April, followed a few weeks later by the stems, tinged with red, the trifoliate leaves giving this plant a distinctive appearance. The narrow, white-petalled flowers open in June, and are held by thin, branched stalks over the crown of the plant, which is a metre (3 ft. 3 in.) tall at this stage. As each flower fades and drops, the calyx brightens to a bronze-red colour and there is a short period when the two displays may be seen on the one plant. In the autumn it dies back to the crown, when it may be cut down. This plant grows well in sun, but it appears to prefer the shade, at least in the south, and it is ideal for a herbaceous planting in the dappled shade or part shade of small trees. Sufficient moisture is essential to its well-being, and if the plant is in a sunny position on a hot, dry soil the foliage is often scorched.

An unusual plant to grow, yet it should not be so, for it was cultivated as long ago as 1758 by Phillip Miller.

It is easily propagated by division, but it is also possible from seed.

Glaucidium   Glaucidiaceae

This should not be confused with the genus *Glaucium*, which is the name of the horned poppies in the family Papaveraceae.

G. palmatum, a herbaceous perennial, is one of the lovely and rare woodland plants from Japan. From the rhizomatous roots the growths appear in late April, each with a pair of palmate and sharply serrated leaves which are a good, light green in colour. By late May the flowers open, consisting of four lilac sepals and a prominent bunch of stamens.

This is a plant which must have the best of woodland conditions—moisture, coolness coupled with humidity, and dappled shade. The soil should be enriched with well-decayed leafmould. The foliage fades and collapses during September, and the position of the plant should be clearly marked to ensure that it is safe from treading feet in the winter.

Propagation is by division in the spring as growth begins.

Glechoma   Labiatae

G. hederacea (*Nepeta hederacea*), ground ivy, is a native often found in damp woodlands over heavy soil, but is also common in deciduous woodlands and tree plantings on the lighter soils where there is build-up of organic material. It is happiest in dappled shade, and although it does occur in the open in grassland, it does not always thrive under these conditions and in some cases has probably survived from earlier times when the area in question was under woodland. Once this plant gains a hold and is happy, it usually spreads rapidly, with the prostrate stems rooting at the nodes.

During the spring and summer the purple flowers are produced on a short spike, the whole plant having the various characters typical of its family. This is a good plant to encourage in natural woodlands, or in the outer fringes of the shade garden, for it can become a part of the natural ground-cover over the soil, thus conserving moisture and life generally. In addition it proves to be a good indicator of the suitability of the site for other plants. In woods and tree groupings which are rather poor through impoverishment or neglect, or where such plantings have been established within recent times, the appearance and build-up of this plant can be taken as an encouraging sign that an organic, woodland type of soil with the appropriate flora and fauna is developing.

This species can be introduced quite easily by planting rooted pieces in the autumn or spring.

Haberlea
Gesneriaceae

In many respects these are similar to ramondas, and they will thrive and flower under the same conditions, liking a moist soil during the growing season of the autumn, winter and spring. Like ramondas too, they are not in the least concerned if all but the innermost leaves are dried to parchment during a summer's drought. The growths are tufted and fit well into long crevices, and it is thus an ideal plant for walling and vertical rockwork, but it loves to be able to root deeply. *Haberlea* have the tubular flower which is common to the Gesneriaceae. *H. rhodopensis*, from the Balkans, is one of the most popular species, the flowers being a soft lilac in colour.

Propagation is by seed or root cuttings, taken in the spring.

Hebe
Scrophulariaceae

This is a large genus of sun-lovers which are mainly from New Zealand. They vary in height from quite large shrubs, 2 m. (6 ft. 7 in.) or more in height, down to very small species which hug the ground closely and form tight hummocks of growth. Many, however, will grow surprisingly well in part shade, especially the larger-leaved species and hybrids—*H. speciosa* cultivars for example—but in the main they show a great dislike of dry conditions caused by tree roots. *H.* × *franciscana* 'Blue Gem' stands alone in being able to withstand even quite dry and shady conditions, for instance among widely spaced conifers. It is, unfortunately, of doubtful hardiness as are many others, particularly the larger-leaved hebes, and can be relied upon only in the warmer counties.

Hedera
Araliaceae

H. helix, common ivy, is well known as a native climber, and also as an excellent ground-cover plant for shade. It is surprising how well it will creep on the surface, through trees and shrubs, forming a complete coverage, even in dry situations and under the dense canopy of such trees as *Quercus ilex*, holm oak. As a colonizer it appears to be most at home on soils which are bare or sparse of foliage; it generally makes little progress when in direct competition with strong-growing herbage and grass.

One advantage of the ivy is that it can be cut back quite severely, either to make room for other plantings, or if it becomes too invasive. Without this treatment, areas which remain undisturbed will grow on, for ivy roots freely into the soil at points as it creeps along. However, it is mainly surface rooting, and the use of a very strong fork is all that is needed to clear areas as required.

Beneath trees the growths collect dead leaves, a great advantage in that this helps to conserve and stabilize the leaf fall. The effect of the fallen leaves through the winter may be unsightly, but new growths will quickly hide this during the remainder of the year. One disadvantage of extensive areas of ivy beneath trees is that vermin such as rats and mice will find shelter and breed in the canopy which this plant forms; but this is true with many other ground-cover plants and the vermin can be quite easily controlled. Also, a thick covering of ivy beneath large, old trees which might be dangerous will do much to prevent people from sitting beneath them, but of course a regular inspection of such trees is necessary, with action if there is any danger.

There are many forms of *H. helix*, but a number of these are not as strong-growing as the ordinary one in difficult situations. Nonetheless, a mixed grouping in the shade, including such variegated cultivars as 'Glacier', makes an attractive planting for a dull corner.

H. colchica 'Dentata Variegata' is a very strong grower, and wonderful as a ground-cover subject for brightening up areas of bare soil beneath evergreens where little else would grow.

The secret with ivies in a difficult situation, is to plant them in the best positions available in the area; when established the runners can even be turned to grow into the less promising areas.

Helleborus   Ranunculaceae

Provided that they are respected and are given a little consideration these plants are easy to grow. Most are very hardy and develop their flowers and foliage early in the year. Moreover they do well in light shade, in fact they appear to prefer it. They will grow well on a variety of soils, including the heavy clays and chalky soils, indeed in the wild many of the species are frequently found over chalk. Hellebores are impatient of the light, sandy or gravelly soils, mainly because they dry out so quickly in the spring just as the plant is ready to grow after flowering. They are in the buttercup family and this goes a long way towards explaining their dislike of very dry conditions. However they will survive dry spells, especially those which occur during the late summer and of course when they are fully established. Hellebores are almost always visible above the surface and are therefore excellent to use as markers.

H. niger, Christmas rose, from Europe, produces white flowers on short, dark, red-brown stalks over the Christmas period or early in the New Year. The flowers have a choice appearance with large yellow central stamens. Often at the time of flowering *H. niger* is leafless but in the spring an established clump will produce a good carpet of dark, glaucous green leaves which are held close to the ground—an ideal contrast with other plants, for this foliage often lasts through to the bad weather and even to the spring. Some prefer to cover the flowers with cloches to prevent them being splashed with mud during rainy periods, but this can be avoided by means of a carefully positioned pebble layer forming a complete coverage round and among the growths.

H. orientalis is a variable species from Greece and Asia Minor, but there are many hybrids, originating both in gardens and in the wild, which masquerade under this name. Most of them have leaves which die down during the winter or early spring and throw up heads of drooping flowers in the spring, some much earlier than others. The blossoms vary in colour from white to deep plum red, but are always spotted and in shades of green. The whole group is loosely termed the Lent roses.

Among the many cultivars, four have been selected which are variants of *H. orientalis*. 'Queen of the North' has a good display of white flowers which appear very early in the year. 'White Swan' is a little later with large nodding white flowers often produced with the new leaves, the whole being very impressive and luxuriant. 'Abel Carrière' has deep maroon-coloured flowers with bright yellow stamens, which are held on red-spotted stems. 'Macbeth' has very dark flowers of the deepest plum red, thus the yellow stamens show up very distinctly: it is a variety which makes an interesting contrast in a mixed group or singly.

There are a number of other species and hybrids which are worth growing, including two native species—*H. foetidus* (see Plate 15) and *H. viridis*. *H. corsicus* (*H. argutifolius*) is a most impressive plant with spiny foliage which is strong and lush and pea-green in colour. It has an impressive panicle of light-green flowers, often grows up to 700 mm. (2 ft. 4 in.), and is suitable as a feature plant beneath large deciduous trees and shrubs.

Hellebores have many other uses in the garden and woodland —they will grow well in dappled shade, part shade, or in shade, provided it is not too dense. They may be planted in groups or drifts, but are also effective if placed singly, especially if a distinctive variety is chosen in each case. Along the length of the shrub border or beneath old apple trees are suggested locations, but there are plenty of others. They will succeed in the sun, but the moisture content of the soil is a more critical factor. In exposed positions the flowers and young leaves may be singed a little by wind frosts but the still radiation frosts, despite the fact that the flowers hang limply until they thaw out, appear to do them no harm.

Propagation is normally by division in the spring after flowering, when growth begins. The crown and roots are tough, but with patience they may be divided with intact root systems. Hellebores, without exception, resent disturbance and every care must be given to the divisions to ensure a speedy recovery; for example they must never dry out and must be watered if necessary until they can fend for themselves. Seed provides another means and it should be sown as soon as it is ripe, but the results may be very variable. It is often possible to dig up one or two-year-old seedlings from nearby established clumps and these may be saved. A beautiful effect is obtainable from a group or drift of mixed seedlings of the Lent roses, for example, but it is not safe to put a name on any of them.

Concerning *Helleborus* generally, once the old foliage becomes unsightly it may with advantage be removed as this will improve the effect of the flowers and new leaves.

Heloniopsis
Liliaceae

The discovery that *H. japonica* is an evergreen from Japan, and is in the family Liliaceae, makes it sound very exciting, as indeed it is. The clump of broad leaves lasts the winter through, with fresh, lighter green leaves appearing in the spring to make it all the more pleasing. Also in spring, the short spikes of flower, pink with prominent stamens, appear with all their refinement, but even after these fade the bright green leaves remain, forming a close and pleasing hummock.

This is a plant for dappled shade, part shade or shade, in a border or place where such a choice plant can be looked after properly, but shelter from the cold, searching winds of winter is desirable. The soil should be on the light side, but well stocked with decayed leafmould.

Propagation is by division in the spring as the new growth appears.

Helxine   Urticaceae

H. soleiroli, mind-your-own-business, mother of thousands, a member of the nettle family, is native to the Balearic Isles, Corsica and Sardinia. It forms bright green mats of creeping growths which root at the nodes. The evergreen foliage is made up of rounded leaves of various sizes, which fit closely together to form a complete coverage. The plant has the appearance of another mat-producing subject, *Arenaria balearica*, but that has showy little white star-shaped flowers; those of the helxine are very small and a yellow-green. *Mentha requiennii* is another plant which is very similar, and where this is valued, the helxine should be avoided.

It is a very useful plant for growing in crevices, in rock gardens, walls, paving, and banks in shade, as it gives a mature appearance very quickly, but the position must be damp. A limited period of drought does not appear to damage the plant unduly, provided that it is in the shade. Once established and happy, the tiny growths creep out in every possible direction where they can gain a foothold, and may be considered by many to be invasive. However, helxine can be curbed, with patience, and it will pick out the spots where other plants which love shade and moisture would be happy too.

The plant is not fully hardy and formerly it was found only in glasshouses, but often, if caught by the harshness of the winter, it will usually break into growth again in the spring.

H. soleiroli, which has become naturalized in the south-west, is good for stabilizing damp, shady banks. Small rooted pieces are easily torn off and established in a moist soil.

Hemerocallis   Liliaceae

This is the day lily genus—a common name which really means

something, for they are in the family Liliaceae and the flowers are lily-like, each one only lasting a day. As the flowering stems carry many buds, they blossom over a long period through the summer.

These herbaceous plants are normally quite easily grown and are suited to sun, dappled shade and part shade. In the colder parts of the country a border against a west-facing wall is ideal, but otherwise they are suitable for many other purposes in the more formal sections of the garden, for example, a herbaceous planting in dappled shade or part shade. Having an informal charm, they are also in keeping with a setting among lightly spaced trees in dappled shade; it is usually necessary to cultivate them in prepared areas, as they seldom do well in competition with grass. *H. flava*, probably from eastern Asia, is a dainty, yellow-flowered species which is ideal for this purpose, but there are many more species and cultivars; they should be seen at flowering time before a choice is made.

Hemerocallis will grow well in a wide variety of soils but one word of warning should be given—they will not thrive and flower well under extended dry conditions.

Propagation is by division during the dormant season.

Hepatica   Ranunculaceae

Hepaticas are closely related to the genus *Anemone*.

H. triloba, from Europe, Asia and North America, is a plant for dappled shade, either in the woodland, beneath groups of trees, in shrub borders, or even in shaded borders against walls. The sticky clays and heavy soils seem to suit it best, provided that abundant supplies of organic material are added—the type of soils on which the wild snowdrop and daffodil are found growing naturally are ideal. It will also thrive on chalk.

Among the attractions of Hepatica are the dark green and lobed leaves, which are clustered neatly round the centre of the plant. From the spring after flowering, they last through the summer and autumn. The anemone-like flowers, often grouped in the centre of the plant, are most commonly blue, but are also found in colours ranging from white to purple, double forms included.

Propagation is by lifting and separating the roots in the autumn, but they resent disturbance and this should not be done more often than is necessary.

Heuchera
Saxifragaceae

The genus *Heuchera* is made up of many showy species and hybrids which are sun-loving, but *H. americana* will thrive and flower well in dappled shade. The evergreen foliage and the mode of growth are typical of *Heuchera*, the leaves being green with a dull bronze colouring by the main veins. The new leaves, as they develop with the flower spikes in the early spring, are flushed with shades of pink and bronze. By early June the inflorescences have fully developed and form an absolute forest of thin stems and flowers 600 to 800 mm. (2 ft. to 2 ft. 7 in.) high. Individually the brownish-green flowers are insignificant, but each has a prominent cluster of stamens, and the effect of a drift at this stage is quiet, but dainty and interesting. Even when the flowers have withered and dried, the appearance is pleasing and remains so for several weeks.

It is an ideal plant for grouping in the border or island bed in dappled shade, although it will grow well in the sun. In common with the other heucheras it requires a light and well-drained soil.

Propagation is by division in the spring, or by cuttings of individual crowns during the summer.

Hosta
Liliaceae

These popular foliage plants, coming mainly from Japan, are vaguely plantain-like, the leaves having a similar, marked venation. There are many species, varieties and cultivars, and the consequent confusion in nomenclature has been further complicated by hybridization. It is important, therefore, before a choice is made for the garden, to see the plants in growth and leaf.

H. crispula (*H. albomarginata*) (see Plates 3 and 13), has small leaves which are light green, with a neat margin of white, making them quite conspicuous, even in the half light at dusk. The leafy flower spikes, appearing at first like miniature globe artichokes, rise during late May and, after extending to a height of 300 mm. (1 ft.), produce flowers which are a very pale lavender. This neat and attractive display lasts for three or four weeks, but when the effect becomes ragged, the stems should be cut down to improve the appearance of the planting. This species will stand more sun than many, but it must not be allowed to dry out.

H. fortunei 'Albopicta' is variegated, the shoots appearing above the surface in late April, but even at this stage the colouring is noticeable. By late June, when the foliage is at its brightest, the leaf surface appears as if hand-painted in shades of dark to light green in an irregular margin, with yellow in the centre, the various colourations tending to extend along the interveinal areas. By mid-July, however, the variegation is hardly discernible, although the slender spikes of lilac flowers, 800 mm. (2 ft. 7 in.) high, are quite effective. As a finale, by the late autumn the petioles stand with the flower stems, while the leaf blades hang to the ground, a most unusual and interesting effect. The cultivar 'Aurea' has foliage which is yellow in the spring (see Plate 7).

H. lancifolia appears above the soil in March, with thin green and crowded shoots from crowns which form low hummocks on the surface. The narrow foliage is a good shiny green, with a very prominent venation. The rays from a low sun produce an unusual effect from the varied reflections on the raised, interveinal surfaces. The placement of the leaf surfaces round the crown is also interesting, for they all radiate from the centre of the clump, pointing outwards. The foliage is 300 mm. (1 ft.) high, so a clump or drift can be brought to the front to be appreciated. After the small spikes of lavender flowers have dropped, the bracts remain green, while in the autumn the foliage turns a deep yellow and brown.

H. plantaginea, from China, has a very pleasant and light green foliage which is distinctive enough. It will keep in good condition until the autumn, when it will slowly die off to a rich yellow, the oldest leaves first while the younger ones are yet green, a very beautiful effect indeed. The leafy spikes of white flowers are at their best in September, and these too are very beautiful.

H. sieboldiana (see Plates 2 and 13) is an impressive plant, forming a good, strong clump 1·3 m. (4 ft. 3 in.) in height. The bold glaucous foliage, with a conspicuous venation, carries this plant well, even if it is in the background. In July a disappointing display of whitish flowers is produced but later on, in December, after the foliage has coloured in the autumn to a deep yellow and lies broken in a thick layer on the ground, the old flowering stems stand up straw coloured and quite striking. This species loves a dappled shade, shelter, and a rich, moist soil.

H. tokudama 'Variegata' appears above the ground in late April and produces white flowers during the summer. At first the

rounded leaves are glaucous green, but as they mature the variegation becomes more evident when the foliage is seen against the
light; later on, as the colour intensifies, it is among the finest of our
variegated plants. This plant must have shelter, shade, and good
growing conditions. By contrast, H. *tardifolia* is a smaller grower,
with dark green and shiny foliage and short, crowded spikes of
lilac-coloured flowers, which open in late September.

Taking the genus as a whole, they all prefer some form of shade
—dappled shade, part shade or shade, with a soil which is moist
throughout the growing season. Even so, to some extent they are
tough plants, and will withstand short periods of drought, or intense sun, but the foliage may suffer through flagging or scorch.
They are ideal plants to have in groups or drifts (see Plates 3
and 13), in the woodland or shade garden, but they are also
suitable in more formal borders, and in town gardens where their
foliage looks very well against a background of stonework, or
brick walling.

Propagation is by division as growth begins in the spring.

A full account of this genus will be found in the article '*A
survey of the genus Hosta in cultivation*' by C. D. Brickell, *Journal of
the Royal Horticultural Society*, vol. XCIII, September 1968, part 9,
365–372.

Houttuynia
Saururaceae

H. *cordata* an unusual plant, found from the Himalayas to Japan,
has a choice and rather unusual appearance, and yet is strangely
familiar, with foliage and growth which is almost like that of
Polygonum. The heads of white flowers, produced during the
summer and autumn, become prominent as the foliage which
forms a background turns to a bronze-purple. This is a bog or
marsh plant in its natural habitat, but it will thrive and spread in
a moist border or position in part shade.

Propagation is by division during the dormant season.

Hyacinthus
Liliaceae

Bedding hyacinths, with their densely packed, colourful and
highly scented flowers are well known. They are also very popular
for indoor cultivation in bowls and pots. They may be grown in
beds and borders outside where, in addition to growing well in

full sun, they will respond in shade, but it is generally considered to be too expensive to do this on any scale. They are also suitable for culture in outside window-boxes and tubs and have a special appeal for the town garden when grown in this way. The compost for the containers should be well drained, while if possible a cold, draughty situation should be avoided. When they are grown in containers after flowering they should be left for as long as possible to ripen the bulb for the next season, but it may be thought desirable to change over to summer display plants before the bulbs have died down completely; in this case they may be carefully removed and heeled in to complete their ripening. Later, after being lifted and dried, they may be cleaned up for planting in the garden.

Bulbs treated in this way will not produce a first-class flower spike again, but they can be planted up to form a group in beds and shrub borders, where they will give pleasure for many years; the vivid colours would not fit in well in a purely natural setting. The bulbs will slowly deteriorate over the years, but they can be replaced as successive batches are available for planting.

Bulbs which have been grown indoors can also be planted out, but it is better if they are given the protection of a frame or glasshouse, with feeding and watering until they die down and ripen.

Hydrangea   Hydrangeaceae

Hydrangeas bring welcome colour into the garden at the end of the season, and many will thrive in some form of light shade. While this genus is lacking in the numbers and variety found in *Rhododendron*, its range offers something to suit most purposes. Hydrangeas can be grown in either a formal or informal situation, singly or in groups, and are thus suitable for the smallest or largest gardens. They will grow in a wide variety of soils although for the good, blue colouring an acid medium is needed. This may be achieved where necessary by treatment with aluminium sulphate, or a 'blueing powder'.

The Hortensia group is very popular, with many widely grown cultivars; all have large heads of sterile flowers. Many people prefer hydrangeas in the more graceful Lacecap group, particularly in an informal setting. These have flat heads of fertile flowers surrounded by showy flowers that are sterile. Such cultivars as 'Bluewave', and 'Lanarth White', both in this group, are wonderful plants in light dappled shade.

With a flowering period which stretches from the latter part of the summer into the autumn, a display of a different nature is provided by the dead flower heads, and this carries on through the winter. One form which is found wild in Japan, *H. macrophylla normalis*, is among the best for winter effect, for the light brown and polished stems are conspicuous among the old, dead inflorescences, an effect which is made more colourful in the spring when the terminal buds show a beautiful green.

H. paniculata, from Japan and China, has terminal and pyramidal inflorescences which develop to maturity during the late summer, but in a mild November there are often a few late heads in display. The late autumn foliage effect is frequently a very good yellow, a pretty sight when the younger leaves are still green. A dark soil or a leafmould dressing adds to the attraction, as the leaves fall and lie on the ground. *H. quercifolia*, from North America, has distinctive, lobed foliage which is a soft green.

Among the larger growers is *H. sargentiana*, from China, which reaches 3 m. (10 ft.) or more. It has a stiff habit, with a strong central axis, while once it is established it suckers vigorously. The young growths and petioles are covered by a surfacing of coarse and fleshy, hair-like structures, while the leaves, especially on the undersides, are covered by soft hairs. As the summer wears on, the flat flower buds terminating the growths become apparent, and through the system of branching these are thrown out and held in a most dramatic way. At maturity, the large flat heads of closely packed, fertile flowers are a pale lilac in colour, the sterile ones being white. Even after the flowers are over, they are presentable, the centres with green, developing fruits, and the outer sterile flowers also green. Later these droop and then turn to face up, as if about to put on some new and even bolder display. A truly magnificent plant to feature in the dappled shade, and a fine contrast plant to have with old walling as a background.

While hydrangeas in general fit perfectly into an informal position among trees, there are climbing species which, in their natural woodland habitat, will grow through the canopy into the light and air above. Of these, the best known is *H. petiolaris*, climbing hydrangea. In the garden it may be planted in a position where it can climb trees, but it is also suitable for a shaded or part shaded wall. It is self-clinging, producing clusters of aerial roots like the ivy. Another use for this species is for covering old tree stumps, where it produces a rounded mound of growth, the flowering laterals turning up to the sky as the leading growths creep over the surface. Sometimes it will develop into an effective ground-cover subject.

This species flowers during the early summer, but, in common with many others, the old flower heads are held during the winter. This makes it a most attractive feature, for the old heads show up so well against the light, but rich, brown and polished appearance of the young wood. The older wood is also dark in colour, being gnarled with matted roots and growths as they age further. In the early spring there are more glories to come, for as the buds become prominent they are light green in colour, but tinged with cerise pink.

This is a short account of a wonderful genus. Many of its members do well in the sun, but fortunately there are more which like at least some shade. One note of warning is that these plants are impatient of dry conditions, and will wilt very quickly, and even die, if they suffer drought for any length of time.

Hydrastis   Berberidaceae

H. canadensis. This North American plant is seldom seen in gardens, yet, although not showy, it has a lovely woodland effect and is easily grown, given the right conditions. The dark and hairy anemone-like foliage, at first folded for protection, appears above the surface during April with the tiny flower buds. Development is very rapid, and within two to three weeks the flowers are open, being held just above the foliage at a height of 200 mm. (8 in.)—they are white and 15 mm. ($\frac{1}{2}$ in.) in diameter, with prominent stamens. The palmate leaves are pale green and form close attractive clumps which remain in good condition until early autumn. Then various shades of yellow and bronze appear with the green, until finally the plant dies back to the rhizomes beneath the soil.

A plant for the dappled shade of deciduous trees with a soil which is moist, but well-drained and rich in decayed leafmould. It is advisable to plant it in an informal group or drift near the front where it can be seen easily.

Propagation is by division as growth starts in the spring.

Hypericum   Hypericaceae

This genus, found mainly in the northern hemisphere, holds one
of the most efficient ground-cover subjects in the whole range of
available plants, *H. calycinum*, rose of Sharon, which comes from
south-east Europe and Asia Minor. Growing only up to 300 mm.
(1 ft.) high, it spreads by means of short rhizomatous growths,
and will colonize freely, in full sun, part shade, dappled shade or
full shade. It will grow well in many positions, including banks
and beneath trees, but it will not invade established grassland. Nor
will it put up with such deplorable conditions under dense trees
as will *Ruscus aculeatus*, butcher's broom, or *Hedera helix*, ivy,
which reign supreme above all others in this respect. *H. calycinum*
begins flowering in late June, and by early August the bulk of the
blossoms have fallen, but often, where it is happiest, there may be
a few flowers into October. The fruits are attractive, the calyx,
which is retained, being a light green and showing up distinctly
against the dark foliage. Another attractive period is the spring,
as the new growth breaks forth. Then the leaves are light green,
tinged with bronze—a wonderful effect when raindrops glisten
on the surfaces. This young foliage is more prominent if the old
growths are cut down to near ground level early each spring as
the buds break, when the area should be weeded and lightly
mulched with fine organic material. It is a good plant for a shaded,
dry wall but is very invasive and may take over completely.

   H. androsaemum, tutsan, is a native species which grows up to a
metre (3 ft. 3 in.), being found mostly in damp, but open woodlands. During the summer and autumn the flowers and fruits
make this an attractive shrub to grow in dappled shade.

   Apart from these two species a number of others, especially *H.
× inodorum* (with *H. androsaemum* as one parent), and *H. ×
moseranum* (with *H. calycinum* as one parent), will grow and flower
in shade, but they appear to be happier and flower more in the
sun. Hypericums have the advantage under deciduous trees that
they break into leaf early, before the overhead canopy.

Ilex   Aquifoliaceae

I. aquifolium, common holly, is the most adaptable of small trees,
growing well in full sun, in an exposed position on the coast, and
in the dense shade of such large deciduous trees as the beech.

Being a native it is used to our climate but it suffers badly in very dry conditions. As far as soils are concerned, it is not too fussy, although like so many other trees, it shows considerable impatience with prolonged, boggy conditions, such as exist on the worst of the low-lying clays.

In shade the holly tends to grow thinly, but is much more satisfactory than the yew under these conditions. Seedlings are often to be found in nature, beneath and between trees, particularly in the gulleys formed by the rain running down the trunks. That they are seedlings which have germinated *in situ* is not without significance, for the tap root, with its original lateral system, has remained intact. It is a different matter with transplants, which are never as good or as drought tolerant. Often it would pay to sow *in situ*, in a protected bed, for this beautiful evergreen tree is ideal for screening purposes in the shade. So is its American counterpart, *I. opaca*, which should be more widely grown.

Impatiens   Balsaminaceae

This is a surprisingly large genus with well over 200 species which are mainly tropical. A few, including the native species *I. noli-tangere*, will grow well in dappled shade, part shade and shade, provided that the soil is permanently wet. It is well worth growing in an informal setting and being self-seeding will normally appear year after year. So will *I. glandulifera*, a strong-growing species, from the Himalayas, which reaches to 1 to 2 m. (3 ft. 3 in. to 6 ft. 7 in.) high and has showy purple flowers. The many common species, cultivars and strains which are tender are known as busy lizzies, and they must have protection and be grown in a warm house during the cold months. They are, however, suitable for bedding out during the summer months, and will flower quite well in the shade, provided that there is sufficient shelter with a moist soil. They are suitable for beds and window-boxes.

Kirengeshoma   Saxifragaceae

K. palmata is, to those who do not know this plant, full of surprises. It belongs to a family that contains many plants familiar to us, yet this beautiful species with a September flowering period, introduced from Japan as long ago as 1891, is little known and rarely seen. Immediately the question is raised—is it fussy?

If the truth is given—yes, it is a little, for it does best in a rich, lime-free soil, in dappled shade where it is cool, with moisture available as it is required.

The growths from this herbaceous perennial, when they first appear above the soil in mid April, are almost hydrangea-like. However, soon they are more distinct, producing pale green, opposite leaves, palmate with interesting, serrated edges. The stems at the area of the nodes are zoned with dark purple, while the cluster of leaves at the growing point display their pale under-surfaces. A well-grown clump or drift, even in May when only 300 mm. (1 ft.) or more in height, is very distinctive.

By late July, with the growths over 1 m. (3 ft. 3 in.) tall, the plant is even more impressive, the stems, black by this time, are more visible, while the terminating flower buds show good development. A few weeks later the blossoms open—they are a soft, pleasing yellow and reminiscent of drooping abutilon flowers, being held in loosely branched and arching panicles. This is a good plant for a large drift in the middle to the back of a planting in the shade garden, or beneath large rhododendrons.

Propagation is by division.

Lamium Labiatae

L. maculatum is mainly a European species, but many of the forms and cultivars which are grown in gardens have a broad, silky, white stripe down the centre of each leaf and are especially attractive in the spring and autumn with the newer foliage (see Plate 16). The plant will grow properly only in a deep and moist soil, well stocked with decaying organic material. It will thrive in dappled shade or part shade and is suitable for light shrub or rhododendron plantings, a herbaceous planting in light shade (see Plate 16) or for a lightly shaded part of a town garden, being attractive against stonework. Once it dries out this plant soon loses its fresh appearance. It is not a very aggressive subject as far as shade is concerned, and often does not grow well beneath even the lightest of evergreens, partly due perhaps to the dry conditions that can occur there.

Propagation may be easily carried out by cuttings or division during the dormant season, when large clumps may be dug out of established drifts, leaving some to fill in with afterwards.

(See also *Galeobdolon*.)

Lathraea Orobanchaceae

L. clandestina is a most attractive parasite found in many parts of the Continent, and it has also become naturalized in parts of this country, being mainly found on the roots of trees.

The white growths appear above the ground in clusters in the very early spring, and by late March they are 80 mm. (3 in.) high, with lilac-coloured flowers which create quite a bright effect, especially in the fading light. Once established, this species will spread along the roots of the host plant, coming up through groups of neighbouring plants, providing some attractive combinations and doing no harm at all. It will remain showy for several weeks, giving early colour until it is overgrown by other plants and dies back. It is readily established by planting a developing cluster in a proposed site, above the root of the selected host plant.

Leucobryum Leucobryaceae

L. argeneum (*L. glaucum*), bun moss, is abundant in the south-east where it is found on hills and raised ground where the soil is poor and leached, often beneath beech trees where little else will grow. (One of the most extensive and beautiful carpets of this moss is found in the Savill Gardens, Windsor.) It is dense and tufted, forming close hummocks, and the colour is an almost silky green. If the moss is present, and one wishes to encourage it, thin out the trees if necessary, as too dense a canopy will result in a heavy leaf fall. It may also be necessary to remove some of the lower branches of the trees which have been left, and there must be no undergrowth. This ensures that fallen leaves blow away to other parts, for treading feet and rakes would injure the moss. Also relentlessly pull out anything else which attempts to grow, so that leaves will not be held up when they fall and that the nutrients will leach away slowly. The same advice applies to other mosses, although the conditions vary according to the species.

Leucojum Amaryllidaceae

This is a genus of bulbous plants closely related to the snowdrops. *L. aestivum*, summer snowflake, a native, is a strong grower with narcissus-like foliage which grows up to 500 mm. (1 ft. 8 in.). The white flowers, with a green tip to each petal, hang like bells when they open during April to May. A moist, heavy soil is preferred, but the species will do well in other types provided the site is decidedly moist. Its demand for a sufficiently moist site takes priority over everything else, and it will do as well in full sun as in light, dappled shade. It is impatient of a dry late summer and autumn, for it produces new roots and growths very early. It is a good plant for an informal setting in wet areas, and for a damp border in the shade.

L. vernum, spring snowflake, from central Europe, which flowers in February and March, requires a damp soil which is rich in organic material, and is better suited to a shaded part of the rock or bog garden. Both species often take two to three years to settle down and return to full flowering after disturbance.

Propagation is by separation of the bulbs early in the dormant season.

Lilium   Liliaceae

Lilies are too well known to need a description; they form the most important genus in the family. There are sun-lovers among them, for example *L. chalcedonicum*, but at the other end of the scale there are a few, such as *L. rubellum*, which demand a dappled shade. The vast majority love to have the lower part of their stems and the soil beneath shaded, and they have these conditions when grown in the shade of shrubs, with the upper part of their stems and the flowers in the sun. The shoots of some, for example *L. regale*, are prone to frost damage as they emerge from the soil in the spring, thus the overhead shelter provided by shrub growth has an added advantage. However, the vast majority of lilies are very accommodating, and proof of this is in the way some species and hybrids will naturalize or spread, regardless of being in varying degrees of shade, or even in full sun. *L. martagon* provides one example: it will seed and naturalize freely on a heavy clay soil under trees and in the open. On a similar soil the rhizomatous bulbs of *L. pardalinum* will creep through even solid clay into both sun and shade. The suitability of the soil and probably of moisture availability, have an important part to play. This is so with *L. canadense* which must have more than its share of rotted leaves and no lime. In point of fact, most lilies prefer a neutral or slightly acid soil. There are a few lime-lovers, *L. monadelphum* and *L. henryi* being among them.

The foliage of all lilies is attractive, particularly from the time when they emerge from the soil until flowering, but it is also very variable. Full advantage should be taken of this when the selections are made and the positions decided upon. As examples the following may be quoted: L. × *aurelianense*—clumps of reddish growths appear in March; L. 'Bellingham Hybrid'—during April the crowded shoots are beautifully green; L. 'Black Magic'— shoots are a dark purplish green and are attractive as a contrast; L. *centifolium*—developing shoots are strong and bronze-green; L. *henryi*—growths are strong with dark stems; L. *pardalinum*— forms a strong, effective clump but in the spring the growths vary in the rate of development. On the more advanced growths the unfolding leaves are held at various angles, causing varied surfaces of reflected light; L. *pyrenaicum*, the earliest species to flower, often in May, is crowded with stems and pea-green leaves, but the growing tips are lighter; L. *speciosum* is the last species to flower and afterwards goes into autumn colouring, a pale brown.

The reader is advised to see the different species in various stages of growth as well as in flower before making a choice, and it is advisable to start in a small way, building up on experience. It is important to ensure that stock is healthy and, in particular, free of virus troubles. After any necessary preparation and enrichment of the site, the lilies can effectively be planted in groups which need only be small to begin with. L. *superbum*, which has reflexed orange flowers on 2·5 m. (8 ft. 2 in.) high stems, is effective in small numbers, with just a few flowers showing through from the back among the shrubs. The planter must ensure that the stem-rooting species and cultivars are planted deeper than those which root at the base only; this will vary according to the size of the bulb. Lilies prefer a sheltered position, but even so the taller groups often need staking; hazel branches are the neatest and most effective for this purpose.

Propagation by scales, although specialized, is a good means of increase, but it should be noted that most lilies resent disturbance and may take two or three years to recover.

Liriope   Liliaceae

This small group of late summer-flowering subjects is becoming very popular, both for use under glass and outside.

L. *platyphylla* (formerly L. *muscari*) is one of the best for outside use. The violet flowers open during the latter part of August, being tightly packed like beads on the rather stiff and crowded spikes, a perfect contrast to the dark green, grass-like foliage. The display is maintained until the really cold weather begins, when the flowers dry up and drop when touched. The foliage sometimes weathers a little because of this and as well as in the interest of keeping the display on for longer, it is better for the plant to have some shelter from the worst of the winter's winds.

Liriopes will grow well in sun or light dappled shade. They are good plants for use as ground-cover among freshly planted shrubs, for they will carry on for many years as the main occupants grow, despite the fact that they themselves are shaded. They may not flower as well, but if this fact is accepted, they may even be taken into a fair degree of shade—with rhododendrons in light oak woodland for example. Another use for them is in a mixed, partly shaded border. They are surprisingly tolerant plants and will grow and flower well in a wide range of soils.

Propagation is very easy by division in the late spring.

Lonicera   Caprifoliaceae

Although the majority of species of honeysuckle can be relied upon to give a good display in the sun, many of the shrubby species are suitable for growing in light, dappled shade. The climbing types will grow and flower well in part shade, and a number are suitable for a north-facing wall. Included among these is *L.* × *brownii*, a fine plant both in flower and fruit. Returning to the shrubby species, *L. fragrantissima*, an early spring-flowering species, is suitable for a north-facing wall, and will remain an evergreen in this position in all but the coldest of areas.

It is, however, to the semi-evergreen *L. pileata* that we turn for an example of an outstanding, larger growing, ground-cover shrub. It grows to over a metre (3 ft. 3 in.) tall, with a strong spreading and dense growth. The foliage is dark green, but the reflective surfaces have a lightening effect, while the new foliage is light green. This is a very reliable shrub to grow as under-cover beneath deciduous trees, and it will withstand dry periods on a light soil.

Lunaria   Cruciferae

L. annua, honesty, from south-eastern Europe, is widely grown in our gardens, but in places it has escaped into the countryside. It is usually biennial in nature, growing a metre (3 ft. 3 in.) high in the second year when the red-purple flowers, in structure typical of the family Cruciferae, are produced. The heads of white and papery fruits, which follow as the plant dies, are in popular use for winter decoration indoors. This plant will grow well in dappled shade, part shade or shade, and is particularly well suited near old buildings, walled gardens and in town gardens, where it will lend much to the atmosphere of quietness and maturity. Odd seedlings will often appear and thrive in the cracks between paving slabs, and in impossible positions at the bases of walls and buildings.

Although there are many strains which vary in colour, there is nothing to match up to the common species.

Macleaya   Papaveraceae

M. cordata (*Bocconia cordata*) is full of surprises for those who do not know this plant. It is a herbaceous perennial, belonging to the poppy family and grows up to a height of 2 m. (6 ft. 7 in.), each stem ending in a conspicuous panicle of small, pinky-beige flowers lasting for several weeks, around or after the midsummer period. However, the attraction of this plant lasts over a much longer period, for as growth commences in the spring, the clusters of neatly lobed leaves are made conspicuous by a blue colouring, which remains, at least in part, on the undersides of the mature leaves during the remainder of the spring and summer—a source of joy to the eye each time they are gently blown by the summer breezes.

To find this perennial among shade plants may surprise those who, quite rightly associate it with sunny herbaceous borders. Yet it will give a good account of itself in a position of part shade, for example in a herbaceous planting near or under small trees, or on a west-or east-facing border. Many such borders and plantings are to be found in town gardens too, where it provides contrasts and gives pleasure during the season.

It is propagated by division in the spring.

Magnolia   Magnoliaceae

The need for some form of shade in this genus of beautiful trees and shrubs is limited to a very few species and hybrids, although the shade from early morning sun and shelter from cold easterly winds will protect the tender blossom and growths. However, this is not always possible, and often as a planting matures many sun-loving species end up in conditions of part shade, but surprisingly they do not suffer a great deal either in growth or flowering.

The one species which prefers a position in the dappled shade of a very light woodland or tree planting is *M. wilsonii*, a beautiful species from western China. A moist but well-drained soil and a mild, humid climate suit it best. The hybrid, *M.* 'Charles Coates' often appears to be happiest in a position of light dappled shade, especially when it is grown in dry sunny areas. It must be remembered that magnolias themselves often cast quite a dense shade through the summer months. Account should be taken of this when selecting a position for a young plant. The practice of planting them among smaller shrubs often proves disastrous later on.

All magnolias will grow well on a moist but well-drained soil which is slightly acid. However, a few, such as *M.* × *highdownensis*, may be grown on alkaline soils, provided that the rooting medium is abundantly supplied with moisture and organic material. More experiment is needed on these lines with alkaline soils.

× **Mahoberberis**   Berberidaceae

A small group of bigeneric hybrids involving the two genera, *Mahonia* × *Berberis*. Possibly the best one for shade is × *M. aquisargentii* (*M. aquifolium* × *B. sargentiana*), and for this a dappled shade is best—it is interesting that both parents will do well in such a position. The new growths, with a variable foliage produced during the summer, are attractive, being shiny and bronze in colour. The habit is bushy, and it is a slow grower, eventually reaching a metre (3 ft. 3 in.) in height.

Mahonia   Berberidaceae

This is quite a large genus of evergreen shrubs closely related to *Berberis*, the most important difference being that the foliage is pinnate and the stems spineless. The flowers in various shades of yellow are generally in racemes which terminate the growths.

M. aquifolium, Oregon grape, is commonly grown in gardens, increasingly so as ground-cover plants have become so popular and useful. Planted between trees and shrubs, at 500 mm. (1 ft. 8 in.) apart, they will soon fill up all the space available with suckerous growths, overcoming such pernicious weed as *Oxalis* with ease. Thus we have a subject which can be kept down by careful pruning to 500 mm. (1 ft. 8 in.), or less. It flowers in the early spring, has a dark green but glossy leaf surface which is often bronzed and attractive during the winter, and it is not at all fussy—sun or shade (provided that it is not too dense), and on any reasonable soil.

There are other, more choice, mahonias which are wonderful plants to grow in dappled shade with an informal setting; *M. bealei* and *M. japonica*, for example, have beautiful foliage, and delicate, early flowers. *M.* 'Charity' is magnificent, with thickly clustered and rigid ascending stems, these being dramatically marked with leaf scars and longitudinal cracks. In addition the downward sweep of the impressive foliage, and the beautiful racemes of flowers and fruits, make this a most outstanding plant. It is an ideal plant for a key position in a setting of dappled shade, and what a fine contrast to other foliage!

The shaded border with a brick or stone backing is another position to be considered for these plants, which for foliage effect alone are outstanding. In the milder areas, *M. lomariifolia* could be tried in a position in the shade. It is an impressive, large-growing shrub with small leaflets.

Maianthemum   Liliaceae

M. bifolium, a small, but pleasing, herbaceous perennial is very rare as a native.

In June spikes of white flowers, in which the stamens are prominent, rise above a carpet of cordate, fresh green leaves, the height being 150 mm. (6 in.). The fruiting heads which follow later are white with red spotting. This plant is never showy, but it has a delightful air of informality and will always please. If happy it will form a thin drift and may be left to spread at will, by means of the rhizomes which it freely produces. A plant for the dappled shade of the woodland or shade garden, it is also suitable as ground-cover in shaded shrub borders and among rhodo-dendrons, and will even run into quite dense shade, provided there is sufficient moisture. It requires a well-drained soil, but one which is moist and rich in leafmould or peat.

F

Matteuccia   Polypodiaceae

M. struthiopteris, ostrich fern, from the northern hemisphere, is
an attractive and distinct fern in all its stages of growth (see Plate
13). The fronds, which develop from the dormant crowns in late
March, are a clear and delicate green, so beautiful with the low,
early morning or evening sun behind them. At first upright, the
fronds are often 700 mm. to 1 m. (2 ft. 4 in. to 3 ft. 3 in.) tall, and
finally open out to produce an overall vase-shaped effect (see
Plate 13). It is an impressive stage, more so when the plant is
viewed from above, for at the base the midribs are dark while the
crown, deep in the centre, is black. It is well worth having one or
two plants near the front, so that this effect can be admired without treading on the bed and causing consolidation. The upright,
fertile fronds appear from the centre in late April, uncoiling and
developing until they reach 1 m. (3 ft. 3 in.) in height; they have
a distinct appearance with a darker midrib. In the autumn the
sterile fronds turn to a bronze or rich brown, eventually collapsing, but the fertile ones remain standing, later turning to a very
dark brown colour. The effect is decorative, and becomes so much
a part of the winter's scene that they may well be left until
February, when they should be cut back to within 70 mm. (2½ in.)
of the crown, so that their positions are clearly indicated. For this
reason it is a good marker plant.

This fern will grow in the sun in a very wet position, but it is
also perfectly happy in dappled shade or shade. It should have a
moist, peaty soil and is suitable for informal situations in the
woodland or shade garden. One use is in drifts which run into the
background, appearing to extend into the distance among bushes
and trees. However, even a single plant in a small garden will add
much to the character and interest of the planting. It is also
effective against rock-work in a shady and moist corner, particularly if it is of limestone.

Propagation is by offsets, which appear by established crowns.
These should be removed in the spring and be planted irregularly
between 800 mm. and 1·2 m. (2 ft. 7 in. and 4 ft.) apart—if
planted too closely the beauty of the individual plant cannot be
seen as clearly.

Meconopsis
Papaveraceae

This genus contains, among other species, the well known blue poppies, of which *M. betonicifolia* is the best known. Almost without exception, the species are exacting in their requirements, and must have the right conditions if they are to even survive. It is true that where a variety of meconopsis can be grown well, the successful culture of a whole range of shade and woodland species is possible, including many of the more difficult ones.

M. cambrica, Welsh poppy, is a native perennial and is found in rocky and shaded places in the west and south-west, always where the soil is well drained but moist, and almost without exception this is an essential condition for this genus as a whole. This species is, however, much easier to establish than many, and if it is really happy it will spread extensively by seed, so that it is necessary to weed out most of the seedlings at an early stage. The species makes an early start, and by late March there is a good covering of fresh green foliage, which is especially pleasing in the early morning, when dew is on the edges of the leaves. The four-petalled, yellow flowers, which are held singly on stems 400 mm. (1 ft. 4 in.) high, appear during May and June, but often there is a second crop during the late summer. Should the weather be dry after flowering, the foliage looks rather tired, but it soon recovers after refreshing rains and then can be cleaned up.

This plant is not really suitable in a border; but if used in this position it should be near the front, where the vast numbers of seedlings it produces can be thinned out. It is essentially a plant for shady rock and stonework, and is often happiest in a position of its own choosing. This species can be quite easily established in the first place by pressing a little seed into the crevices, but if this is difficult a pellet of heavy soil may be used to provide a suitable sowing surface.

M. betonicifolia, from western China, has a neat crown which is quite decorative as the new leaves develop in the spring. Then the varied effect as it is seen from different angles is especially pleasing, with the brown, hairy petioles and midribs showing up distinctly as the undersides are exposed to view. By late April, the mature crowns start to run up to flower, the first sign being the filling out of the centres with erect leaves. The flowers open a few weeks later; they are soft blue in colour, often with the faintest trace of a purple sheen in places, and with a beautiful, fragile appearance, the petals being crinkled. The prominent cluster of golden yellow stamens lends to each blossom an individual beauty, which can be appreciated even from a distance. The display is also enhanced by the foliage, carried up to the full height of the flowering stems, which may be 1 m. (3 ft 3 in.) or more. There is a white-flowered variety—*M. betonicifolia alba*—which produces a lovely effect in fading light against a dark background. In common with most of the *Meconopsis*, this species prefers a cool, moist, well-drained and acid soil, to which a plentiful supply of well-rotted organic material, preferably leafmould or peat, has been added.

This species adopts a perennial habit, but there must be sufficient moisture and food available for the formation of a new crown, after the production of a crop of seed. On the other hand, a plant that is starved and dry will concentrate all its resources on seed production, after which it will die out. The practice of cutting off developing spikes in the first year of flowering will do much to ensure the development of a perennial habit.

M. grandis, a perennial species with a wide distribution from Nepal, Tibet and China, is similar in many respects. Colours vary from poor shades of blue to violet, but there are a number of good cultivars, which may be propagated by vegetative methods in the spring.

M. paniculata is a monocarpic species, forming impressive crowns of deeply cut and hairy foliage, which at maturity extend into magnificent heads of nodding yellow flowers, each with a cluster of orange-yellow stamens. The topmost flowers open first, the hairy buds extending down the length of the leafy stems. The species flowers over a period of several weeks, during which the lower foliage remains in good condition. When flowering is completed, the plants become very untidy and may be pulled up, with the exception of any which have been selected for seed. *M. napaulensis* is perhaps the most commonly grown in the monocarpic group but like many others it varies considerably (see Plate 4).

M. regia, another monocarpic species with yellow flowers, also has bold foliage. This is most impressive in a low sun and the varied shades of green, produced by light and shadow according to the position of the serrated leaves, is outstanding. Many of the hybrids also have an attractive crown, for example *M.* × *sarsonsii* (*M. integrifolia* × *M. betonicifolia*), with foliage covered by straw-coloured hairs, which are even deeper on the midrib and petiole.

M. dhwojii is a plant for the front of the border, where it can be seen easily, for in the rosette stage it is very beautiful indeed. The finely cut leaves have a glaucous appearance, and are generally a light green, but with flushes and blotches of dark purple in places. The foliage is hairy and darkly spotted to a varying intensity, and the spots apparently originate at the base of the hairs. Rime frost, or rain drops, which cling to the hairy petioles and leaf surfaces provide an added attraction. Flowering takes place during late May and June: the nodding, yellow blossoms with rich, golden stamens, are held on long hairy stalks. With an overall height of 500 mm. (1 ft. 8 in.), it is suitable for planting among low shrubs. A month or so after flowering the plant becomes untidy, and with the exception of plants selected for seed, it may all be pulled up, for it is a monocarpic species.

As a general rule for the propagation of *Meconopsis*, seed* provides a good means of increase, and is the one and only method with the monocarpic species (although these notes do not apply to *M. cambrica*). The importance of ensuring that the source of the seed is good and true to type cannot be over emphasized, for a number of the species hybridize very freely, and precautions should be taken to prevent this happening with plants which have been selected for seed. The seed is best sown towards the end of February in a temperature of 15° C, reducing this a few days after germination. The plants should be kept growing, to be ready for planting outside in May. They should be taken through the pricking-off and potting stages, and a good batch of plants may need 130 mm. (5 in.) diameter pots by the time they are planted out. For successive batches to be available for planting as replacement, a number should be propagated in this way each year.

The perennial species may sometimes be divided, either in spring or autumn, but there must be more than one crown or

---

* Those who intend to raise these plants from seed will be interested in the article 'Germination responses of *Meconopsis* species' by P. A. Thompson, Jodrell Laboratory, Royal Botanic Gardens, Kew. *Journal of the Royal Horticultural Society*, vol. XCIII, August 1968, part 8, pp. 336–43.

head of foliage which can be separated with roots attached. The whole operation of lifting, dividing and planting should be carried out with great care, and if any tap roots are present the hole should be deep enough for them to be planted at full length. The only means of propagating clonal forms and hybrids true to type is by vegetative methods, and it is sometimes necessary to detach the basal growths, and root them like cuttings.

When selecting a site for flowering it should be remembered that in the southern part of the country most of the species prefer a cool and shaded site, where the air is humid. Under these conditions the blossoms last for much longer than when in full sun, and the plants are much happier. In the north, however, they thrive with a greater amount of sun, but nevertheless remain good plants for the shade. The type of shade to which they are adaptable depends upon the site and area, but dappled shade and shade may be considered, with a possibility of part shade in some localities.

On a large site one or more drifts may be required, but on a smaller scale groups or even individual plants would be in keeping. Mixed grouping with primulas is effective, in either a large or a small garden, while a grouping of primulas and meconopsis alongside each other, with a mixture of the two on the edges where they meet, is also very good (see Fig. 11).

The planting site should be well prepared with a good depth of soil, and the addition of plenty of organic material, including if possible, a good portion of well-rotted manure. In most cases the plants should be set out at not less than 500 mm. (1 ft. 8 in.) apart, in order to reduce the risk of rotting through overlapping foliage, but regular spacing should be avoided. The actual planting should be carried out carefully, ensuring that the base of the crown is level with the finished surface.

Maintenance consists of spring mulching, taking care that the leaves are not covered, or the base of the crowns partly buried. A cover of such plants as celandine, anemone and crocus gives a far more natural appearance if left to grow among the crowns, but some form of control may be necessary to reduce competition, particularly in a dry season. During the autumn leaf-fall the crowns should be kept free of heavy and thick layers of fallen leaves but consolidation, especially in wet periods, can be prevented by taking off the worst with a long-handled rake. Losses through flowering and exhaustion may be made up with fresh plantings, when the varying stages of development will prove interesting. Occasionally it is advisable, however, to give the site a rest from meconopsis for a few years, and to make a new planting with primulas or other suitable subjects. Staking, however neatly carried out, spoils the effect of these plants, which should appear as natural and informal as possible, and provided a sheltered site is selected it should not often be necessary.

There remains the problem of whether or not to cover the crowns with glass for the winter, as a protection from rain and snow, which may cause rotting; first, is this necessary? Certainly it is often needed in industrial areas and within the spread of large cities, especially for those species which have large, hairy crowns. The need for covering must be finally decided by trial and error, veering on the side of safety until some experience has been gained. If protection is necessary, this should be taken into consideration at planting time and the size and positions of the clumps be determined so they may be covered quite easily with frame lights. These should be positioned and tied down on pegs, with the sides open to allow free circulation of air through and over the crowns.

Finally it must be emphasized that there is a need for experiment with these plants, for as they grow it will be found that their behaviour is variable, even on different sites in the same garden, while in gardens over the country at large their behaviour often contrasts so much that they could be different plants.

Melittis   Labiatae

M. melissophyllum, a native which has all the appearance of being a dead-nettle (*Lamium*), is, in fact, in the same family. The clumps of opposite-leaved growths with square stems appear in early March, an attractive period for the plant. The serrated and hairy leaves have a good green colour with a prominent venation.

The flowers, produced during June when the plant is up to 500 mm. (1 ft. 8 in.) in height, have an open throat, a distinct hood with a broad, nicely marked and spotted lower lip. The colour varies from white to rose-pink with a deeper spotting. By early August the foliage yellows and the plant becomes a little unsightly, particularly if a dry period sets in. However, it is often possible to cut the plant back, still leaving some furnishing growths at the base. It is not a showy plant, but an interesting one, suited for the dappled shade of the woodland, the shade garden or even a border planting. This is a plant for those to try, who have soils and sites which would be too dry for such as trilliums, meconopsis.

Propagation is by division as growth is renewed in the spring.

Mercurialis   Euphorbiaceae

If flower display is considered, the native species *M. perennis*, dog's mercury, must be one of the most insignificant in the family Euphorbiaceae. Yet it is very pleasant to find it in the early spring in woodlands and copses among primroses, wood anemones and other plants. It is usually found in dappled shade on soils which are sufficiently retentive of moisture, at least during spring. The plant is a rapid colonizer, spreading by means of underground stolons early in the season—if it is too hard and dry for this there will be very little spread. Later in the season, as the foliage hardens and turns a darker green, the plant is well able to withstand dry conditions. Its presence indicates that quite a wide range of early developing and maturing subjects will also thrive, but it is not indicative of permanent dampness throughout even a normal season. It is to be found in a wide range of soils and over chalk and therefore cannot be used as a guide for ericaceous subjects. It should not be introduced or allowed to spread into 'cultivated' areas.

Muscari   Liliaceae

The grape hyacinths are closely allied to the scillas, in the same family, Liliaceae. The species most commonly grown is *M. armeniacum*, from Asia Minor, but there are many others, including the well-known cultivar 'Heavenly Blue' which is a strong grower producing a 230 mm. (9 in.) high flower spike of dark blue flowers in April. A number of species are more suited to the rock garden or alpine house. The species and cultivars of *Muscari* are at their best on a light, well-drained soil, in quite a sunny position, and if given shade it must be only a very light, dappled shade or part shade, otherwise they will gradually die out.

The foliage of many species appears in the autumn, and lasts through the winter and spring until June, when it dies back. During this period it often becomes untidy, especially if the winter is a bad one. It should not be removed before it dies down or the bulbs will suffer. Mulching should be carried out before the new leaves appear.

It is suggested that a limited quantity be grown to begin with, and an increase made later if desired. If they are grown in grass this should not be too vigorous, but even so they are not always successful, for cutting or mowing must be withheld while the bulbs are in leaf.

Propagation is by seed and offsets, which are dug up during the dormant season.

Myosotis Boraginaceae

To the number of good plants for shade in the family Boraginaceae, certain of the *Myosotis*, forget-me-not, may be added. Of these *M. palustris* (*M. scorpioides*), water forget-me-not, a native, is outstanding. It will thrive by a stream or pond, or in a very wet situation with full exposure to the sun or a light dappled shade. It is therefore a good plant to run from sun to shade, perhaps on the edges of a stream.

The form *M. p. semperflorens* flowers over a long period during the late spring and summer. Both this and the parent species can be propagated by seed sown in June, by summer cuttings, and by division in autumn.

Narcissus Amaryllidaceae

This vast genus of bulbous subjects with countless hybrids and cultivars, includes the commonly termed daffodils, a name which alone covers a very wide field. Many have been raised for a specific use, for example the cut-flower industry, but they are mostly very accommodating and thrive in almost every garden in the land, and in a great variety of situations and soils.

The majority will thrive in various degrees of shade—in deciduous woodland (see Plate 10), among groups of deciduous trees and in deciduous shrub borders, to mention only three settings. In common with so many other bulbs which grow and flower well in the shade of deciduous trees, they are able to build up their bulbs for the next season before the leaf canopy is too heavy, and on some soils before it is too dry. The great advantage is that narcissi are perfectly happy in the open, even in full sun, and they can be used to achieve continuity, as with grass, in a position or planting which is in both shade and sun.

It has already been indicated that their moisture requirement is important to them, and they must have sufficient water during the early part of the year, and up to the stage in May or June when the foliage dies down and the bulbs undergo a short period of ripening. In the normal year there is sufficient moisture, but it is noticeable that, on the dry soils particularly, there is often a marked reduction of the flower display in the year following a dry spring. One of the haunts of our native daffodil, *N. pseudonarcissus*, is on the retentive and heavy clay loams of Surrey, which gives an indication of the importance of moisture to this species. It is not alone in this; it is true of all plants that naturalization is only full and complete when regeneration takes place by seed from established plants.

N. cyclamineus, from Portugal, is one of the earliest to flower, often in February, and it can be naturalized if conditions are suitable. One of the most successful positions for it is in the more open parts of deciduous woodland or tree plantings where the soil is a sandy peat and moist, especially during the autumn, winter and spring.

It is successful in shaded parts of the rock garden. Being so small, only 150 mm. (6 in.) at the most, it will not compete with long grass. The small, clear, yellow blossoms have a long and narrow trumpet with perianth members which are reflexed. Once established it will spread freely by seed, provided of course conditions are suitable. The narrow foliage adds greatly to the charming effect which a drift or small group produces.

N. pseudonarcissus, our native wild daffodil is typical of the larger-growing species. The flowers are pale yellow, reaching a height of 350 mm. (1 ft. 2 in.) with the foliage. This species (in common with the larger growers, including the commercial hybrids), can be naturalized in grass, provided it is cut only after the foliage has died down. A choice has to be made in the first place: is the naturalized planting to consist of species only, or are hybrids to be used—if so which ones, for some are stronger and more colourful than others? Not only size and colour, but also the period of flowering must be considered. The latest to flower are in the *N. poeticus* group. One answer to this problem is to confine the species and the more natural-looking hybrids to informal plantings, using the highly bred cultivars in groups among shrubs and in borders. However, it is a matter of taste. It is important to realize that a change of mind after a start has been made may cause difficulties. Whatever the setting the species or cultivars should be grouped together, not mixed. The reader is advised to explore the vast field in the first place by visiting as many gardens and shows as possible, and then to gain experience by trying a few initially. When introducing new bulbs it is important to ensure they are as free as possible from pests and diseases, in particular of narcissus eelworm and narcissus fly.

Planting should be done as soon as possible in the autumn, for rooting takes place freely during this period, while the soil is warm. The depth of planting depends upon the size of the bulbs, that for the larger ones being 100 mm. (4 in.). The distance apart also varies with size; the larger growers may be 120 mm. (5 in.) apart. Those to be naturalized should be thrown on to the surface and planted where they fall. The removal of the developing seed capsule after flowering is helpful and should be carried out on the large flowered hybrids; with such species as *N. cyclamineus* or *N. pseudonarcissus* they may be left to encourage the establishment of naturally sown seedlings.

Nicotiana Solanaceae

This genus contains a group of beautiful, flowering plants, which as far as culture is concerned are raised from seed, and treated as half-hardy annuals. Although they are commonly seen in bedding schemes in full sun, these plants thrive in dappled shade or shade. *N. alata* (*N. a. grandiflora*, *N. affinis*), is the sweet-scented tobacco plant, a perennial from Brazil, with long tubular white flowers, reaching a height of 800 mm. (2 ft. 7 in.). This is a plant to have by a door, window, path or patio where the beautiful scent as the flowers open at dusk can be fully appreciated. How refreshing for the owner of a town garden at home after a tiring day's work!

Among the hybrids which have appeared over the years, are the more recent developments in which the flowers remain open by day, although many are not as strongly scented. The range now includes dwarf strains, and colours which vary from mauve to white. Many are suitable for shaded window-boxes. The strain 'Lime Green' with yellow-green coloured flowers is suitable for the shade garden or the woodland garden, if used carefully and sparingly.

Nomocharis   Liliaceae

There is satisfaction in growing a difficult plant under the right conditions, but there is very little skill attached to this. Knowledge and talent are involved when a difficult plant is grown under exacting conditions, and the more adverse these are, the greater the triumph of success. Often this is realized through the gardener's refusal to give up, coupled with his ability to work with nature.

This is true of nomocharis, for in addition to their demand for a moist, peaty and well-drained soil, they must have coolness, a condition which the gardener must take into account when he selects the site. Furthermore, the coolness must be fresh and not stagnant, a condition more likely to be found on the higher ground and in the country.

Like many lilies, to which they are very closely allied, if they are in a sunny position the lower part of the stem should be shaded by a suitably placed shrub. Otherwise they should be planted in light, dappled shade. They are suitable for the more cultivated parts of the shade garden and for the peat garden. Although they can be propagated by vegetative methods, the advice is to leave successful plants alone to be enjoyed, using seed, which although slow is reliable.

Omphalodes   Boraginaceae

From this genus, which has the 'forget-me-not' flowers so typical of many of the borage family, *O. cappadocica* is outstanding as a rock garden plant. It has short, pointed leaves with prominent venation. The flowers, which are produced during late spring and early summer on 200 mm. (8 in.) stems, have the intensity of blue colouring which is so common in this family. Often, if sufficiently moist, a thin scattering of blossom continues through the summer after the main display.

This plant needs a moist rooting medium, full of peat or leafmould (the latter being preferable) and a position in dappled shade or part shade, where only the morning or evening sun reaches it.

Propagation is by division in the spring, as soon as the new leaves appear.

Ophiopogon   Liliaceae

Although these are close relatives of the liriopes, they have no
great floral beauty, and often the flowers are hidden in their grass-
like foliage. They are nevertheless very good plants for furnishing.

O. intermedius, from the Himalayas, forms a thick and compact
growth, both in full sun and dappled shade. It is particularly
effective when in drifts or groups, for if the plant is happy and
thriving, the coverage is complete. The foliage has a bluish appearance, especially when viewed in low morning or evening
sun, which seems to bring out this colour in its reflective rays. It
is very effective when grown beneath a small tree with ornamental
bark, such as silver birch. Being an evergreen it is useful during
the winter, and when it is covered with rime on a frosty morning,
it has an entirely different but pleasing appearance. It is noticeable
how the foliage bends over towards the light when it is in a
shaded position.

A warm, well-drained soil is preferable. If it is in a very cold
and exposed situation, the foliage may be badly bleached during
the winter, even in the warmer parts of the country. It is not a
plant for cold parts.

Propagation is by division in the spring.

Orixa   Rutaceae

O. japonica. This unusual deciduous shrub reaches a height of 2
to 3 m. (6 ft. 7 in. to 10 ft.), but has a very spreading habit, sending out long branches which root freely where they come into
contact with the soil. It is ideal for forming a thicket of growth
beneath deciduous trees in dappled shade, growing well in poor
soils which are often dry in the summer. For fruiting, both the
male and female plants are needed, but this species is far from
outstanding in this respect.

Ornithogalum   Liliaceae

This is a genus of bulbous plants. *O. nutans*, drooping star of
Bethlehem, is quite a common species, from Europe and Asia,
and will grow well in dappled shade and part shade. The green
and white flowers are produced on a short spike during late April
or May. This species starts into growth early and the foliage dies
down quickly, even before the seed fully ripens. It is an ideal plant

for borders and beds of deciduous shrubs, but will even thrive among woodland grasses under a beech tree, right up to the trunk on the southern side, provided the tree is not too low-branching. It thrives best on a well-drained soil.

A ready means of propagation is to dig up and replant the bulbs during the dormant season.

Ourisia Scrophulariaceae

This is a little-known genus in Scrophulariaceae, a family full of interesting plants, herbs, shrubs and even trees.

In *O. coccinea*, from Chile, the small leaves of this herbaceous perennial appear above the surface during March, and soon form a compact, light green carpet of lobed and serrated leaves, reminiscent of *Primula malacoides*. This is one of the main attractions of this plant, for it is delightfully informal as it readily develops over the floor of a woodland or shade garden. It hugs the ground closely, even if it is rough and uneven, and is only about 100 mm. (4 in.) high. It requires a moist and well-drained soil, full of richness and leafmould, and must be in dappled shade.

During late May or early June the flowers appear just above the foliage, and are scarlet and tubular, being held on short spikes. Some might regard this colour as out of keeping with a woodland or shade association, but it is a matter of taste.

Propagation is by division as the growths appear in the spring.

Pachysandra Buxaceae

This is a small group of low-growing evergreens that has sprung to the fore as ground-cover. *P. terminalis*, a Japanese species, is outstanding in this respect, for the growths, only about 150 mm. (6 in.) in height, form a complete coverage and grow into shade from a position of dappled shade, provided that conditions are suitable. Thus the planting as a whole becomes an association in which all plants are happily growing together. Only the weeder is likely to spoil such an effect at this stage, as the growths are easily crushed if they are trodden on. The leaves are a light green and reflect the light to some extent, thus tending to brighten up the dull corner. The flower buds in the tight cluster stage appear in the late summer and develop slowly through the winter, to open during March and April. Composed mainly of whitish stamens, they are not showy, but an extensive carpet has an interesting effect. The cultivar 'Variegata' is a bright subject, but is not such a strong grower, and is more suitable for a border where more attention can be given. If it proves to be a good grower in the area it can be propagated and given a tougher assignment.

This species is at its best in a light soil that is well stocked with organic material and moisture and does not dry out. In a hot and sunny position, bleaching often occurs.

P. stylosa var. *glaberrima* (*P. axillaris*) is not such an effective carpeting plant, but it has distinctive and large, almost *Aucuba*-like leaves, while the flowers are quite conspicuous in spring. Shelter is essential, otherwise the leaves become discoloured and torn during winter. It is an interesting subject for a shaded border.

Parthenocissus   Vitaceae

This genus is closely allied to the genera *Ampelopsis* and *Vitis*, a group of climbers in the family Vitaceae. Many of the species grow quite well in part shade or shade, although the majority are happier in a warm position in the sun. However, there is one self-clinging species, *P. henryana*, which is happier with part shade or even shade, for example on a north wall. The shelter of a wall also appears to suit it better, as there it will build up a spur system if pruned in early winter. Its attraction begins in early April as the new bronze-green growths appear. As this foliage matures during the summer, it has a variegated appearance, with a prominent silvering along the midrib and main veins. Combined with this effect is the bronze of the young foliage as it appears during the summer. The late autumn colouring is in shades of a fairly bright cerise pink, while the midrib remains prominent.

It makes a wonderful climber for the walls of a sheltered passage or patio.

Peltiphyllum   Saxifragaceae

P. peltatum, from California, is one of the most extraordinary plants in the family Saxifragaceae. It is most at home by the waterside where abundant supplies of moisture are available for the free production of the giant and rounded leaves, which rise to 1 m. (3 ft. 3 in.) high, giving it the very apt name of the umbrella plant. The leaves spring from rhizomes which develop over the surface during summer, but the plant flowers in spring before these are produced. The effect at this stage can be described as fantastic rather than beautiful, for the heads of pink blossoms similar to those of the bergenia, are held high on rather stiff and bare stalks. Their distribution is random and made more effective by ensuring that the soil surface is free from weeds and dead leaves. A thin mulching should be applied before or after flowering.

Propagation is by division during the dormant season. It is hardly a suitable subject for a very small garden, being more in keeping with a large informal layout. It will grow well in sun, dappled shade and part shade.

Pentaglottis   Boraginaceae

P. sempervirens (*Anchusa sempervirens*), is a tough subject which thrives in a great variety of situations—in sun, dappled shade, part shade or shade, although it appears to shun large trees and woodlands and is often found in gardens near buildings, annoying the gardener as he tries to keep the area clean and orderly. It will thrive in a variety of soils but prefers the warmer, better-drained ones, showing considerable impatience with the cold heavy clays.

The plant produces a cluster of broad basal leaves which are coarse and hairy. During the late spring a number of semi-erect growths are produced which bear beautiful bright blue 'forget-me-not' flowers backed by attractive green foliage. This is all very beautiful and pleasing until a few weeks later when flowering is completed and the plant concentrates upon the production of a heavy crop of seed. Then the whole effect is one of such extreme untidiness that the gardener is only too pleased to cut the growths down to the ground at the earliest opportunity in order to encourage the second crop of flowers that often follows. It is not a plant to introduce lightly, for apart from its rather bedraggled appearance at a time of year when all should be fresh and green, if conditions prove suitable it will spread rapidly by seed, and once established it is almost impossible to eradicate. When an attempt is made to dig it out, small pieces of the thong-like and brittle roots will most likely be left behind. These have no difficulty in forming adventitious buds from which they will grow out quickly, to form a cluster thicker than ever. Nevertheless, this plant may with justification be considered for part shade on a very light and poor soil which dries up rapidly in the spring, and where irrigation and soil improvement are out of the question. A position like this is too dry for any but early maturing plants.

Propagation is by seed or by root cuttings taken in November.

Petasites   Compositae

This genus of vigorous perennials must never be introduced into the small intensive area, for with their rhizomatous roots they will quickly take over and be very difficult to keep in check. They are plants therefore for the larger, informal garden or thin woodland. When they have to fend for themselves, they are far more selective, and conditions in part shade, where the ground is moist, appears to suit them very well.

Unless you have a suitable site and situation the advice is to go out into the country to enjoy them; their distribution, however, is very localized. The flowers are produced very early in the year before the leaves, and are most strongly scented. *P. japonicus*, which has become naturalized in places in this country, bears dense heads of white flowers.

The cultivar 'Giganteus' has even larger inflorescences (see Plate 5).

Phyllitis   Polypodiaceae

P. scolopendrium (*Asplenium scolopendrium*), hart's-tongue fern is a native evergreen fern (see Plates 6 and 7) which loves the shade and shelter of rocks, banks and walling.

It must have moisture, both in the atmosphere and at the roots, to do well—if too exposed, sunny or dry the fronds are short, often bleached yellow, or even scorched. The mature fronds may be up to 600 mm. (2 ft.) long, strap-shaped and dark green, while on a vertical face they tend to hang down—a beautiful sight in many old lanes in the West Country, a region it loves as it is milder there with a high rainfall. The new fronds, at first whitish and very hairy, appear during April, developing in the crown at the base of the old fronds, which remain green for the whole of the winter into the spring. It is worth having a plant or so near the path, so that the beauty of this fern may be appreciated at all seasons. This species is available in many cristated forms; some are neat and are very decorative; whether planted singly or in groups they may serve as markers. These ferns have a prominent venation, which is displayed clearly in places where the under-surfaces are brought into view—a beauty of form which many like to study closely. Often the fronds of the cristated forms, 'Gibbosum' for example, are shorter than the type, and these are therefore suitable for the smaller feature or garden.

Plant young, small specimens in the autumn, and once this fern is established and really happy it will soon spread and colonize naturally by spores. If just the common form is preferred, do not introduce any cristated forms, for these will also reproduce freely by means of spores. It is an easy fern to establish given dappled shade or shade, moisture at the roots at least (a well-drained and not boggy situation), and also shelter.

In a woodland or shade garden it will help to create an atmosphere of informality and maturity, but it is also suitable for other types of garden, while in the town garden the glossy, dark green leaves will be specially appreciated during winter.

Pieris Ericaceae

Members of this genus require the same conditions as many rhododendrons, especially as far as the soil is concerned. They are at home on a moist but well-drained, acid and peaty soil, and will not lightly tolerate the extremes, be they chalky soils (which may be fatal), dry soils, or wet and cold clays. Often however, improvements may be made to give the soil the right properties.

They will thrive in an open, sunny position, especially in a cool and clean country air, but at the risk of damage from frosts and cold winds. Brought into the dappled shade of the woodland, particularly among rhododendrons and like plants, they add greatly to the variety of form and interest.

P. formosa forrestii is magnificent in the right setting, particularly in the spring when in growth and flower. The young leaves at this period are red, making a beautiful contrast with the dark green of the mature foliage. The old seed heads or fruits remain attached for months afterwards, adding to the interest and beauty of this plant. Even during winter it is decorative and full of promise, for the future flowers, in bud form, are held prominently on compound racemes, with their dull-pink petioles and main stalks. The white, bell-shaped flowers are slightly fragrant. Added to all this is the effect of the bark which is often shaggy, and looks quite dramatic on the older specimens. There are a number of well-known cultivars which are also good garden plants.

Poa Gramineae

P. nemoralis, wood poa, wood meadow grass, is a native, found commonly in woods and other shady places, on soils which are moist for the greater part of the year. It may be used for shady places in gardens, either for lawns or natural stretches of grass. Often it is available only in mixtures, unless special arrangements are made with a seedsman, but special mixtures containing this species give very good results, for the initial coverage is speedier. Later the most suitable species for the position predominates.

In a very dry position beneath deciduous trees only *P. annua*, annual meadow grass, is capable of surviving, for it is able to germinate in the autumn and reach the flowering stage before the leaf canopy is mature again.

A spring sowing of grass seed beneath trees is preferable to an autumn one, because fallen leaves impede the growth of the young grass.

Podophyllum Podophyllaceae

These extraordinary plants, grown mainly for their foliage effect are all herbaceous perennials, dying down at the end of the growing season to a system of rhizomes by which they spread.

With all the species the excitement starts in spring as the growths emerge. Taking *P. peltatum*, from North America, as an example: by early April the first white shoots appear, soon to be followed by two drooping leaves which are at first held on a short stalk with an almost mushroom-like appearance. There is a prominent white patch at the junction of the leaves with the petiole, almost as if this part is designed to bear the brunt of the wear and friction as the shoot emerges. The flower bud appears early too, being a light bronze-green turning almost to green. During June the flowers open white, but unfortunately they are hidden by the bronze-green foliage, for each stem from the crown is forked into two leaves and the flowers are produced in the axils of this fork. The oval fruits, which ripen to a red colour in July, are also hidden. The foliage dies down in the autumn, when the plants may be cut down, leaving the lower part of the stems to indicate the position of the clumps.

P. hexandrum, from western China, has very strong, lush, shiny green foliage with bold serrations, which lend well to a woodland appearance. The leaves, 500 mm. (1 ft. 8 in.) in diameter, may reach a height of 2·0 m. (6 ft. 7 in.) or more. With *P. emodi* the leaves, usually blotched when young, often exhibit some interesting variations. The foliage of *P. versipelle*, from western China, may colour to a reddish bronze in the autumn. All the species are plants for the dappled shade of the woodland or shade garden. They thrive best in a deep, rich and moist soil with shelter. They should be planted in a drift or group not too far from the front, so that the emerging growths can be closely examined.

Propagation is by division in the spring as growth commences.

Polygonatum   Liliaceae

P. multiflorum, common Solomon's seal, is a native. The green shoots grow rapidly during April with attractive pea-green leaves, eventually arching over to reach up to 800 mm. (2 ft. 7 in.). The long, bell-shaped flowers, which open in May, are a beautiful and pure greenish-white and hang down in small axillary clusters along the leafy part of the stem. Flowering is usually completed by the end of June, but the foliage remains in good condition until the autumn, when it turns to a clear, light brown.

P. × hybridum (*P. multiflorum* × *P. odoratum*), from Europe, is a stronger grower and reaches 1 m. (3 ft. 3 in.) high, with the upper third of the stem arching over to assume a horizontal position. The plant is pleasing from the time the crowded shoots first break the surface. *P. verticillatum*, from eastern Europe, is distinctive, producing thin, crowded stems 2 m. (6 ft. 7 in.) or more in height. The narrow leaves are in whorls, almost lily-like, with small, greenish flowers, while the fruits, which ripen to red in August, are like small currants. Even in the spring when this species first appears above the soil it is distinctive, for at this stage the strong, cream-coloured shoots are neatly marked with lines of brown-pink fleckings.

There are a number of other beautiful species; *P. punctatum*, from India, Nepal and China, is only 150 mm. (6 in.) high, with spotted, pinkish-white flowers which resemble an ericaceous subject, while *P. biflorum* from North America is possibly the best one for naturalizing if it is happy, for it then extends towards more direct sun or into deeper shade. These plants are very much in keeping with the atmosphere and conditions which prevail in the dappled shade of the woodland or shade garden, but they will also thrive in a shaded border. With their quiet charm and beauty, they have much to contribute towards the peace and serenity that should reign in the town garden. They like a soil which does not dry out too quickly.

Propagation is by division of the rhizomatous mass in the dormant season.

Polygonum   Polygonaceae

This genus at first sight appears to contain ideal subjects for shaded features, but there are important reservations. First, many species occur in the wild where they are never short of free moisture at the roots, often in a hillside gully or a depression. Secondly, if the larger ones succeed well, they often become very invasive and colonize wherever conditions are suitable. Among these are such giants as *P. cuspidatum*, from Japan, which may reach a height of 3 m. (10 ft.) and has become naturalized in this country. They have a place, but only in the larger, more natural garden where there is ample scope for them to run riot, both in dappled shade and full sun. Really a wide strip of mown grass is needed between them and any nearby precious plantings.

P. campanulatum, from the Himalayas, is among the best species for dappled shade, and while it will spread freely into large clumps, it can be checked quite easily by forking the growths out. Even during winter and early spring, the leafy growths hugging the soil are attractive, with a marked herringbone system where the veins are sunken.

During spring and early summer growth is rapid, and by the time the flowers open in July their height may be 1·5 m. (5 ft.) in dappled shade, but less in full sun. The leafy growths branch extensively as they reach full height and produce short spikes or clusters of cream flowers, tinged with pink. The buds are a deep pink and the two together produce a light, dainty effect which can light up the dullest of corners. Flowering continues until late August, but with the onset of winter all that remains is a mass of dead stems which need clearing with care so that there is no injury to the basal growths. A light mulching is helpful at this stage, while a very thick covering of fallen tree leaves may need to be raked off.

This is a plant for an informal setting in the dappled shade of the woodland or shade garden—in a drift or a small group according to the scale. A sheltered position is preferable, for the growths are readily damaged by wind.

Propagation is by division.

Polypodium   Polypodiaceae

P. vulgare is a rhizomatous native fern which creeps on the surface when growing in a crevice or below if it is rooting into a mould, soil or rotting tree stump. In mild areas the fronds often remain green through the winter, the new ones appearing in May. It is found wild in many parts of the country but thrives best in areas of higher rainfall where the roots are able to extract sufficient moisture for the greater part of the year from a shallow rooting medium where ranker-growing subjects would not be found.

This fern prefers some shade, and is found beneath deciduous trees in a variety of situations including rocks and banks and on rotting stumps. In wetter areas it often occurs as an epiphyte on deciduous trees, particularly oak, where the bark furrows are deep, and again in a variety of situations giving part shade or shade, such as walls and old thatch. Always the rooting medium is open and moist, at least for long periods. If it is found in a sunny position where it gets no shade at all it is usually on an exposed hill where driving mists and rains occur frequently, but here the fronds are usually very short.

Provided that there is sufficient moisture and shade, this fern can be readily established. Rotting tree stumps or a rocky crevice are ideal, although it can be grown in a suitable border with other shade-loving plants. If it is desired to establish this fern in a stretch of old walling, plant it at the base and it will spread by spores to the crevices between the bricks and stones, unless of course the cement is too hard.

There are a number of cultivated forms, some crested, *P. vulgare*, 'Cornubiense' has light green fronds which are much divided. It is a very pleasant fern.

Polystichum   Polypodiaceae

P. setiferum, soft shield fern, is a native. Although the type species is an excellent fern, we turn to the cultivars which have very finely divided fronds. When the plants are large and healthy they are among the most outstanding of ferns. Among many very good examples there is the cultivar *P. setiferum* 'Diversilobum

Stipulatum'. It has an attractive growth pattern: the crowns become active during late April or early May. As the fronds develop they appear to unroll, the tips being curled like a very ornamental shepherd's crook. The developing pinnae, on either side of the light apricot-brown and hairy midrib, slowly unfold, being a yellowish-green at first. Those nearest the tip are the last to develop, and tightly packed in the earliest stages they appear as buttons. So the wonderful growth develops; one is never tired of it, and certainly it is worth putting one or two crowns near the front where they can be appreciated. Later of course the fronds mature; light green at first, they become darker with age. Like so many of this group, this cultivar is at its best in dappled shade, and if it is given a little additional shelter, the fronds often remain green into the early winter.

In the early spring they should be cut down to within 100 mm. (4 in.) of the crown, to enable the display by the developing fronds of the new season to be seen to the best advantage. A dressing of leafmould should be applied at the same time, both for the plants and to improve the appearance of the surface as a background for the developing frond effect. Like most ferns, they thrive best in a soil which is moist and rich in decaying organic material. Propagation is by the offsets which appear from time to time.

Primula
Primulaceae

One essential condition common to all primulas is that they must have sufficient moisture at the roots. A large number like to hunt for this through a deep, well-drained soil which is moist and cool, and stocked with grit and organic material in the form of leafmould or peat.

P. marginata, a species with serrated leaf edges and intense lilac flowers is an example, but it is happiest with this rooting medium deep down in a rock crevice in a sunny position. By contrast, *P. edgeworthii*, which prefers this type of rooting medium, will thrive best in dappled shade.

P. nutans, from Yunnan in China, is one of a more exacting group. In June it produces heads of pale, mealy, lavender-blue flowers, which are almost bell-shaped, on 300 mm. (1 ft.) high stems. It is a late starter, with the crowns beginning to grow in late April, thus demanding extra care during weeding. Despite the fact that the foliage remains in good condition until late autumn, this species often fails during the following season. The stock should therefore be maintained by raising a quantity each year from seed. Many of the more difficult species which are shade-loving are suitable for the peat garden or walling, but even so they thrive better in the north where it is cooler.

P. *viali* is rightly considered a very desirable species, but for good results extra attention must be paid to cultivation. It is essential to start with good healthy plants, to choose a moist and cool site with dappled shade and, if the species is to be grown for longer than a year or so, it is necessary to have a young batch coming along each year for gapping up. This plant also is a late starter, and when growth begins during May the foliage is up-right, suggesting that the area between the crowns could be used for an early flowering and maturing subject such as *Eranthis hyemalis*.

The moment of glory for this plant is when the flowers on the narrow and pyramidal inflorescence begin to open, giving the whole an orchid-like appearance. The unopened buds heading the spike are red, while the lower ones which are open are deep lilac. Blossoming continues through June and July, but even then the spikes remain attractive with the red and green colouring of the calyx showing through the withered flower remains.

There are many primulas including cultivars and hybrids which by contrast are comparatively easy to grow, provided the soil is well drained and moist with plenty of peat or leafmould added.

In P. *sieboldii* early foliage is an appealing feature as it first appears, often in February. It is delicate and almost fern-like. Later the serrated edges become more obvious as the growths appear in irregular drifts and clusters, showing up very plainly against a soil darkened with leafmould. By April the flowers, which resemble phlox, appear in a head on 200 mm. (8 in.) stems and have a perfect background in the fresh, green, crowded leaves. There is a wide variety of choice, from white to magenta, but the form 'Alba' is really beautiful, especially at dusk when the white and irregular drifts remain conspicuous as the light fails. However, wonderful as the display may be from any of these cultivars, it must be recognized that the blossoms lack a certain daintiness associated with primulas. Planting up a small group to begin with in a carefully chosen position is advised. If more are required, plants may be lifted and divided in the early spring as growth begins. This species is happiest in dappled shade, and is perhaps more suited to the shade garden than the woodland garden. It makes an ideal border plant for the town garden.

P. denticulata, from the Himalayas, is another easy-to-grow primula provided it is given the correct conditions—and if it does not look healthy and strong it is just not worth having. At its best it sends up lush, pale green, primrose-like leaves and rounded heads of flower. Often this stage is reached in the very early spring, when severe weather may cause some damage, but in a sheltered position will be largely avoided and growth may be earlier. After flowering, a general tidy-up is required and will help a lot in maintaining a presentable appearance until the autumn, when the foliage dies back once more to a crown on the surface. The flowers vary in colour from lavender to mauve, although there are also many strains and cultivars, including 'Alba' and 'Rosea'. Generally they may be raised from seed, but a definite form must be propagated vegetatively by division or root cuttings. Moisture is all-important to this primula and it will as willingly grow in a boggy position as in a well-drained deep and moist soil, but the flowers last far longer in dappled shade, part shade, or even shade.

The Candelabra Primulas are a large and popular group easily recognized because the flowers are in whorls, tier upon tier up the length of tall stalks which may reach 700 mm. (2 ft. 4 in.) or more high. They will grow in sun or shade, but prefer dappled shade or part shade. The species and hybrids in this group love a position where water is permanently close to the surface—the banks of a stream, pond or lake, even a bog. Such a high water table is not absolutely essential, but the only alternative is a good depth of soil, permanently moist and well supplied with decayed organic material, which acts as a sponge in holding the reserves of water so essential to the thirsty rootlets. Let them suffer from a lack of this essential and they quickly deteriorate, and may die out completely.

These plants have an air of informality which is seen to best advantage in a group or drift (see Plate 9), but they can be just as effective on a small scale provided a suitable background and surroundings are built up. This group lends itself very well to a mixed planting with other plants such as lilies, trilliums and iris,

The choice of species and hybrids in this group is a very wide one. *P. japonica* is a strong and rather coarse grower compared with the others. The flowers are an off-shade of red, but there are a number of good cultivars including for example 'Postford White'. Unfortunately virus infections appear to have gained a foothold among them; the leaves become fern-like and growth and flowering rapidly deteriorate. Once stock becomes infected, it is better left out of the collection completely. *P. aurantiaca* has orange blossoms during June, which are followed by a later but smaller display if the seed crop is removed before it develops and matures. (All primulas benefit from this treatment; leave just sufficient of the best forms to provide seed for the future.) *P. bulleyana* has deep orange-coloured flowers in July, with foliage which is quite erect and close. It is worth growing for the foliage effect alone. *P. pulverulenta*, with deep wine-red flowers, has strong, upright foliage which contrasts well with the fallen leaves of the late autumn (see Plate 9). *P. helodoxa*, with deep yellow flowers, is one of the daintiest of this group. All are happiest in the dappled shade where the flowers are a better colour and last far longer than in the sun, especially in the south. A sheltered site helps to create a good humid atmosphere and minimizes wind damage to the stems when they are heavy with blossom.

The Sikkimensis group is made up of the real moisture-loving primulas. Indeed, *P. florindae* is never happier than when growing in a bog where water is actually standing for long periods. The foliage with long petioles and the clear yellow flowers, hanging rather untidily in a head on a stem which is almost a metre (3 ft. 3 in.) high, give the plant a graceful yet informal appearance. A drift or group shows up very well from a distance or in fading light, a thought for those who return home late from work. The flowering period is a long one, over June and July. On the other hand *P. sikkimensis*, similar in many ways is smaller, and flowers two or three weeks earlier. Both will grow in the sun, but seem to be happier in light, dappled shade or part shade.

P. secundiflora is a perfect plant to use for contrast in this situation, with its heads of purple flowers—a redeeming feature for a plant which has such unexciting foliage. All the species in this group can be grown without boggy conditions provided the soil is moist, although perhaps *P. alpicola* is the best one to use under these conditions. The heads of flowers are creamy-yellow, held up strongly at a height of 300 mm. (1 ft.) and producing a subtle effect, especially if intermingled with lilies or meconopsis. This is a variable species as far as colour is concerned. The form 'Alba' is very good as a contrast among other primulas, but a large group on its own gives such a startling effect that it is rather disturbing in a shaded area where the quieter colours should prevail.

Our much loved native primrose, *P. vulgaris*, is in the Vernales section. It is common enough in many parts of the country, but only on soils which have a suitable moisture content during the greater part of the year. They expect and will tolerate a dry period during the latter part of summer, but of course this does not happen every year. Positions which frequently dry out during the spring and summer months are not likely to be successful with primroses. On such a site, often over sand or gravel, much can be achieved by the introduction of clay, either by digging this in to some depth or by filling a prepared hole 300 mm. (1 ft.) deep, having just sufficient soil over this for planting. The outline to this excavation should be irregular in an informal setting. Often over gravels a filling of chalk has the same effect. Shade is also an important factor and the primrose is often found under deciduous trees and woods, but it will thrive equally well in other positions with varying degrees of shade—dappled shade, part shade or even shade. In the West Country it is often found in open grass-land, but usually on slopes away from the sun.

There are a number of other species and hybrids in this group that will thrive under similar conditions. However, most if not all of these require good standards of cultivation as regards division when needed and top-dressing, thus leaving the field clear for the primrose and other British species to spread as they will. The hybrid polyanthus are also happy in dappled shade, part shade or shade and are suitable for planting in the more formal parts of the garden in beds and borders (including shrub and herbaceous borders), as are most of the others in this group (see Plate 16).

If propagation is attempted it is important to ensure the best method is used. In many cases for this species, seed propagation is the best. Seed should be sown as soon as ripe. The viability of primula seed is soon lost if it is kept in storage for any length of time. Division is a good method with many but it must be carefully carried out. Primulas form a fresh set of roots at the base of the new crowns as they develop after flowering. Once they have formed and become established it is really too late to split them up. There will be no extensive activity from the crown until the new growths form in the following spring. The secret is to carry out the operation at the right time and to do it carefully.

Those who intend to raise these plants from seed will be interested in the article 'Germinating Primula seed' by P. A. Thompson, Jodrell Laboratory, Royal Botanic Gardens, Kew, *Journal of the Royal Horticultural Society*, vol. XCIII, March 1968, part 3, pp. 133–8.

Prunus   Rosaceae

This large genus displays a considerable variation in its sun requirements, but at least two of the evergreen species, and a few of the deciduous ones, are tolerant of a degree of shade, in some cases beneath deciduous trees. *P. laurocerasus*, common laurel, cherry laurel, probably the best-known evergreen species, is available in many forms, but the larger growers with extensive root systems are better able to compete with trees for the available moisture. They are particularly useful for giving furnishing and shelter, on a wide variety of soils which are unsuitable for such acid soil lovers as rhododendrons. The smaller forms, quite good as ground-cover subjects in shade, are not very successful in dry situations. The same applies to a hedge of even the larger growers, for under constant pruning their root system is very shallow and restricted.

P. lusitanica, Portugal laurel, is hardier and more shade tolerant and, given the situation, will send branches right out into deep shade. Both this and the smaller forms of *P. laurocerasus*, such as 'Otto Luyken', are ideal for patio and tub culture, where their evergreen nature is especially appreciated, and their response to pruning, to restrict them in size if this is necessary, is ideal.

P. tomentosa, downy cherry, forms a spreading clump of growth, 2 m. (6 ft. 7 in.) or more in height, and is very happy in an informal planting beneath scattered deciduous trees, even on a light soil. The Morello Cherry will grow and fruit well, either trained or free standing, in the shade of a building, or against a north wall. This group which is of hybrid origin is grown for its edible fruit.

Pulmonaria   Boraginaceae

The plants in this genus, like so many in the family Boraginaceae, are quite easy to grow given the right conditions.

P. officinalis is universally loved and has the common name of soldiers and sailors. It is not as commonly found in gardens as one might expect, especially since it was introduced into this country from the Continent many hundreds of years ago. It has become naturalized in places, and perhaps for this reason some consider it too common to cultivate in their gardens. However, the search for ground-cover plants has brought it to the fore. In a drift or as a single plant, it is appealing in spring as it comes into flower on leafy stems which may be 300 mm. (1 ft.) tall. The flowers which are at first deep pink as they open, turn to blue with age. Good forms have foliage which is very clearly spotted white.

P. saccharata, from Europe, flowers when 230 mm. (9 in.) tall, during April and May and, as in the former species, the colour changes from deep pink to blue with age. The new foliage from the crown develops as the flowers fade and, provided that it is not too dry, remains in good condition until the autumn. In fact, both this and *P. officinalis* will keep their foliage through the winter if the weather is kind. There are a number of forms or cultivars with variegated foliage, in which shades of creamy-white play a prominent part. These, in particular, are much better if they are shaded from the midday sun, for there is a tendency for them to scorch rather badly, particularly if it is dry. These forms are attractive against a dark and definite background, logs or tree stumps for example, while the foliage shows up distinctly in the fading light.

Neither of these two species, although they prefer the shade and grow well in it, will creep freely beneath such bushes as rhododendrons. However, *P. angustifolia* (see Plate 11), again from Europe, will do just this, although like the others it is impatient of very dry conditions. The multitude of blue flowers start to open a few weeks after the foliage appears above the soil in the spring. The effect is so pleasing and thrilling that the plant in full blossom never fails to attract attention. Pulmonarias can be planted in dappled shade, part shade or shade in a variety of situations, always to give pleasure, provided that the soil is reasonable and does not dry out completely.

Propagation is by division, preferably as the new growth appears in the spring. Plant at 500 mm. (1 ft. 8 in.) apart.

Pyracantha Rosaceae

Collectively the shrubs in this genus are referred to as firethorns. In common with many other plants in the family Rosaceae, these form short flowering shoots or spurs, and the ability to do this is related, in part at least, to condition and maturity, although the ripening influence of the sun may be a balancing factor at times. The fact that pyracanthas are evergreen helps to compensate for lack of direct sunlight. Thus the hardiest species and cultivars are suitable for growing against a north-facing wall. Included among these is the well-known *P. coccinea* 'Lalandei'.

Pyrola Pyrolaceae

The family of this small genus is closely related to the Ericaceae. Collectively known as the winter greens, the family consists of low and creeping evergreens which, in the garden at least, like to move forward into fresh ground full of moist peat and partially decayed organic material, which they find rewarding.

P. rotundifolia, a native, will form a thick drift of rounded leaves. The evergreen foliage of winter is brightened in the spring by tufts of fresh, green leaves which herald the appearance of the 300 mm. (1 ft.) high spikes. The flowers, white, flushed with rose-pink, have an orchid-like appearance. Another, but equally delightful, effect is carried on well into September with the lengthening fruit spikes, for the stigma remains attached to each fruit, giving a spurred and orchid-like appearance.

It is a good plant to have near the front, to be appreciated with others which like a moist peat and dappled shade. By having the plant in such a position, not only can it be appreciated from close quarters, but also the fallen leaves of autumn can be removed from the low clusters without treading on the soil.

Propagation is by careful division as the new growth appears in the spring.

Ramonda Gesneriaceae

This is a hardy genus in the family Gesneriaceae, which is made up mainly of tropical and warm temperate plants.

R. *myconi*, from the Pyrenees, is the most commonly grown

species in this small but important genus of shade-lovers. The plant takes the form of a beautifully shaped and perfect rosette, which hugs the rocks or ground closely. The flowers similar to those of *Saintpaulia* (African violet) are produced on reddish stalks which arise from the axils of the older leaves. The flowers are held up towards the light, no matter what position the rosette may be in, and often it is on a vertical face of rockwork. The combination of the rock colouring with the green and hairy foliage forms a perfect background for the lilac-shaded flowers, which have a quaint orange 'beak' in their centres.

This is an ideal plant for a dry retaining wall in shade. The rooting medium should be extensive, and sufficiently moist during winter and spring periods. During summer, however, after flowering is completed, it can dry up almost completely. The outer leaves may wither and die, but the plants will retreat to their innermost growth buds and live this period through, to break out as strong as ever as soon as the autumn rains begin. They are none the worse for the experience.

Propagation is by seed or leaf cuttings taken in the spring.

Ranzania   Podophyllaceae

R. japonica is one of the many desirable but uncommon woodland plants from Japan. The Solomon's seal-like growths appear above ground during April, with very thin stems and alternate leaves. These are a good green, oval and pointed, with an interesting parallel venation. The plant produces small, pale lavender flowers on the head of the growth during mid to late June.

It is suitable for a bed of choice plants in the coolness of a dappled shade. The soil should be moist and full of leafmould.

Propagation is by division as the growths appear above the soil in spring.

Rhododendron   Ericaceae

This genus, a very large and complex one, is made up of many, many species, hybrids and cultivars. They show great variation in almost every respect, and yet there are a few essentials common to the vast majority. These are mainly concerned with growing conditions. They must have a well-drained medium, but one which is moist and acid. As far as shade is concerned, some are more demanding than others, but the climate and the area generally also come into the picture. Many of the dwarf rhododendrons require sunny and open conditions.

The large number requiring shade must, for the sake of their health and well-being, be part of the environment and help to create the necessary shelter and shade, although of course additional and supporting tree and shrub plantings are usually needed. When a site is being considered, it is important to take into account any existing features and to remember that in most cases where the average annual rainfall is a light one, drought is likely to be the main enemy.

Where there is a choice of the types or species to grow, it is advisable to start off with the common species or hybrids, for generally these are easiest to grow. If a marked preference gains ground at a later stage, the surplus can always be sold or given away, as the one characteristic common to all, is a fine and fibrous root system, very close to the surface; provided that this is dug out with care, and when replanted is not buried deeply, it will be found that they transplant quite easily. Large sections of *Rhododendron* have an evergreen foliage, which is tough when mature, and they are slow to die if conditions are not suitable. Often they pine away over a period of years, and while this gives no excuse for complacency or neglect, it allows time for a mistake in positioning to be corrected. One must watch the amount of annual growth, for this is a sure measure of the health of the plant.

The deciduous rhododendrons, often referred to as azaleas, are well worth a place in light shade, preferably dappled shade (see Plate 13). Not only is there a great variety of colour; in some cases they are scented, while the autumn colour effects are often very beautiful. Even after the leaves have dropped, the mixed planting of deciduous rhododendrons will have considerable interest, for the various branch systems show up distinctly, some for example being more twiggy than others. With some the remnants of the old fruits remain attached, forming conspicuous and interesting heads of open capsules which are almost star-like, and light brown in colour. Again, variety may be introduced into such plantings by irregular drifts or groups of evergreens or semi-evergreens, and often these are low-growing to give further variation. In the early spring, the flower buds become more and more conspicuous, but the variation in the rate of development throws the different branch systems into further relief.

Out of flower, a carefully balanced rhododendron planting can be interesting with the variation in foliage, form and habit of growth. This can be enhanced further by a suitable selection of shade-loving plants. Even before most of the rhododendrons flower during spring and early summer months, drift plantings of *Eranthis hyemalis*, the winter aconite, will give lovely sheets of colour, while a variety in *Cyclamen* will give foliage and colour, again during the dull periods. There are, of course, many other plants which could be considered, but it is important to take height and soil conditions into account before a final selection is made. In addition to increasing interest, a ground-cover planting helps to create the right environment for rhododendrons, for the roots are shaded and are thus cooler.

The policy of including plants other than rhododendrons in such a planting may be extended to the smaller-growing trees. The silver birch is one obvious example, but the range is much wider than is generally appreciated. The mountain ash section of the genus *Sorbus* may, for example, be considered. They are not thirsty and strong-growing trees, while the canopy is light and effective. Some, such as *S. aucuparia* 'Beissneri', have effective light, copper-brown stems. Magnolias may be considered for a choice, but it must be remembered that their canopy of foliage is often heavy during the summer. In considering plants to establish among rhododendrons, it is important to choose subjects which will not rob them of moisture, or harm their delicate root systems. It is important too, when planting up between rhododendrons, not to dig too closely to them, but to move just sufficient soil to establish the plants.

Ribes   Grossulariaceae

It may be surprising to find a genus which grows so well in full sun even mentioned in this work. However this is partly for the benefit of R. *sanguineum* 'Brocklebankii', a cultivar of the flowering currant, which has quite a bright yellow-green foliage and forms a compact bush a metre (3 ft. 3 in.) or more in height. Some form of shade is desirable, otherwise the foliage scorches badly in hot, sunny periods. Even with shade this is likely to happen during long, dry spells. This is to some extent a neglected genus, and it is likely that many more of the currants would do well in shade with a moist soil. One has only to remember the old private garden

G

practice of growing a late crop of red currants on a north-facing wall.

Rodgersia   Saxifragaceae

This genus of large and impressive foliage plants must be well grown in a deep, rich and moist soil to be seen at its best. Although these plants are frequently grown in the sun, they will also thrive in dappled shade or part shade. It is important that the setting in which they grow is scaled to their size, with sufficient depth for them to be planted either singly or in a drift towards the mid-distance or in the background, preferably with a screen of tree trunks and foliage at the back. Properly positioned, they help to give the impression of space, as there are often large gaps among the leaves and stalks, giving views through and beyond, perhaps to ferns. If grown in a small garden, and there is no reason against it, the plant must be very carefully positioned.

R. *aesculifolia*, from China, starts its growth in April, the shoots at first being an attractive bronze. As the handsome foliage develops to 700 mm. (2 ft. 4 in.) in height, it has a distinct horse chestnut-like appearance. The small white flowers are held in compound spikes 1·7 m. (5 ft. 8 in.) high, being most effective against a dark background. Even after the flowers have fallen the heads are attractive into the autumn, as the pale green calyces remain at the bases of the paired green capsules. R. *pinnata* 'Superba' has foliage with a striking, dark green lustre, while the large inflorescences consist of white and pink flowers. Later the developing fruits assume a reddish-brown colour. R. *tabularis*, from China, has yellow-green, plate-like leaves which have an attractive lobed and serrated edge. This account of grandeur and magnificence could be continued, describing the effect of light and shadow playing among the giant leaves of the various handsome species such as R. *podophylla* (see Plate 12) and cultivars.

Propagation is by division just as growth restarts in the spring.

Rosa   Rosaceae

The members of this vast genus and complexity of hybrids and cultivars are known so widely just as roses, and are recognized as sun lovers. However, a number of the climbing roses in particular grow and blossom well when trained on a north-facing wall. They are particularly effective against an old stone wall. Among the cultivars suitable for this position are: the climber 'Etoile de Hollande', a deep red which is very fragrant, and the old noisette rose, 'Madame Alfred Carrière', white tinged pink and scented.

Ruscus   Liliaceae

This small genus is closely allied to *Asparagus*, which it resembles in some ways, particularly as it sends up new growths in the spring.

R. *aculeatus*, butcher's broom, a native evergreen, forms a close stool of stiff growths, the leaves being reduced to scales, their function being taken over by flattened stems which are called cladodes. This is a plant that will thrive even in the shady and often dry conditions found beneath horse chestnuts and holm oaks. Such an environment would prove impossible for most shade-lovers, but this species is tough and hard, and slow to establish. Perhaps too, the fact that the cladode surfaces are reflective plays an important part in the success of this plant under these conditions, for by this means the light is thrown to the innermost depths of the clump, where the less fortunate growths benefit.

It is rather a small grower, being up to a metre (3 ft. 3 in.) high, but it has a certain attraction and is at times even dramatic, especially when during the early part of the summer, the young, light green growths show up distinctly against the dark green of the old. The flowers are small and inconspicuous, but their bright red berries are quite showy on the female plants. There is a superior fruiting form with larger, dull red berries.

R. *hypoglossum*, from southern Europe, will also grow in dimly lit situations, although it will not tolerate such poor conditions as the former species as the cladodes are flat and broad; again the star-shaped flower is inconspicuous, but with a small leaf which is held at an angle, giving an interesting but curious effect. Like the former species, it loves the shade, and will even bleach in the sun. After a very rough and severe winter the evergreen foliage is often in poor shape, so the worst of the foliage may be removed as the new appears in the spring.

Both species will thrive in most forms of shade, although a full and complete canopy may be a little too much for them, especially during the early years. In such cases they can be established just within the edges of the shaded area, to creep in later.

Propagation is best carried out in the spring, by division as the new growth commences.

Sanguinaria   Papaveraceae

S. canadensis, from North America, is a little plant with all the appearance of a woodlander. It is referred to as blood root because of the colour of the sap in the roots (although the leaves and stems also contain blood-coloured sap).

Growth starts during April with the appearance of the glaucous leaves, which are neatly folded to protect the flower; both are apparent even at such an early stage. Not only are the growths unusual, but the way in which they are scattered evenly over the entire area occupied by the cluster or drift is appealing, especially if set against a dark soil or leafmould dressing. As the foliage unfolds it is a light grey-green and deeply lobed, similar to that of *Macleaya*. By late April the flowers open—they are single, consisting of several narrow and pure white petals with golden anthers. There is also a cultivar, 'Flore Plena'. Even after the flowers have dropped the foliage remains in a fresh condition until the late summer. Then as it fades, the older leaves first colour to shades of brown and yellow and, with the younger ones still green, it gives a good early autumn display.

It is a suitable plant for the dappled shade of the woodland or shade garden, where the soil should be deep, moist, but well drained and plentifully stocked with decayed organic material. It is a good plant to have in a group or drift near the front, because it is so interesting. The foliage is distinctive and thus provides a good contrast with other plants such as *Hosta*.

Propagation is by seed, which should be sown as soon as it is ripe; by division in the autumn and by root cuttings in the early spring.

Sanicula   Umbelliferae

S. europaea, wood sanicle, is an unexciting, native perennial which yet adds much to a woodland setting as it grows among other plants. From a rosette of palmate leaves, small and close umbels of white or pink flowers are held on stems 200 mm. (8 in.) long, giving little indication that it is closely related to the genus *Astrantia*. Apart from its quiet charm, it is a good 'indicator' plant, for it is usually found on the loams and better soils over chalk, where there is moisture and often a good organic content. It is seldom seen on thin and dry soils, and is indeed hardly likely to succeed if introduced to these. Of course this does not mean that no other plant will be successful if it is not found—it is just one more indicator. Sometimes it is found beneath beech in quite dense shade.

Sarcococca   Buxaceae

This group of smaller shrubs in the box family comes mainly from China. They have become very popular as they are such wonderful plants for furnishing, because of their evergreen foliage, and their small size, being very suitable for the average garden. Indeed there are few plants which match them, for they will thrive on a wide variety of soils, with a considerable amount of shade.

S. confusa forms a dense shrub up to a metre (3 ft. 3 in.) high, but is of course thinner in the shade. It flowers very early in the year, and the blossoms are small and white, but very fragrant—a great favourite with early flying bees. The foliage has a light green, glossy surface, and while it is not especially compact, it can be pruned carefully to prevent it from bearing down on to nearby, smaller plants.

S. humilis is the best species for a shady place, and it will even grow, perhaps rather reluctantly, beneath the shade of a mature but quite dense conifer, such as *Cedrus libani*. Under these conditions the plant is likely to suffer from a lack of moisture, not light. The growth is very dense and fairly upright. The shrubs are only 500 mm. (1 ft. 8 in.) high, with a suckerous habit, which results in their filling in completely over the years.

While these two species are the best for shady places, there are limits to the range of positions which they can cope with. Beneath a dense canopy of holm oak or common beech, common ivy is much more reliable. There are a number of other species which are fine for dappled shade, including *S. hookerana digyna*, which has a graceful foliage and habit, and *S. ruscifolia*, with broad, dark green foliage and red berries, which hold during the winter while the new flowers for the following season are open.

Cuttings provide a ready means of propagation.

Saxifraga   Saxifragaceae

This genus is, for a writer on shade plants, just about as complicated as it can be When simplified (always a dangerous practice) it is by no means a genus of hot sun-lovers.

There is at least some justification in dealing with the outstanding woodlanders first. *S. fortunei*, from China and Japan, will give nothing but pleasure through the seasons, and it flowers during the latter part of October. From the time the leafy shoots emerge in the spring the plant is attractive, with brownish-red stipules to the shoots and folded, shiny leaves similar to those of begonias. As the plant develops during the summer, the variable nature of the foliage becomes apparent, in both shape and colour, some leaves being a rich green, others being lighter. The white flowers with strap-shaped petals hang in compound racemes—they are a great favourite with the late wasps. The growths are tufted, finally reaching 500 mm. (1 ft. 8 in.) high. It is an attractive plant to have near the front, either in a group or as a single plant, especially with a dark leafmould background.

S. pennsylvanica, from North America, is an entirely different plant, but one which is interesting and well worth growing as a contrast to others, singly, in groups, or in a drift. The foliage is coarse and hairy, while the flowers, borne in June on a 1 m. (3 ft. 3 in.) high spike, are small with reduced, greenish petals and orange stamens with a prominent disc. It spends the winter in an almost rosetted form, with rather broad leaves. Finally in the spring some of the surviving leaves are tinged with pink, and give quite an interesting effect.

Both these species are best in dappled shade in an informal setting, the latter plant appreciating a little more shelter. There is no reason at all why they should not be grown in a border of interesting plants in the shade.

The Robertsonia section of this genus is to a great extent typified by *S. umbrosa*—a native. London pride, *S. × urbium*, is a hybrid of this and is of course almost too well known to need description. This plant is best in a border in shade, and forms a nice fresh and compact rosetted growth, provided that there is sufficient moisture. It is not as happy under trees, hating the autumn leaf-fall and the winter's drip. When growing among shrubs, it will make little effort to run into the shade of the lower branches. There are a number of closely related species and hybrids. In addition to border use, they are ideal plants for the shady crevice in the rock garden or dry retaining wall. When growing on a vertical face, the spikes of flower, which rise from the mature rosettes, arch up with a beautiful sweep to display the flowers to the best advantage.

Of the remaining groups, the Mossy saxifrages, which form evergreen carpets with a mossy appearance, are at their best in shade or part shade, but they are impatient of being dried out at the roots, nor do they like overhanging branches, for the same reason as the preceding group.

However, each gardener should experiment for his own particular site, for even the Encrusted, Kabschia and Engleria saxifrages, recognized by many as sun-lovers, have been taken with success into partly shaded positions, particularly in the hot, airless valleys of the south, where they certainly appreciate shade from the midday sun. Owners of east- or north-facing cliffs or dry retaining walls should not despair, for with trial and error some surprising results may be obtained.

The herbaceous types may be propagated by division, but often the best means with the evergreen cushion ones is by cuttings, taken as the new growths mature after flowering.

Schizophragma   Hydrangeaceae

S. integrifolium is considered by many to be the best species in this genus, the plants being very similar to *Hydrangea petiolaris*, to which it is closely related. They are wonderful, self-supporting, wall subjects, and can be successfully grown on a north-facing feature. They can also be used as climbers against large trees, or again, over old tree stumps in shade.

The flower heads, produced during the summer, have large white bracts which appear to 'drip down' from the branch systems, for they are oval and point down. Later the inflorescences turn a light brown, which stands out against the foliage. In late autumn the foliage gives a display of autumn colour before the leaves drop. This is often a gradual process, the main veins being first margined with yellow, while the areas between are still green. This is viewed to full effect against the tracery of light brown branches and the supporting stone or brickwork.

Scilla   Liliaceae

Now that our native bluebell, *Endymion nonscriptus*, and closely allied *E. hispanicus* have been taken from this genus, only one or two outstanding species for shade are left.

S. bifolia, from Europe and Asia Minor, can be considered; it is often in flower in February, to be followed by *S. siberica*, from Russia, and other countries. Both species need to be grown among shrubs, in a bed or border, where they can be looked after properly. They are easy subjects to grow especially in a light, well-drained soil, but they are very accommodating and will grow in a wide range, including calcareous media. Unless the position is very well suited to them, the foliage, needed to form the bulb for the next season, will be swamped by other low-growing plants. Both species are blue flowered, but *S. siberica* is deeper in colour and more showy. Some of the other species would be worth growing.

They may be propagated by lifting during the dormant season, and also by seed. Any coloured forms must be propagated vegetatively.

Selaginella　　　　　　　　　　　　　　Selaginellaceae

This is a very large genus of moss-like plants, and they are found in many parts of the world. Various degrees of moisture are essential for their success, but generally even the foliage must never dry out completely. *S. kraussiana* was commonly grown in greenhouse collections, but has sometimes established itself outside in the milder parts of the country, originating no doubt from surplus material or cleanings which were thrown out on to rubbish tips.

It is a suitable plant to try in the mildest areas, choosing a sheltered and shady position. It loves the shelter of a loose-growing ground-cover such as *Galeobdolon luteum* 'Variegatum'; another suggested position is in the sheltered recess of a dry retaining wall (see Fig. 9). If need be, further shelter may be provided within this recess by placing the plant in a pot of peaty soil. This may then be placed within a larger pot which is then covered by a sheet of glass. If the outer containing pot is watertight so much the better, for the pot with the plant may be left standing in 20 to 30 mm. ($\frac{3}{4}$ to $1\frac{1}{4}$ in.) of water, making regular attention unnecessary.

Shortia Diapensiaceae

These beautiful woodland plants are quite exacting but are well worth the extra effort which is needed to grow them, provided of course the necessary conditions can be provided.

S. uniflora, from Japan, is a low-growing evergreen which at flowering time is no more than 130 mm. (5 in.) high. One of the main attractions is the flowers, which are produced during April to May. They are held singly on short stalks at various angles below the horizontal, while the five petals are joined at the base to form a short tube. Because of this they are frequently likened to bells, but a great deal of their charm lies in the fact that they have a beautiful pink colouring with the lobes of the petals having a cut edge. In the autumn the shiny green leaves are tinged with shades of reddish brown—an attractive feature against a dark soil.

S. uniflora grandiflora has larger flowers, and there are also several cultivars.

S. galacifolia, from North and South Carolina, is similar in many respects, but the foliage is even more attractive during the autumn and winter as it turns to a deep plum-red. These plants require something deeper than dappled shade, a position where perhaps only a low weak sun reaches them; one beneath a deciduous tree canopy on a north slope where it is cool, suits them very well. There are of course other positions which give shade and cool conditions, for example the rock garden. The peat garden also holds possibilities, for they love an acid, peaty soil, but it must not be too compact, and should remain permanently moist. Shelter is also necessary, particularly from the north and east. Good growing conditions are always necessary for these plants, particularly in the spring as the new leaves form.

They may be propagated by careful division when growth begins.

Skimmia Rutaceae

Although they will grow well in the sun, and often in exposed positions, these are wonderful plants for dappled shade and part shade, and are very useful for furnishing and general interest, being evergreen and slow growing, they will survive in quite poorly lit conditions beneath deciduous trees, although they will to some extent at least lose their close habit. They appear to prefer the better-drained soils, while *S. reevesiana* shows some dislike of calcareous soils, unless they are well stocked with peat.

S. laureola, from the Himalayas, has all the appearance of a woodland plant, with bright green and reflective foliage, which is one of its attractions. The clear, yellow-green flowers are held in terminal clusters in May, but even in the bud stage in early spring they are very prominent. With *S. japonica* the leaves are held more upright, and the whole bush is very compact. When the star-shaped blossoms open, they appear terminally, backed up by foliage which has a rosetted appearance. The berries, held by the female plants, remain on the bushes for months, to be hidden partly by the fresh, green growths and even the flowers in the following spring. There are many cultivars, including 'Rubella', with dull red flower buds which are showy from the late summer until the following spring, when they open white.

A number of seedlings of *S. japonica*, grown in a group, show an interesting variation in both habit and leaf colouring. They are ideal plants to introduce into a rhododendron planting.

Smilacina Liliaceae

S. racemosa, from North America, is very similar in growth to the Solomon's seal (*Polygonatum*), an important shade-loving genus to which it is closely related. The season's growth starts in late March when the stout, erect asparagus-like shoots reach approximately 500 mm. (1 ft. 8 in.) high before the leaves unfold. It is a dramatic stage, for the rate of growth is rapid and the stems are thickly placed. A few weeks later the flower buds appear—they are a creamy green and on a multiple panicle which terminates the arching stems 700 mm. (2 ft. 4 in.) high. The stem is well furnished with simple yet bold and clear foliage. As the flowers open white the heads assume a feathery appearance—conspicuous and yet so subtle, contributing much to a shade planting.

By early June the flowers fade, but the foliage remains and is green until late in the autumn, with the stalks still attached, and often with a thin scattering of lavender-purple berries. At the end of the season the stems may be cut down to 150 mm. (6 in.), leaving the bases to serve as useful markers.

This is a plant for the dappled shade of the woodland or shade garden, where it is effective either in a drift or a small group. It prefers a rich, but well-drained, lime-free soil.

Propagation is by division of the rhizomatous mass during the dormant season.

Speirantha   Liliaceae

S. gardenii is an unusual but easily grown plant, from China, with an almost bulbous appearance. During autumn, winter and spring the plant is most distinct, with bold, stiff, evergreen leaves which form a thick clump 500 mm. (1 ft. 8 in.) high. During April the flower spikes appear, an attractive stage with the white flower buds showing up plainly against the green leaves. An even more beautiful stage follows a few weeks later, when the flowers open. They are white and star-shaped, with narrow petals and prominent stamens, placed thinly with long, white stalks on a stem which never rises beyond the leaves. Many of these are new and thus fresh and green, and the appearance of the inflorescences against such a background is perfect.

After blossoming the plant remains with good foliage until the next flowering period comes round, and there is very little to do apart from the mulching and pulling off the dead leaves. It some-times produces a few fruits, but these are not attractive.

This plant prefers shade, be it the dappled shade of the wood-land or shade garden, or a border in the shade. When grown in the sun, especially in the south of the country, the leaves lose their intense, green colouring. Shelter is also desirable, otherwise the leaf tips turn yellow during periods of cold east winds. On a large scale, it is a good plant for a drift—an excellent marker, but it must be placed very carefully, for the foliage at times appears hard with a partially reflective surface—one could easily have too much of it. Singly or in small groups for the small garden, in town or country, it is a wonderful plant.

The soil requirements are simple, for a well-drained medium, enriched at planting time with decayed manure, suits it very well.

Propagation is by division in the spring. Plant at 500 mm. (1 ft. 8 in.) apart.

Stylophorum   Papaveraceae

S. diphyllum is an unusual but easily grown herbaceous perennial from North America. In the spring the almost glaucous basal

leaves are deeply lobed, their attractive appearance being enhanced by a scattering of glistening raindrops, and a background
of dark soil. The first hairy flower buds form when the growths
are only 150 mm. (6 in.) high, while the deep yellow, poppy-like
blossoms, approximately 45 mm. (1¾ in.) in diameter, are usually
open before April is over. Flowering continues as height is gained
often up to 600 mm. (2 ft.), but by late July the plants often
present a poor appearance. However, the stems may be cut down
to 150 mm. (6 in.), new basal growths appearing in the autumn.

An interesting plant for dappled shade or shade, in formal or
informal situations, it is at its best in narrow drifts running across
the planting, so that it is hidden by other subjects as it passes out
of flower. A moist and rich soil gives the best results, while
shelter will ensure that the growths are not damaged by wind.

Propagation is by seed which is sown as soon as ripe and
wintered in a cold frame.

Symphoricarpos   Caprifoliaceae

The members of this group of vigorous and hardy shrubs are
wonderfully adaptable, taking the best positions in the sun, or the
poorest corners in the dappled shade of deciduous trees in their
stride. They will not do well in full shade, beneath a large beech,
for example. *S. rivularis*, snowberry, is one of the commonest,
producing a heavy crop of white fruits which are most conspicuous, even on a dull November day. *S. orbiculatus*, coral berry,
with small pink berries, has a very dense habit, and will form
impenetrable thickets beneath trees.

Symphytum   Boraginaceae

Of all the ground-cover plants which are to be found in the
borage family, this genus may hold the best all-rounder—*S.
grandiflorum*, a low-growing plant from the Caucasus.

Throughout the winter the close mat of foliage holds the
ground that it has covered in the previous growing season, con-
tinuing to grow and root from the nodes on older stems during
mild spells. In the early spring the process is speeded up, with
fresh green leaves edged with bronze, and the flowers at first peep
rather timidly in clusters on a short stalk above the foliage. In bud
they are a dull, pale red, opening out to a cream yellow; the

various stages are held on each cluster, a pleasing habit common
to many other members of the boraginaceous tribe.

So this plant will creep forward, into the dappled shade of
deciduous trees and up to the very tree trunks, leaving behind a
close mat of foliage which suppresses all weeds. There is hope
for those who garden on the drier soils beneath trees with plants
like this, and what an interesting and intriguing plant for the
town garden!

Taxus   Taxaceae

T. baccata, yew, will grow reasonably well in light shade, for
example, between widely spaced oaks, where the lower branches
have been removed and where at times the sun reaches them.
However, on dry soils in such a situation, growth is often very
thin, and under drought conditions many will lose the greater
proportion of their needles. The prostrate and low-growing forms
are better than the taller ones in the shade of large trees, especially
if there is side light, with only a low sun reaching the plants.

A yew hedge is most impatient of overhead shade from trees,
doubtless because the excessively dry conditions which prevail at
times are associated with their impoverishment. Such conditions
are most unkind to the shrubs, with their unnatural and restricted root systems thwarted and starved by constant and close
clipping. The holly is the superior hedge plant under these
conditions.

Tellima   Saxifragaceae

T. grandiflora, from North America, is an alluring little plant,
which will naturalize quite readily on a variety of soils, provided
other conditions prove suitable. The palmate leaves, neatly lobed,
are light green and often faintly bronzed when they are young.
These develop in the early spring from the crown, which rests at
ground-level, and have an almost rosetted habit. The greenish
flowers, opening in May, are held in racemes which are 300 mm.
(1 ft.) high. It is a plant for the dappled shade in the woodland
garden, in the shrub border as ground-cover, or in a shaded
border, or in a town garden.

Propagation is by division as the crowns become active in the
spring.

Teucrium   Labiatae

T. chamaedrys is a low-growing evergreen, producing spikes of
pale rose-coloured flowers during late summer. A drift, with the
crowded, upright inflorescences, produces an unusual overall light
green sheen, but in dappled shade the effect varies as the angle of
light changes through movement. This is an ideal plant to use as
ground-cover in a newly planted shrub border. When it grows
tall and straggly, it can be cut back quite hard in the spring, for
it will break out freely. It is a popular plant with bees when in
flower.

Thalictrum   Ranunculaceae

The thalictrums are often regarded as herbaceous border plants,
where their finely divided foliage and clouds of small flowers provide a wonderful contrast to the showy composites and their
even more flamboyant associates.

    T. dipterocarpum, from western China, may be grown in full sun
where the inflorescence, producing a pale blue and misty cloud
when it is in flower during the midsummer period, is much
appreciated in herbaceous borders. But it is equally at home in
light woodland plantings in dappled shade and part shade, and
for the foliage alone it is well worth a place. When it appears in
April it is almost fern-like, later assuming a light, pea-green
colouring. Still later, if the plant is happy the finely divided
foliage extends; the perfect plant to lighten a dull corner or a
heavy effect. A group in the mid distance, several feet away from
the front is quietly conspicuous. Staking early is advisable, using
a few well-placed hazel sticks, for the plant in flower will eventually reach a height of 1·5 m. (5 ft.) or more. A position well away
from the front will allow for this height, and the staking will also
be less conspicuous.

    During September the foliage turns to a pale yellow, the older
leaves first, thus producing a changing effect as the green colouring is lost and the plant sinks deeper and deeper into the months
of dormancy which lie ahead. Then, when it is in full autumn
colour, the standard of the staking shows up clearly—with care
this can be good, making all the difference to the general appearance of the planting.

    Although this species has moved far from the marshes and bogs, so dearly loved by some remote ancestor, the plant retains at least some of the passion for moisture, as is the case with more than one group of the Ranunculaceae. It just will not put up with drying out, and prefers a deep soil well-laden with decayed organic material.

Propagation is by division during the dormant season.

Thelypteris Polypodiaceae

T. dryopteris (*Gymnocarpium dryopteris*), oak fern, is a dainty, little native fern found abundantly where there is moisture, shade and neutral or acid conditions among rocks and in woods, although under cultivation a slightly alkaline soil is suitable provided that peat is added. The thin petioles arise singly from a creeping rhizome which is just beneath the soil surface, while the fronds are divided into three and turn at right angles to grow parallel to the ground, forming a neat but close and level canopy sometimes reaching 300 mm. (1 ft.) high.

The thin new fronds, a delicate, light green, appear in late April, for this fern dies back to the rhizome each autumn. If it is happy the colony will increase in size year by year, and it can be quite exciting to see at this stage just how far it has spread.

Care is always necessary when weeding through these ferns, but particularly at this stage, for the developing fronds can easily be mistaken for weeds. This fern retains its fresh, green appearance through the season, while a lovely effect is produced later when the newer fronds have a pale copper-green colour at first. The dead fronds should be left in the autumn until weeding and mulching are completed, for they serve as useful markers.

A delightful fern for the shade, perhaps in some selected corner where very little sun reaches it, but it must not be heavy shade. Against stone the fronds are beautiful and therefore, in addition to the woodland, a border against a wall or a rock garden could be considered. In addition to shade, moisture and a peaty soil which is not badly drained are suitable.

Propagation is by careful division of the rhizomes when dormant.

T. phegopteris, beech fern, is also a native, with a rhizomatous system which creeps beneath the surface of the soil, sending up fronds along the lengths, these sometimes reaching to 300 mm. (1 ft.) high. The fronds are a delicate green and slightly hairy, and appear during May. This is so late that care is necessary to avoid damage from tramping feet, and it is necessary to be patient until they appear. By the late autumn the fronds die down to the rhizomes.

It is a plant for the light dappled shade, in a woodland, shade garden, or rock garden, where little sun reaches it. The soil should be peaty and moist, but not badly drained.

Propagation is by division in the spring.

Thuja   Cupressaceae

T. plicata, western red cedar, is normally found growing in an open and sunny position although it is a good subject for dappled shade beneath a thin canopy of deciduous trees. It is also one of the best conifers for a heavy clay soil.

Tiarella   Saxifragaceae

This is one of the smaller of the genera in a family which contributes a number of good shade plants. They are all herbaceous perennials and shade-lovers.

T. cordifolia, from North America, is the best-known species. It has 230 mm. (9 in.) high spikes of small, white flowers with prominent stamens which open during May. The cordate leaves, grown in tufts, have an appearance similar to those of *Ribes* and colour up to a beautiful bronze in the autumn. This delightful woodlander is suitable for many positions in dappled shade or shade (see Plate 10), and will thrive on a wide variety of soils, provided they are moist and rich. It is suitable for a retaining wall in the shade, and is an interesting little plant for a town garden.

Tricyrtis   Liliaceae

Any of the ten species in this small genus from the Far East are worthy of a place in dappled shade, or part shade, although in the north they will grow well in the sun. They are suitable for a herbaceous planting in the shade, or in a group in the shade garden.

From the moment the growths appear above the ground in the spring, they are distinctive, resembling those of *Tradescantia* growths. Some, such as *Tricyrtis macropoda*, are deeply spotted, with an attractive venation, giving the foliage an appearance similar to that of orchids. The leaf tips of some species are looped, as if about to form a tendril for climbing. The flowers, which are held in a head, are cup-shaped and resemble lilies. The stamens and stigmas are very prominent, occupying a strong central position, while the colouring varies, with a light background and a deeper blotching. This characteristic has given them the unfortunate name, toad lilies.

T. formosana var. *stolonifera* is particularly outstanding and is in display during October. The flowers are lilac with a deep violet spotting. By the time the last of these fade, the growths are a metre (3 ft. 3 in.) high, and hold a cluster of seed capsules which remain firm and clear in outline, even after the foliage and stems have withered and dried brown in the winds of winter.

Propagation is normally by division of the rhizomatous roots, but seed provides a good alternative means.

Trillium   Liliaceae

These are choice but not too difficult woodland plants, being distinct with three leaves surmounted by a flower on a common stalk.

In *T. grandiflorum*, from North America, the bronze growths appear above the soil by early March and soon the leaves unfold with the soft yellow buds showing even at such an early stage. By mid-April the flowers open, white with yellow stamens on a short stalk; in the background is the lush green foliage—it is a lovely plant at this stage. Reaching up to 400 mm. (1 ft. 4 in.) high, it is a plant for the front, but is also effective in a drift running towards the centre of a planting. The cultivar 'Roseum' has a pink tinge to its flowers, while the very rare 'Flore Pleno' is white, many petalled, but with a definite, almost tubular centre.

T. sessile is an extraordinary plant which emerges from the soil with a strong almost arum-like growth. The leaves, which open out, are green, mottled with lighter and dark, almost bronze, blotches, while in addition the strong venation produces a variety of reflective surfaces. The purple and maroon flowers, springing directly from the leaf centres, are thin-petalled and like magnolia flowers—a perfect contrast to the foliage. The whole plant at this stage is more reminiscent of a tropical plant from the depths of some South American jungle. After flowering, the withered and shrunken petals produce a curious effect as they stand as centre pieces to this exotic, foliage. There are other treasures in this genus, for example: *T. cernuum*, with fruits which turn a dull purple; and *T. erectum*, which is among those species which have nodding flowers.

Trilliums are plants for the cool, dappled shade of the woodland or shade garden and thrive best in a well-drained but moist medium, which is slightly acid and well supplied with well-decayed leafmould or peat. *T. grandiflorum* is the easiest grown species and will thrive among shrubs in a damp site.

Propagation is by division in the early spring, or by seed.

Tsuga   Pinaceae

T. heterophylla, western hemlock, is an excellent conifer for a position in dappled shade beneath a light woodland canopy, especially in those areas which have a moderate to heavy rainfall.

Uvularia   Liliaceae

This small genus of woodland plants from North America has the general appearance of Solomon's seal and is in fact in the same family.

U. sessilifolia develops rapidly during March with thin, crowded growths. The green-white flowers, which intensify to cream, hang among the fresh green and narrow leaves and are almost bell-like as the petals clasp along their length to form a tube. When flowering has finished there is a display of interesting fruits on stems which have grown to 300 mm. (1 ft.). During the early autumn the foliage often colours to a beautiful clear yellow. *U. grandiflora* has glaucous green growths over 300 mm. (1 ft.) high, with lemon-yellow flowers made up of strap-shaped petals.

These are plants for the dappled shade of the woodland or wild garden, where they will thrive in a soil which is rich in decayed organic material. They should be planted in a group or drift near the front, for these are interesting plants to view at close quarters. Careful staking with a few shortened pea-sticks set within and on the edges of the clump is helpful, since the growths are often laid flat by rain and wind, but it must be done at an early stage when the shoots first appear. The thick mass of rhizomes may be divided quite easily if desired, during the dormant period.

Vancouveria   Berberidaceae

This is a small genus from North America. Although they are not in any sense showy the two species commonly grown are interesting. Some similarity with the epimediums can be seen and indeed they are related to them, being in the same family.

V. planipetala is evergreen and once established under the right conditions it grows freely, creeping about in shaded places—even beneath such evergreens as rhododendrons provided the canopy is not too heavy. During late May and early June the small, nodding white flowers are produced on pinkish stems that grow to 300 mm. (1 ft.), giving a delicate and pleasing effect. The foliage, which hugs the ground, is very shiny and thus reflects the light—a point in its favour for brightening a dull, shady spot. At times the plant appears to be almost mahonia-like.

After flowering the young leaves develop, a lighter green than the more mature foliage, and this again provides an interesting effect. Another display period is during the autumn and winter when the dark green foliage is seen against a pattern of fallen leaves. Should the plant be covered by the leaf-fall for a time this will do no harm, provided a wooden rake is used with care. *V. hexandra*, a deciduous species, does not give this trouble, but the evergreen is worth the extra effort involved.

These plants like a sandy, peat soil which is cool and moist. They may be propagated by careful division in the spring, but *V. planipetala* in particular resents disturbance and may take two to three years before it grows away freely.

Viburnum   Caprifoliaceae

V. tinus, laurustinus, is often a large-growing shrub. It has a dense, twiggy, evergreen habit, and is very popular for screen and boundary planting. It will succeed in sun or shade, provided it is not too heavy, and this makes it a very useful plant indeed, for it is hardy and suffers only in the severest of winters. Not only is it suitable for planting in the dappled shade of deciduous trees, it will also thrive amongst conifers—for example, *Pinus nigra*—provided these are widely spaced with light filtering through from high crowns, and with long, clean trunks. The white heads of flower are produced through the winter and spring, while after a good summer, the heads of blue fruits add to the attraction as the pink buds open for the following season.

Other evergreen species and cultivars also prove suitable in the lighter shade. One of the most outstanding of these is *V. davidii*, a native of western China. The bush has a low, spreading habit, being from 1 to 1·5 m. (3 ft. 3 in. to 5 ft.) high, while the leaves have a distinctive appearance with three main veins that are almost parallel. The flowers are borne in terminal clusters through the summer, and if several plants are together the scattering of oval blue fruits is attractive during the winter. *V. rhytidophyllum*, from west and central China, is a large and fast-growing evergreen which produces creamy clusters of flowers in the late spring (see Plate 2).

Vinca   Apocynaceae

The world's flora has been sifted through many, many times in search of ground-cover plants, but in the final selection the well-known and much-loved periwinkles are still among the few. The two species which are most common are *V. major*, from the Continent, and *V. minor*, a doubtful native, but one which can be found growing freely in the wild.

V. major, greater periwinkle, is a very vigorous grower, and the arching, tangled growths will form a dense cover, 300 mm. (1 ft.) thick, in sun, dappled shade or shade. There are a number of forms, among them 'Variegata', which has a bright variegation of creamy white. The odd suckerous shoot, coming up among other plants, is very attractive. The foliage colour of this form is a pea-green with a white edge, but with the type the young growths are light green in colour against the darker and older foliage.

V. minor, lesser periwinkle, is a smaller grower, but it can be used for the same purpose, as ground-cover, although being less vigorous it can be brought more to the edge. Even so, the long trailing shoots, which will stretch over a path, can become very untidy; there is then a need for careful pruning, taking off the shoots individually, so that an informal and not a clipped edge is left. There are some beautiful forms of this too, including 'Variegata', which also has a variegation of creamy-white.

These are wonderful plants for almost all types of shade, except full shade where it is often also too dry. They have so many uses in the garden, and they will send runners out into quite dense shade beneath bushes. They can be propagated quite easily by lifting and dividing established plants during the autumn.

An established drift will provide cover for mice, especially during the winter. If this is suspected, the growths may be either thinned or cut down completely as a control.

Viola   Violaceae

Among the many garden plants in this genus everybody would surely find one worthy of a place in his or her garden.

V. odorata, sweet violet, is a native and is found commonly in many parts of the country, particularly where the soil is calcareous or has a tendency towards this—over chalk, soft limestone or as the result of some other cause; for example, there are soils in certain coastal areas which contain a high proportion of broken sea shells handed down from the past, when deposits from the sea bed were pushed up on the shore through glacial action. While a well-drained position is important, this plant must have sufficient moisture, especially through the growing and flowering season. This is why so many fail with it, but not only drought is troublesome to it—this species, in common with many others in this genus, can have too much sun when it either yellows and hardens or is sucked dry by red spider mite. In both cases it loses that fresh and green appearance so desirable with violas generally, and dies. At the other extreme it can easily be killed by misdirected kindness, for example, it may be planted with care in a specially made-up pocket in a deep and shaded place in the woods. In such a position the plant has to contend with drip from the overhead canopy during the winter and drought and dense shade during the summer—all potential killers. One of the positions where it is likely to succeed best is in part shade on a retaining bank or wall facing east. There, provided with a neutral or calcareous soil and dappled shade from a nearby herbaceous plant from midday onwards, it is likely to thrive and spread, provided there is sufficient moisture, this is why this plant does so well in the West Country, where the rainfall is heavier. However, there are many other suitable positions in part or dappled shade; it is often found in nature, thriving behind grass and other herbage against a hedge.

There are a number of very well-known cultivars, including such old favourites as 'Princess of Wales', which was at one time grown commercially on a large scale for bunching. There are one or two white forms, but the most common colour, and often one mostly sweetly scented, is violet.

Many of the other species require similar conditions, but are usually grown in the more cultivated parts of the garden, including the rock garden and in selected positions such as shrub borders. *V. cornuta*, from the Pyrenees, will establish itself very readily and will even increase and spread into other parts of the garden, particularly into the shady and moist corners. The flowers are quite large and graceful, being pale violet, with white at the base of the lower petal. There is a white form, 'Alba', which is very beautiful and will come true from seed. This is a particularly good subject for patios, window-boxes and town gardens, provided it can be given shaded and cool conditions. It will flower throughout the summer and autumn, if there is sufficient moisture for it to keep growing, otherwise it will run to seed and die out very quickly. Only when the foliage is fresh and green are violas healthy.

Pansies, available in many different colours, do best in a moist and rich soil with shade from the midday sun. This is hardly surprising when it is remembered that *V. tricolor*, a native and one of the parents of this group, is often seen at its best among other plants, or beneath fruit trees in a deep and moist kitchen garden soil, where it may be looked upon as a weed.

Most violas will propagate readily from seed, but the chances of hybridization are so great that vegetative propagation of correctly named stock or selected forms is advisable. Cuttings taken in September are ready for planting out in the spring.

Bedding violas are often sown outside in April and are grown for planting in their flowering positions during the autumn, when the summer bedding is cleared. Sowings made under glass during the early spring produce plants which flower during the summer. These are ideal for planting in the shade, perhaps in a narrow border against a wall, but they will also thrive in many other shaded places, including window-boxes, patios and town gardens. Sometimes they are grown quite successfully among roses, although on a large scale this presents difficulties with spraying.

The culture of the rarer species is more exacting, many requiring moraine-like conditions.

Viscum   Loranthaceae

Lathraea clandestina, a parasite, has been included in this work, and it seems only reasonable therefore for *Viscum album*, mistletoe, to be included also. It is recognized by many as a partial parasite, its leaves being green and capable of manufacturing some food at least, while without any doubt it is a plant for dappled shade. The apple is accepted as one of the most common host trees, but it will grow on many other deciduous subjects: it is seldom found on evergreens and conifers.

The method of establishing this plant is to choose a medium-sized branch on the tree selected as host, for it is preferable if the bark is smooth and has not reached the mature, furrowed stage, and is not too thick. A very shallow and sloping incision is made into the bark on the lower side of the limb, and one or two fully ripe berries are smeared over it and are held just within the cut.

Mistletoe prefers the southern part of the country, but a required level of humidity may be an important condition for its success, especially in the early stages.

Xanthorrhiza   Ranunculaceae

X. simplicissima, yellow root, is an interesting deciduous shrub, which grows to 600 mm. (2 ft.) high, with a suckering habit. The flowers are at first sight most unlike those of the buttercup, but nevertheless it is in the same family. They are small and purple, being produced on panicles in the spring, but after the petals have fallen the remainder is green through the summer as the fruits develop. However, the foliage is the outstanding feature of this plant, for it is so dainty and yet full of character, being pinnate and deeply toothed. The colour is also a fresh green, and interesting, for the interveinal areas are markedly paler than the zones running by the main veins. Often too, the foliage turns to yellow or copper shades in the autumn. A good plant for the dappled shade in open, but damp woodland.

Appendix I

Easy Reference Table of the Genera and their Uses

This table has been drawn up to give the reader a means of quick reference to the likely genera in which plants may be found for the various uses. These are suggested uses only, for tastes in the matter of planting vary considerably; for example, to have such shrubs as yews growing as free-standing specimens against a north-facing wall might be considered by some to be a waste of valuable space. In some cases, too, species within a genus vary considerably in their requirements. I must therefore leave it to the reader to make the final decision.

Those suggested for growing as free-standing specimens, without any tying against a wall, are marked in the table with an asterisk.

It is emphasized that the hardiness of plants should be taken into consideration when a selection is made.

	Informal Tree Group and Woodlanders	Shade Garden	Shaded Border	Shaded Herbaceous Plantings	Shaded Rock Garden	Shaded Dry Retaining Wall	Shaded Patios and Paving	Window-box Culture	Tub Culture	North-facing Wall (Woody Plants and Climbers only)
Acanthus	✓	✓	✓	✓	—	—	—	—	✓	—
Acer	✓	✓	✓	—	✓	—	—	—	—	—
Aconitum	✓	✓	✓	✓	—	—	—	—	—	—
Actaea	✓	✓	✓	—	—	—	—	—	—	—
Adiantum	✓	✓	✓	—	✓	✓	—	—	—	—
Adlumia	✓	✓	—	—	—	—	—	—	—	—
Aesculus	✓	✓	—	—	—	—	—	—	—	—
Ajuga	✓	✓	✓	✓	✓	✓	✓	✓	—	—
Alchemilla	—	✓	✓	✓	—	✓	✓	✓	—	—
Allium	✓	✓	—	—	—	—	—	—	—	—
Andromeda	—	✓	✓	✓	✓	—	—	—	—	—
Anemone	✓	✓	✓	✓	✓	—	—	✓	✓	✓
Anthriscus	✓	✓	—	—	—	—	—	—	—	—
Antirrhinum	—	—	✓	—	✓	✓	—	✓	—	—
Aquilegia	—	—	✓	✓	✓	✓	✓	✓	✓	—
Arabis	—	—	✓	✓	✓	✓	✓	✓	✓	—
Arctostaphylos	✓	✓	✓	✓	✓	✓	—	—	—	—
Arenaria	—	—	—	—	✓	✓	—	—	—	—
Arisaema	✓	✓	✓	—	—	—	—	—	—	—
Arisarum	✓	✓	✓	—	✓	—	—	✓	—	—
Armeria	—	—	—	—	—	—	—	✓	—	—

	1	2	3	4	5	6	7	8	9
Arum	✓	—	—	—	—	✓	✓	✓	✓
Aruncus	✓	✓	—	—	—	✓	✓	✓	✓
Arundinaria	✓*	✓	—	—	✓	—	✓	✓	✓
Asarina	—	—	✓	—	✓	✓	✓	—	—
Asperula	—	—	—	✓	✓	✓	✓	✓	✓
Asplenium	—	—	—	—	✓	✓	—	—	—
Asteranthera	✓	—	✓	—	—	—	—	—	—
Astilbe	—	—	—	✓	✓	✓	✓	✓	✓
Astrantia	—	—	—	—	—	✓	✓	✓	✓
Athyrium	—	—	✓	✓	✓	✓	✓	✓	✓
Aubrieta	✓*	—	✓	✓	✓	—	—	—	—
Aucuba	✓	✓	—	—	—	✓	✓	✓	✓
Berberidopsis	✓	—	—	—	—	—	—	—	—
Berberis	—	✓	—	—	—	✓	✓	✓	✓
Bergenia	✓	✓	✓	—	✓	✓	✓	✓	✓
Billardiera	✓	—	✓	—	—	—	—	—	—
Blechnum	—	—	—	—	—	✓	✓	✓	✓
Bletilla	—	—	—	—	—	✓	✓	✓	✓
Boykinia	—	—	—	—	—	✓	✓	✓	✓
Brunnera	—	—	—	—	—	✓	✓	✓	✓
Buxus	✓*	✓	—	—	✓	✓	✓	✓	✓
Caltha	—	—	—	—	—	✓	✓	✓	✓
Camellia	✓*	✓	—	—	—	✓	✓	✓	✓
Campanula	—	—	✓	—	✓	✓	✓	✓	✓
Cardamine	—	—	—	—	—	—	✓	✓	—

	Informal Tree Group and Woodlanders	Shade Garden	Shaded Border	Shaded Herbaceous Plantings	Shaded Rock Garden	Shaded Dry Retaining Walls	Shaded Patios and Paving	Window-box Culture	Tub Culture	North-facing Walls (IV only) Plants and Climbers only
Cardiocrinum	✓	✓	—	—	—	—	—	—	—	—
Carex	✓	✓	✓	✓	—	—	—	—	—	—
Carum	—	—	✓	✓	—	—	—	✓	✓	—
Cassiope	✓	✓	—	—	✓	—	—	—	—	—
Caulophyllum	✓	✓	—	—	✓	—	—	—	—	—
Cephalotaxus	✓	✓	✓	—	—	—	—	—	✓	✓*
Cercidiphyllum	✓	✓	✓	—	—	—	—	—	—	—
Chaenomeles	✓	✓	✓	—	—	—	—	—	✓	✓
Chamaecyparis	✓	✓	✓	—	—	—	—	—	✓	—
Chamaedaphne	✓	✓	✓	—	✓	—	—	—	—	—
Chamaepericlymenum	✓	✓	—	—	—	—	—	—	—	—
Chelidonium	✓	✓	—	—	—	—	—	—	—	—
Chionodoxa	✓	✓	✓	—	✓	—	—	✓	✓	—
Cimicifuga	✓	✓	✓	✓	—	—	—	—	—	—
Circaea	✓	—	—	—	—	—	—	—	—	—
Clintonia	✓	✓	✓	—	—	—	—	—	—	—
Codonopsis	—	✓	✓	—	—	—	—	—	—	—
Colchicum	✓	✓	✓	—	—	—	—	—	—	—
Convallaria	✓	✓	✓	✓	✓	—	✓	✓	✓	—
Cortusa	—	✓	✓	—	✓	—	✓	—	—	—
Corydalis	✓	✓	✓	✓	✓	✓	✓	✓	—	—

Cotoneaster	✓	✓	—	✓	—	✓	—	✓	✓
Crinodendron	✓	—	—	—	—	—	—	—	✓*
Crocus	✓	✓	✓	✓	—	✓	✓	✓	—
Cyclamen	✓	✓	✓	—	—	✓	—	—	—
Cypripedium	✓	✓	✓	✓	—	✓	—	—	—
Cystopteris	—	✓	✓	—	—	✓	—	✓	—
Danae	✓	✓	—	—	—	—	—	—	—
Daphne	✓	✓	✓	—	—	—	—	—	—
Daphniphyllum	✓	—	✓	—	—	—	—	—	—
Dennstaedtia	✓	✓	—	—	—	—	—	—	—
Dentaria	✓	✓	✓	—	—	—	—	—	—
Dicentra	✓	✓	✓	✓	—	✓	—	—	—
Digitalis	✓	✓	✓	✓	—	—	—	—	—
Diphylleia	✓	✓	—	✓	—	—	—	—	—
Disanthus	✓	✓	—	✓	—	—	—	—	—
Disporum	✓	✓	✓	✓	—	—	—	—	—
Distylium	✓	✓	✓	✓	✓	—	—	—	—
Dryopteris	✓	✓	✓	✓	✓	—	—	✓	—
Endymion	✓	✓	✓	✓	✓	—	✓	✓	—
Epimedium	✓	✓	✓	—	—	✓	✓	—	—
Eranthis	✓	✓	✓	✓	—	✓	—	—	—
Erythronium	✓	—	✓	✓	—	—	—	✓	✓*
Escallonia	—	—	—	—	—	—	—	—	—
Euonymus	✓	✓	✓	✓	✓	✓	—	✓	✓*
Euphorbia	✓	✓	—	✓	—	—	—	—	—

	North-facing Walls and Cliffs (Woody Plants and Climbers only)	Tub Culture	Window-box Culture	Shaded Patios and Paving	Shaded Dry Retaining Walls	Shaded Rock Garden	Shaded Herbaceous Plantings	Shaded Border	Shade Garden	Informal Tree Group and Woodlanders
× Fatshedera	—	—	✓	—	—	—	—	✓	✓	✓
Fatsia	—	✓	—	—	—	—	—	✓	✓	✓
Filipendula	—	—	—	—	—	—	✓	✓	✓	✓
Fragaria	—	—	—	—	—	✓	✓	✓	✓	✓
Fritillaria	—	—	—	—	—	✓	—	✓	✓	✓
Fuchsia	—	✓	✓	—	—	✓	—	✓	✓	—
Galanthus	—	—	✓	—	—	✓	—	✓	✓	✓
Galax	—	✓	✓	✓	✓	✓	—	✓	✓	✓
Galeobdolon	—	—	—	—	—	—	✓	✓	✓	✓
Garrya	✓*	✓	—	—	—	—	—	✓	✓	✓
× Gaulnettya	—	✓	—	—	—	—	—	✓	✓	✓
Gaultheria	—	—	—	—	—	—	—	✓	✓	✓
Gentiana	—	—	—	—	—	✓	✓	✓	✓	✓
Geranium	—	—	✓	—	—	—	✓	✓	✓	✓
Gillenia	—	—	—	—	—	—	✓	—	—	—
Glaucidium	—	—	—	—	—	—	—	—	✓	✓
Glechoma	—	—	—	—	—	—	—	—	—	✓
Haberlea	—	—	—	—	✓	✓	—	—	—	—
Hebe	—	✓	—	—	—	—	—	✓	✓	✓
Hedera	✓	✓	✓	✓	✓	✓	—	✓	✓	✓
Helleborus	—	—	—	—	—	—	✓	✓	✓	✓

Heloniopsis	✓	✓	✓	—	—	—	—	—	—	—	—
Helxine	—	—	✓	✓	✓	✓	✓	—	—	—	—
Hemerocallis	✓	✓	✓	✓	—	—	—	—	—	—	—
Hepatica	✓	✓	✓	✓	✓	—	—	—	—	—	—
Heuchera	—	✓	✓	✓	—	—	—	—	✓	✓	—
Hosta	✓	✓	✓	✓	—	—	—	—	—	—	—
Houttuynia	✓	✓	✓	—	—	—	—	—	—	—	—
Hyacinthus	✓	✓	✓	—	—	—	—	✓	✓	✓	—
Hydrangea	✓	✓	✓	—	—	—	—	—	—	✓	✓
Hydrastis	✓	✓	—	—	—	—	—	—	—	—	—
Hypericum	✓	✓	✓	—	—	✓	—	—	✓	✓	—
Ilex	✓	✓	✓	—	—	—	—	✓	✓	✓	✓*
Impatiens	—	—	✓	✓	—	—	—	—	✓	✓	—
Kirengeshoma	✓	✓	✓	✓	—	—	—	—	—	—	—
Lamium	✓	✓	✓	✓	—	—	✓	✓	—	—	—
Lathraea	✓	—	—	—	—	—	—	—	—	—	—
Leucobryum	✓	—	—	—	—	—	—	—	—	—	—
Leucojum	✓	✓	✓	—	✓	—	—	—	—	—	—
Lilium	✓	✓	✓	✓	—	—	—	—	✓	—	—
Liriope	✓	✓	✓	✓	—	—	—	✓	✓	✓	—
Lonicera	✓	✓	—	✓	—	—	—	—	—	—	✓
Lunaria	✓	✓	✓	✓	—	—	✓	—	—	—	—
Macleaya	—	✓	✓	—	—	—	—	—	—	—	—
Magnolia	✓	✓	✓	—	—	—	—	—	—	—	—
× Mahoberberis	✓	✓	—	—	—	—	—	—	✓	—	—

	North-facing Wall (Woody Plants and Climbers only) (Group)	Tub Culture	Window-box Culture	Shaded Patios and Paving	Shaded Dry Retaining Wall	Shaded Rock Garden	Shaded Herbaceous Plantings	Shaded Border	Shade Garden	Informal Tree Group and Woodlanders
Mahonia	✓*	✓	—	—	—	—	—	✓	✓	✓
Maianthemum	—	—	—	—	—	—	—	✓	✓	✓
Matteuccia	—	—	—	—	—	—	—	✓	✓	✓
Meconopsis	—	—	✓	✓	✓	—	✓	✓	✓	✓
Melittis	—	—	—	✓	✓	—	✓	✓	—	✓
Mercurialis	—	—	—	—	—	—	—	—	✓	✓
Muscari	—	✓	✓	—	—	✓	✓	✓	✓	✓
Myosotis	—	✓	✓	—	—	✓	✓	✓	✓	✓
Narcissus	—	✓	✓	—	—	✓	✓	✓	✓	✓
Nicotiana	—	✓	✓	—	—	—	✓	✓	✓	—
Nomocharis	—	—	—	—	—	✓	—	✓	✓	✓
Omphalodes	—	—	—	—	—	✓	—	✓	✓	—
Ophiopogon	—	—	—	—	—	—	—	✓	✓	✓
Orixa	—	—	—	—	—	—	—	—	✓	✓
Ornithogalum	—	✓	✓	—	—	✓	—	✓	✓	✓
Ourisia	—	—	—	—	—	—	—	✓	✓	✓
Pachysandra	—	—	—	✓	—	—	—	✓	✓	✓
Parthenocissus	✓	—	—	—	—	—	—	—	—	—
Peltiphyllum	—	—	—	—	—	—	—	—	✓	✓
Pentaglottis	—	—	—	—	—	—	—	—	—	✓
Petasites	—	—	—	—	—	—	—	—	—	✓

Genus										
Phyllitis	✓	✓	✓	—	✓	✓	✓	✓	✓	—
Pieris	✓	✓	✓	—	—	—	—	—	✓	—
Poa	✓	—	—	—	—	—	—	—	—	—
Podophyllum	✓	✓	✓	—	✓	—	—	—	✓	—
Polygonatum	✓	✓	✓	✓	✓	—	—	—	✓	—
Polygonum	✓	✓	✓	—	—	—	—	—	✓	—
Polypodium	✓	✓	—	✓	✓	✓	—	—	—	—
Polystichum	✓	✓	✓	✓	✓	✓	—	✓	✓	—
Primula	✓	✓	✓	✓	✓	—	—	✓	✓	—
Prunus	✓	✓	✓	—	—	—	—	—	✓	✓*
Pulmonaria	✓	✓	—	✓	—	—	—	—	✓	—
Pyracantha	✓	—	—	—	—	—	—	—	✓	✓*
Pyrola	✓	✓	✓	—	✓	✓	—	—	—	—
Ramonda	—	—	—	—	✓	—	—	—	—	—
Ranzania	✓	✓	✓	—	—	—	—	—	✓	—
Rhododendron	✓	✓	✓	—	✓	✓	—	—	✓	—
Ribes	—	—	✓	—	—	—	—	—	✓	—
Rodgersia	✓	✓	✓	—	—	—	—	—	—	✓
Rosa	✓	—	—	—	—	—	—	—	✓	—
Ruscus	✓	✓	✓	✓	—	—	—	—	✓	—
Sanguinaria	✓	✓	✓	✓	✓	—	—	—	✓	—
Sanicula	✓	—	—	—	—	—	—	—	—	—
Sarcococca	✓	✓	✓	—	✓	✓	—	—	✓	—
Saxifraga	✓	✓	✓	✓	✓	✓	✓	✓	✓	—
Schizophragma	✓	—	—	—	—	—	—	—	—	✓

	Informal Tree Group and Woodlanders	Shade Garden	Shaded Border and Herbaceous Plantings	Shaded Rock Garden	Shaded Dry Garden Retaining Wall	Shaded Wall and Paving	Window-box Culture	Tub Culture	North-facing Wall (Woody Plants and Climbers only)
Scilla	✓	✓	✓	✓	—	—	✓	—	—
Selaginella	✓	✓	—	✓	✓	—	—	✓	—
Shortia	✓	✓	—	✓	—	—	—	—	—
Skimmia	✓	✓	—	✓	—	—	—	✓	—
Smilacina	✓	✓	✓	—	—	—	—	✓	—
Speirantha	✓	✓	—	—	—	—	—	—	—
Stylophorum	✓	✓	✓	—	—	—	✓	✓	—
Symphoricarpos	✓	✓	—	—	—	—	—	✓	—
Symphytum	✓	✓	✓	✓	—	—	—	—	—
Taxus	✓	✓	—	—	—	—	✓	✓	✓*
Tellima	✓	✓	✓	—	—	—	✓	—	—
Teucrium	✓	✓	✓	—	—	—	✓	—	—
Thalictrum	✓	✓	✓	—	—	—	—	✓	—
Thelypteris	✓	✓	✓	✓	—	✓	—	—	—
Thuja	✓	—	—	—	—	—	—	—	—
Tiarella	✓	✓	✓	✓	—	—	—	—	—
Tricyrtis	✓	✓	✓	—	—	—	—	—	—
Trillium	✓	✓	✓	✓	—	—	—	—	—
Tsuga	✓	✓	—	—	—	—	—	—	—
Uvularia	✓	✓	✓	—	—	—	—	—	—
Vancouveria	✓	✓	—	✓	✓	—	—	—	—
Viburnum	✓	✓	—	—	—	—	—	—	✓*
Vinca	✓	✓	✓	✓	✓	✓	✓	✓	—
Viola	✓	✓	✓	✓	✓	✓	✓	✓	—

Appendix II

Glossary of Botanical and Technical Terms

ACID (of soils): opposite to alkaline or lime-containing; below pH 7·0.

ALKALINE (of soils): lime- or chalk-containing (some other soil formations may be involved); above pH 7·0.

AXIL: the angle between a leaf and supporting stem.

BIENNIAL: plant which builds up a store of food in the first year from seed, dying in the second after flowering and producing a crop of seed.

BIGENERIC HYBRID: a sexual hybrid between two species of different genera.

CALCAREOUS: a soil commonly, but not invariably, containing chalk or free lime; above pH 7·0.

CALYX: part of flower structure consisting of sepals, which are often green and leaf-like.

CLONE: a selected form which has been propagated vegetatively; for example, the apple 'Bramley's Seedling'.

COPPICE: certain trees such as sweet chestnut and hazel are grown for the production of brushwood and stakes. As the crop is collected they are cut down to within 300 mm. (1 ft.) or so of ground-level, a process which is repeated at intervals of 5 to 7 years. Such a planting is referred to as a coppice.

CORDATE: base of leaf is heart-shaped.

CORM: a rounded, almost bulb-like, structure which consists mainly of a store of food in solid form.

CRISTATE (of ferns): frond finely crested.

CULTIVAR: a selected and valued form which is propagated vegetatively or by seed. This is sometimes indicated by a capital letter at the beginning of the name and by the prefix cv. (an abbreviation for cultivar); or, the selected name is placed in single quotes, again with the use of the capital for the first letter—e.g., *Erythronium tuolumnense* 'Pagoda'.

DORMANT: no living plant, seed or spore is completely dormant. The term is used to describe the stage when the plant is at rest, with no new growth being visible, for example, a bulb or corm soon after the foliage has died down.

EPIPHYTE: a plant growing upon, but not nourished by, another.

ERICACEOUS: a member of the family Ericaceae.

FAMILY: referring to a plant family; for example, Primulaceae.

FROND: the leaf-like structure of, for example, ferns.

GENUS (plural, genera): a group of plants within a family; for example, *Primula*.

GLAUCOUS: having a bluish colouring, but referring to leaves and stems only, not to flowers.

INDICATOR: a plant, usually a native, the presence of which indicates a definite soil type.

INFLORESCENCE: the flowering portion of a plant.

ISLAND BED: a bed usually surrounded by mown grass, often informal in design and planted up mainly with herbaceous type plants.

KEY PLANT: a conspicuous plant in a prominent position.

LEAF CUTTING: a cutting consisting only of a leaf (often with the petiole attached), as for *Saintpaulia*. A leaf-bud cutting consists of the axillary bud in addition, as for *Camellia*.

MARKER PLANT: a plant of which a portion at least remains above ground during the winter; it can thus be used to indicate the position of others which are hidden from view.

MID DISTANCE: referring to a mid-way position across the width of a border.

MONOCARPIC: a plant which grows from seed, flowers and produces one crop of seeds before dying completely. It may take more than one year to mature and reach the final stage, and thus it is distinct from an annual, which completes the cycle in one year. *Meconopsis napaulensis* is a monocarpic plant.

MYCORRHIZA: fungi which grow in association with the roots of other plants.

NATURALIZED: a planting made in an essentially natural setting so that it becomes a part of the community of plants to be found in that area. The term naturalized refers to alien plants which have become established as part of a flora within an area.

PARASITE: complete parasite—a plant living entirely off the host plant; partial parasite—a plant sustained in part by the host plant, but also manufacturing some of its own food.

PINNAE: the first or primary divisions of a fern frond or the leaflets of a pinnate leaf.

PINNATE: a leaf made up of leaflets arranged on either side of a leaf stalk; there is usually a terminal leaflet.

RACEME: a spike of flowers on a central stem.

RACHIS: the main stem which runs through a pinnate leaf, a divided fern frond or a branched flower head.

RECURVED (of petals): petals which are coiled back to the flower stem.

RHIZOME: a fleshy stem creeping below soil level.

ROOT CUTTING: the roots of a number of plants will when detached form root and shoot systems. The term refers to a root prepared for insertion.

ROSETTE: a formally shaped cluster of leaves at ground level.

SCALE (of propagation): certain bulbous plants with loose fleshy scales may be propagated by scales being detached and kept moist until small bulbils form and grow.

SPATHE: the coloured leaf-like structure or bract which forms part of an arum flower, for example.

STRAIN: a selection of seed or plants which have been carefully bred, perhaps over many years, to reach desired standards.

TOMENTOSE: with a woolly covering.

TRIFOLIATE: consisting of three leaflets.

WHORL: flowers or leaves which form a circle round a stem, all originating at the same level.

Index